Developing Intercultural Competence in Practice

Languages for Intercultural Communication and Education
Editors: Michael Byram, *University of Durham, UK*
and Alison Phipps, *University of Glasgow, UK*

The overall aim of this series is to publish books which will ultimately inform learning and teaching, but whose primary focus is on the analysis of intercultural relationships, whether in textual form or in people's experience. There will also be books which deal directly with pedagogy, with the relationships between language learning and cultural learning, between processes inside the classroom and beyond. They will all have in common a concern with the relationship between language and culture, and the development of intercultural communicative competence.

Other Books of Interest
Foreign Language and Culture Learning from a Dialogic Perspective
 Carol Morgan and Albane Cain
The Good Language Learner
 N. Naiman, M. Fröhlich, H.H. Stern and A. Todesco
Language, Culture and Communication in Contemporary Europe
 Charlotte Hoffman (ed.)
Language Learners as Ethnographers
 Celia Roberts, Michael Byram, Ana Barro, Shirley Jordan and Brian Street
Language Teachers, Politics and Cultures
 Michael Byram and Karen Risager
Motivating Language Learners
 Gary N. Chambers
New Perspectives on Teaching and Learning Modern Languages
 Simon Green (ed.)
Teaching and Assessing Intercultural Communicative Competence
 Michael Byram

Please contact us for the latest book information:
Multilingual Matters, Frankfurt Lodge, Clevedon Hall,
Victoria Road, Clevedon, BS21 7HH, England
http://www.multilingual-matters.com

LANGUAGES FOR INTERCULTURAL COMMUNICATION AND EDUCATION 1
Series Editors: Michael Byram and Alison Phipps

Developing Intercultural Competence in Practice

Edited by
Michael Byram, Adam Nichols
and David Stevens

MULTILINGUAL MATTERS LTD
Clevedon • Buffalo • Toronto • Sydney

Library of Congress Cataloging in Publication Data
Developing Intercultural Competence in Practice/Edited by Michael Byram, Adam
Nichols and David Stevens
Includes bibliographical references and index.
1. Intercultural communication–Study and teaching. 2. Multicultural education.
3. Language and languages–Study and teaching. I. Byram, Michael.
II. Nichols, Adam, III. Stevens, David
P94.6.D48 2001
370.117–dc21   2001030233

British Library Cataloguing in Publication Data
A catalogue entry for this book is available from the British Library.

ISBN 1-85359-537-3 (hbk)
ISBN 1-85359-536-5 (pbk)

Multilingual Matters Ltd
UK: Frankfurt Lodge, Clevedon Hall, Victoria Road, Clevedon BS21 7HH.
USA: UTP, 2250 Military Road, Tonawanda, NY 14150, USA.
Canada: UTP, 5201 Dufferin Street, North York, Ontario M3H 5T8, Canada.
Australia: Footprint Books, Unit 4/92a Mona Vale Road, Mona Vale, NSW 2103, Australia.

Typeset by Exe Valley Dataset Ltd, Exeter, England.
Printed and bound in Great Britain by the Cromwell Press Ltd.

Contents

v

Foreword

This book fits with several aims of the book series Languages, Intercultural Communication and Education, most notably to provide studies of culture acquisition in pedagogical surroundings and to show how language teaching and learning can be structured and their methods developed.

Like many of the publications that are emerging in the field of Languages and Intercultural Communication, this book is both ambitious and unusual. It is not a traditional academic text, nor is it a textbook full of tips and tricks for teachers. It covers the full formal educational range from beginners to trainee teachers, as well as examining resources and new technologies that take learners beyond the classroom. It is not intended as an 'academic' text, although it is written by academics and teachers. Instead it provides a forum for reflection on the experience and practice of learning and teaching languages and intercultural competence. As such it is packed with inspiring and helpfully laid-out examples and descriptions of good, innovative practice from an impressive number of cultures and languages. This book will, I believe, be an invaluable resource for practitioners, who will recognise that there is nonetheless some important theoretical thinking implicit in the practices described.

One of the most striking aspects of the contributions to this project is the fact that, despite the different languages and cultures examined and the different provenance of the contributors, there is a common enthusiasm and excitement regarding intercultural discoveries made with learners, despite the often fraught practicalities that classroom situations and formal educational requirements can impose on innovative ideas. The reflections by teachers and learners have a freshness that is not overly constrained by theoretical reflection, ethical dilemmas or formal educational concerns. Rather the articles share an ability to leave memorable descriptions of learning experiences behind in the mind of the reader. To read this book is to discover whole new worlds of possibility that Languages and Intercultural Communication in practice is opening up world-wide and to be privileged to share in the first discoveries that these brave, even rash explorers have made. The mountains of Bulgaria, the care for the elderly in Denmark, the motivation of demotivated learners through technology, the excitement of virtual dialogue, the understanding of other geographies, the reading of literature, Christmas cards and visual media in new ways all open up possibilities for the learning and teaching of languages and intercultural communicative competence.

Intercultural communicative practice is a messy business. It involves much trial and error, according to these accounts. It does not fit neatly into a schema but it does have encouraging and stimulating stories to tell. The successes of these examples of good and innovative practice are not produced in ideal conditions, with large budgets or by genius teachers with eager learners. They are produced in hard and often difficult material circumstances that beset some educational systems, or in the time constraints that accompany adult learners, or in socially deprived areas that do not necessarily prioritise language learning. And they are produced by practitioners who have themselves developed intercultural communicative competence and have engaged directly with teachers and learners in and of other languages and cultures. The descriptions of intercultural practice have the potential to inspire and to provide support for those developing teaching in the field of Languages and Intercultural Communication.

ALISON PHIPPS

Introduction

MICHAEL BYRAM, ADAM NICHOLS AND DAVID STEVENS

The initial impulse for this book came from the requests of language teachers for examples of good practice. We hope, however, that much of what follows in the chapters of this book will also be of interest to teachers of other subjects that deal with social and cultural issues, whether in learners' own multicultural societies or in the study of other societies. The editors themselves are from different disciplines, and have sought to highlight the potential for disciplines and school subjects to learn from each other.

It is not very difficult to persuade language teachers that it is important to teach language-and-culture as an integrated whole, probably because the cultural dimension, referred to variously as 'background studies' in English, *civilisation* in French, *Landeskunde* in German, has long been part of the thinking of the language teaching profession even if it has not been part of its practice. Indeed many syllabi and guidelines refer to the importance of cultural learning and more recently intercultural competence, but there is still a lack of good practice, and insufficient attention to the cultural/intercultural dimension in teacher education, inspectors' reports and the like.

Perhaps this is an example of the significance of theory. Language teaching has in recent decades been much influenced by linguistics, pure and applied, and the impact on methods has been considerable. The introduction of notional and functional syllabi, the development of 'communicative language teaching' and the appearance of humanistic approaches can all be traced to theoretical work. Although many practitioners may not be aware of the underlying theory, there is no doubt that theory has impact, and that the impact has been on developing new ways of presenting language, of developing linguistic skills, of creating linguistic fluency as well as accuracy, of ensuring that learners know how to use language appropriately according to analyses of socio-linguistic practices.

Yet there is in fact no lack of theorising on the cultural dimension either, and some of it has been established for a long time, not least in

1

Germany where there is a long tradition of discussion of *Kulturkunde* and *Landeskunde*. This is not the place to trace the tradition, however, nor to discuss why the impact was weakened. Nor is it the place to analyse the ways in which social change, in the form of 'internationalisation' and 'globalisation', seems to have created the conditions for taking the cultural dimension seriously again.

What is important is that attempts to theorise and explain the integration of language and culture and the nature of intercultural understanding (for example Kramsch, 1993; Bredella, 1992; Zarate, 1993) have provided a renewed basis for practice. It is clearly not just an issue for the language teaching classroom.

Working Together in Theory and Practice

Our own work has been an illustration of this. It has involved a combination of theory and practice. *Teaching and Assessing Intercultural Communicative Competence* (Byram, 1997b) attempted deliberately to start from a 'top-down' perspective, to discuss what intercultural communicative competence (ICC) means and then to identify ways in which it could be formulated as teaching and assessment objectives. Then as teacher educators we have worked together to introduce trainee teachers of foreign languages, mother tongue and geography to ways in which they can develop interdisciplinary courses for students in schools. This has led us to exchanges with Bulgaria and the Czech Republic, and the former allowed us to discover the exciting work being done in Bulgarian schools, which we felt had to be presented in this book.

The invitations to other colleagues were issued whenever we came across what we thought was interesting work which would inspire other teachers. This happened by chance and there is no claim here that we have found all the interesting work which is developing, often quietly and modestly, in classrooms in many countries. It is, however, not important to be exhaustive in representing such work, even if it were possible, since we are not presenting the chapters of this book as models to be copied but as encouragement for other teachers. It is not possible or desirable simply to copy what one teacher does into another teacher's classroom, not even in the same education system let alone across different education systems. Teaching has to fit the occasion, the learners, the teacher's own style, as all experienced teachers know. The examples given here provide models of another sort, i.e. they embody principles and techniques which can be transferred to other situations, in language classes and beyond.

There are thus some common themes represented in the chapters in this book:

- the emphasis on learners becoming aware of and analysing the cultural phenomena of their own society as much as those of other societies;
- the development of skills of analysis and interpretation of unfamiliar social and cultural data from a foreign society;
- the opportunities to collect data for oneself, either by stepping outside the classroom into the society in which learners live, or at a distance with the help of old and new technology – the postal service is still a rival to the internet in this respect, and the potential of television is still to be fully developed;
- the use of literary texts to stimulate affective as well as cognitive understanding of otherness and the use of students' literary imagination.

The chapters which follow are almost all written by language teachers and focus on societies where the languages they teach are spoken. On the other hand, the chapter by Françoise Vigneron, who is also a linguist, demonstrates work where a foreign language is not involved. Similarly, the chapter by Eva Burwitz-Melzer could be readily adapted to children with English as their first language even though it was developed with learners for whom English is a foreign language. Indeed most of the chapters can be adapted to situations where a foreign language is not involved but where learners are acquiring an intercultural competence and awareness of otherness wherever it exists.

In the foreign language classroom, what was often seen as a problem in teaching the cultural dimension, the lack of opportunity to travel to a foreign country and society, should not inhibit teachers and learners at all. This is not because new technology can 'replace' first-hand experience, but rather because the cultural dimension has become the intercultural dimension. In other words, it is recognised that it is not the teacher's task to provide comprehensive information and to try to bring the foreign society into the classroom for learners to observe and experience vicariously. The task is rather to facilitate learners' interaction with some small part of another society and its cultures, with the purpose of relativising learners' understanding of their own cultural values, beliefs and behaviours, and encouraging them to investigate for themselves the otherness around them, either in their immediate physical environment or in their engagement with otherness which internationalisation and globalisation have brought into their world.

Furthermore, even where opportunity for foreign travel is available, either in the context of learning a foreign language or for example in a geography field trip, it is not self-evident that mere exposure to experience of a different culture will lead to understanding. It can in fact lead to resistance and rejection if the experience is not well prepared pedagogically and here too models of good practice are useful (Byram, 1997a; Byram & Zarate, 1995).

So to some extent teaching the intercultural dimension is a matter of seizing opportunities, being systematic in developing those opportunities – i.e. drawing on theory for help and guidance – and evaluating the results against clear and explicit criteria. This is what the teachers writing the chapters of this book have done, sometimes working alone, sometimes as part of a team. The opportunities come from the specific situation, and sometimes this involves working in the classroom, sometimes going outside the classroom either physically or with the help of technology. Sometimes the teaching materials are of a familiar kind – texts both factual and fictional – and sometimes the materials have to be collected and shaped by learners or teachers themselves. In many cases all of these are features of the lessons and courses described.

We have tried to organise the chapters to represent the writers' main emphasis, but most chapters could have been allocated to more than one section. To enable readers to browse across and beyond the simple classification we have used, there is a brief overview at the beginning of each chapter of its content and purpose. Each chapter also provides a list of references but in addition we asked contributors to tell us which books or articles they thought would be most useful for other teachers. There is in fact no lack and for any teachers coming to the intercultural dimension for the first time through this present book, we hope that they will develop their theoretical understanding, their classroom techniques and their course planning with the help of this list of Further Reading, presented at the end of the book.

Intercultural Competence

The concept of intercultural competence referred to in our title was not imposed on our contributors. They were asked to report on their practice and decided for themselves whether they would make explicit links with theory. Most have done so and some have referred to theory developed by one of the editors. A brief account of the definition of intercultural competence is therefore provided here for ease of reference.

Language teaching has long been dominated by theory transferred from analysis of how people learn their first language, and language teachers have long used the native speaker as a model for their learners and a benchmark against which to measure their linguistic abilities. This may be useful, although still contentious, with regard to linguistic/grammatical competence, but reflection on the nature of interaction between native speakers of a language and foreign speakers of that language, or again between foreign speakers of a language which is serving them as a lingua franca, has led to the recognition that it is neither appropriate nor desirable for learners to model themselves on native speakers with respect to the learning about and acquiring an understanding of another culture.

We have therefore introduced the concept of the 'intercultural speaker', someone who has an ability to interact with 'others', to accept other perspectives and perceptions of the world, to mediate between different perspectives, to be conscious of their evaluations of difference (Byram & Zarate, 1997; see also Kramsch, 1998). Where the otherness which learners meet is that of a society with a different language, they clearly need both linguistic competence and intercultural competence. Here we focus on intercultural competence which is necessary whether a different language is present or not.

The *components of intercultural competence* are knowledge, skills and attitudes, complemented by the values one holds because of one's belonging to a number of social groups, values which are part of one's belonging to a given society.

The foundation of intercultural competence is in the *attitudes* of the intercultural speaker and mediator:

> *Intercultural attitudes (savoir être)*: curiosity and openness, readiness to suspend disbelief about other cultures and belief about one's own. This means a willingness to relativise one's own values, beliefs and behaviours, not to assume that they are the only possible and naturally correct ones, and to be able to see how they might look from the perspective of an outsider who has a different set of values, beliefs and behaviours. This can be called the ability to 'decentre'.

Another crucial factor is *knowledge*, not primarily knowledge about a specific culture, but rather knowledge of how social groups and social identities function, both one's own and others. If it can be anticipated with whom one will interact, then knowledge of that person's world is useful. If it cannot, then it is useful to imagine an interlocutor in order to have an example of what it means to know something about other people with other multiple identities:

Knowledge (savoirs): of social groups and their products and practices in one's own and in one's interlocutor's country, and of the general processes of societal and individual interaction. So knowledge can be defined as having two major components: knowledge of social processes, and knowledge of illustrations of those processes and products; the latter includes knowledge about how other people see oneself as well as some knowledge about other people.

No teacher can have or anticipate all the knowledge which learners might at some point need. Indeed many teachers have not had the opportunity themselves to experience all or any of the cultures which their learners might encounter. There are however *skills* which are just as important as attitudes and knowledge, and teachers can concentrate as much on skills as upon knowledge.

Because intercultural speakers/mediators need to be able to see how misunderstandings can arise, and how they might be able to resolve them, they need the attitudes of decentring but also the skills of comparing. By putting ideas, events, documents side by side and seeing how each might look from the other perspective, intercultural speakers/mediators can see how people might misunderstand what is said or written or done by someone with a different social identity. The *skills of comparison, of interpreting and relating*, are therefore crucial:

Skills of interpreting and relating (savoir comprendre): ability to interpret a document or event from another culture, to explain it and relate it to documents or events from one's own.

Secondly, because neither intercultural speakers/mediators nor their teachers can anticipate all their knowledge needs, it is equally important to acquire the skills of finding out new knowledge and integrating it with what they already have. They need especially to know how to ask people from other cultures about their beliefs, values and behaviours; these can be difficult to explain because they are often unconscious. So intercultural speakers/mediators need *skills of discovery and interaction*:

Skills of discovery and interaction (savoir apprendre/faire): ability to acquire new knowledge of a culture and cultural practices and the ability to operate knowledge, attitudes and skills under the constraints of real-time communication and interaction.

Finally, however open towards, curious about and tolerant of other people's beliefs, values and behaviours one is, one's own beliefs, values and behaviours are deeply embedded and can create reaction and rejection. Because of this unavoidable response, intercultural speakers/ mediators need to become aware of their own *values* and how these influence their views of other people's values. Intercultural speakers/ mediators need a critical awareness of themselves and their values, as well as those of other people:

> *Critical cultural awareness* (*savoir s'engager*): an ability to evaluate, critically and on the basis of explicit criteria, perspectives, practices and products in one's own and other cultures and countries.

It is not the purpose of teaching to try to change learners' values, but to make them explicit and conscious in any evaluative response to others. There is nonetheless a fundamental values position which all language teaching should promote: a position which *acknowledges respect for human dignity and equality of human rights as the democratic basis for social interaction.*

The role of the teacher is therefore to develop skills, attitudes and awareness of values just as much as to develop a knowledge of a particular culture or country, or of different cultures within one's own country.

Irrespective of whether they have drawn on this particular framework, the following chapters will show how teachers have responded to this new role, and with their professional imagination and experience introduced into their work an intercultural dimension which is innovative and which takes teaching a step further.

We think too that the sharp distinctions which have separated language teaching from other subjects can be easily broken down as teachers of languages, whether first, second or foreign, and teachers of geography, sociology, literature and other social and human sciences see their common ground in the understanding of otherness and self which they share as an educational aim.

References

Bredella, L. (1992) Towards a pedagogy of intercultural understanding. *Amerika-studien 37,* 559–94.

Byram, M. (1997a) *Face to Face: Learning Language-and-Culture through Visits and Exchanges.* London: CILT.

Byram, M. (1997b) *Teaching and Assessing Intercultural Communicative Competence.* Clevedon: Multilingual Matters.

Byram, M. and Zarate, G. (1995) *Young People Facing Difference: Some Proposals for Teachers.* Strasbourg: Council of Europe.

Byram, M. and Zarate, G. (1997) Definitions, objectives and assessment of socio-cultural competence. In M. Byram, G. Zarate and G. Neuner (eds) *Sociocultural Competence in Language Learning and Teaching*. Strasbourg: Council of Europe.

Kramsch, C. (1998) The privilege of the intercultural speaker. In M. Byram and M. Fleming (eds) *Language Learning in Intercultural Perspective*. Cambridge: Cambridge University Press.

Kramsch, C. (1993) *Context and Culture in Language Teaching*. Oxford: Oxford University Press.

Zarate, G. (1993) *Représentations de l'étranger et didactique des langues*. Paris: Hachette.

Part 1

In the Classroom

Chapter 1

The International Partnership Project

CAROL MORGAN

This chapter describes a project in which children from two countries prepared materials to send to a partner class in another country. They were asked to focus on the topic of 'law and order' and what it means for them. The explanations and discussions during the preparation and on receipt of the package reveal a developing intercultural awareness and reflection on their own cultural world as well as learning about others.

Introduction

The 'effectiveness' of learning in a foreign language classroom is often seen in terms of the choice of materials which are 'good' with respect to their relevance, linguistic level, authenticity, interest and so on, and 'good' activities that promote interactivity, autonomy and challenge (Ur, 1996; Swarbrick, 1994). Even where learning is concerned with inter-cultural awareness, a materials/activities focus still appears to be dominant (Jones, 1995; Tomalin & Stempelski, 1993).

The project which is described in this chapter where students exchanged self-made materials takes a rather different perspective in focusing on the process and experience of decoding a culture. The two main aims of the project which we trialled were:

- to explore a particular cultural focus in depth, using both home and foreign cultures: in other words to provide an ethnographic experience;
- to mirror the interactive or dialogic experience of learning: in other words to learn with and from others.

The Context of the Project

Our project was trialled twice with two different student age-groups: in an Anglo-French partnership with 14-year-olds and in an Anglo-

Austrian partnership with 17-year-olds.[1] The detailed description that follows is of the first Anglo-French trial but thoughts from the other projects have also been included where appropriate. The first trial had several factors in its favour:

- as a researcher (and teacher) I had funding to cover time and travel to set up the project and to interview students as well as to observe them;
- the teacher in England who participated had worked with me previously on a Master's dissertation on cultural awareness teaching (see Braham, 1995); she and the students in her school were already trained and experienced in cultural awareness activities;
- we were able to locate an interested French partnership school relatively easily;
- a researcher in France worked with me during the project and afterwards as a 'cultural friend'.

(A discussion of how these benefits might be replicated is included in the final section of this chapter.)

Two secondary schools participated in this first trial: one in England and one in France, with one set of students from each school. Both schools were situated in small provincial towns and drew on a largely white middle-class catchment area. Both schools at that time catered for the 11–15/16 age-group and the schools and classes were of mixed ability.

The two age groups chosen were similar: 'Year 9' (13–14 year olds) in England and '*la troisième*' (14–15 year olds) in France. The class of '*la troisième*' may have enjoyed a slightly superior status, since it is the top year of the '*collège*' lower secondary system in France. In England, 'Year 9' is in the middle of the lower secondary band. The difference in status of the two groups may have had some effect on their attitudes to the project. For example, the French students sometimes appeared more competitive. One pupil enquired: 'on enverra trois trucs . . . aux anglais, ou alors, on choisira l'meilleur?' (shall we send three things to the English pupils or shall we choose the best one? – my translation).

The English students were following the National Curriculum guidelines for Key Stage 3 (ages 11–14) (DfEE, 1995) where teachers monitor linguistic ability according to prescribed levels. Culture awareness, though recommended as a desirable competence, is currently not assessed (see Morgan, 1995). The French students in following the *collège* teaching and learning guidelines were likewise encouraged to consider cultural aspects but without this being part of any formal assessment.

Each class was asked to prepare a package of materials to send to their partner classroom in the other country. These materials were to explain and illustrate a particular cultural topic (we chose 'law and order') in the students' own country and were to be written in the students' mother tongue. The same topic was chosen for both sets of students, and the packages were prepared at the same time. In addition 'help-sheets' were prepared in the mother tongue of the receiving classroom (i.e. in a foreign language for the sending classroom). These help-sheets highlighted and explained potential difficulties in the package materials, covering both language and culture problems. In this first trial, I produced these help-sheets myself, using the information I gained from interviewing the pupils about their materials. This activity would ideally be undertaken by the teacher in collaboration with the students.

The key features of the project which emerged were as follows:

- the students had to explore their own cultural context;
- they then had to present this cultural information in a format that would be accessible in the receiving classroom;
- each set of students both sent and received a package of materials focused on the same topic; these packages represented two different cultural approaches to the topic and were in different languages;
- students had much greater freedom than usual in a foreign language classroom because they were writing in their own language and choosing their own medium;
- the materials generated were truly authentic in that the communication was between students of roughly the same age, and the language and constructs being used were not 'filtered' through institutional media (the textbook or the teacher for example);
- the teacher acted as a facilitator in setting up the project, but did not decide on the content and format of the materials.

The choice of topic (law and order) linked into ideas explored in another project (see Duffy and Mayes, this volume) on how best to explore another culture. In this earlier project a list of twelve key areas was identified in sociology upper secondary syllabuses, including 'deviance' with the sub-areas of 'social order/social control' and 'law-enforcement agencies'.

In England the whole Year 9 class participated (27 students). Students worked for a week on preparing materials (two double lessons and one single lesson, three hours in total), and then spent two lessons discussing the package from France a week later. In France I took six students out of three of their normal English lessons (50 minutes each) to help them prepare the materials. Just over two weeks later, the English package was discussed by the whole French class with their teacher and myself and then in separate lesson time (50 minutes) with myself and the six students who had prepared the French package.

In the preparatory sessions and follow-up lessons a variety of linked activities took place and these are described in the appropriate sections below.

Preparing the Materials

Although the materials preparation stage took roughly the same period of time in both classrooms, the situations differed. In the English classroom, this kind of cultural awareness activity was relatively familiar, although students were breaking with their normal National Curriculum timetable. The whole class taking part availed themselves of a wide range of resources. In France for the six students taken out of their class, the activity was unfamiliar and resources were not so easily available.

I was not with the English class during their preparation stage, although I interviewed several students a few days later about what they had done. In France I helped and taught the six students in preparing their package.

In France the preparation stage seemed to divide itself into three different steps: orientation; self-organisation into groups and exploration of ideas and media; and execution of the materials and help-sheets.The whole of the preparation stage was also characterised by a growing awareness and reflexivity.

Orientation

The main orientation activities with the French group took place in the first 50-minute session and here there were three main activities.

Firstly we did an orientation exercise that alerted students to the topic content. We used the five-word ('cinq mots') associative technique pioneered by Cain (1990). Students were asked to write down the first five words they thought of linked to the topic of 'law and order'. The following key words were produced (individual lists are given in Appendix 1:1): *police* (×5), *justice* (×5), *prison* (×4), *discipline* (×2), *legal* (×2) and single mentions of *hierarchy, respect, courts of law, constitution, verdicts, trial, criminals, breaking and entering* and *chasing* (after criminals).

Students were then given the opportunity to explore their own ideas or constructs and to 'get in the mood' for what they were going to do (what

Cuff and Sharrock call 'pre-beginning activities', 1985). These lists also provided useful extra material for the receiving classroom to work with (see the following section). It is interesting that the students' constructs were evident in the texts that they produced later (all the texts featured the police, for example) and also that there was an interest in abstract ideas. Further comments by the French students in this first session confirmed these areas of interest: 'C'est l'ordre dans la vie générale ou dans le collège ou . . .?'; 'Non, dans la vie générale, ça serait mieux'; 'on recherche dans les livres sur la justice et tout ça, et puis trouver . . . faire des photocopies . . .' ('Is it order in general or in school or . . .?'; 'No, in general would be better'; 'we could look in books about justice and all that and find some . . . make photocopies' – my translation).

As well as the topic orientation with the five-word technique, I also discussed at length the notion of school rules – what were the reasons for these and what rules would students make for themselves. Again this exercise alerted students to the topic content and the information was used later in the English classroom as part of the follow-up activities, once the French package had been received.

A third orientation perspective was that of getting pupils to think about their audience. One student commented for example: 'Avec les dessins ça va aller vachement les aider' (having pictures will really be a terrific help to them – my translation). When I talked to the English students later some of them also commented on how they had considered ways of writing for their audience: 'You had to change what you wrote down to make it more simple . . . I suppose I thought about how the French must find it . . . When I was writing it, I thought "Will they understand it?"'; 'I tried to make sure that nothing was too difficult and we didn't use too much slang because they [the French students] might not know some slang or difficult words'; 'We tried not to speak too quickly as well [on the audio tape]. I know if someone was speaking very quickly in French it would be hard to understand it.' I was not present with the English class when they were preparing their materials. However, one could say that these English students were already oriented towards the notion of cultural awareness because of the previous work they had done with their teacher.

Self-organisation and exploration of ideas and media

The six students in France quickly organised themselves into gender and friendship groups (one group of two girls and one group of four boys). This was also the case in the English classroom where there were eight single-gender groups ranging in size from two to four students. There is some wisdom in allowing students to work together in small groups (Morgan, 1996a): students can support each other and extend their ideas in discussion. The French students discussed various ideas (making a film of a court of law, finding songs about law and order, finding out information about the judicial system) before coming up with their final ideas:

- a series of cartoons which portrayed incidents relating to law and order;
- a caricature to demonstrate the opposite of law and order, in this case traffic chaos (see Appendix 1.2).

The students were allowed to make an entirely free choice of an aspect of law and order and of their preferred medium. This was also the case in England where the students produced nine items (one group making two texts). The English texts were:

- a questionnaire to be sent to the French pupils relating to all the other eight English texts, eliciting opinions and asking comprehension questions (Appendix 1.3);
- a video of a sketch portraying a series of traffic offences (Appendix 1.4);
- an audio-taped sketch relating tales of bullying and flouting of school rules;
- a picture-documentary of police uniforms and equipment (both English and American);
- an audio-tape of a series of sketches demonstrating different roles of the police;
- a photo-documentary of the English school demonstrating all the different rules operating there (school rules, rules for the school bus, the role of prefects, school uniform etc.);
- a board game of 'cops and robbers' with questions relating to laws on age-limits for smoking, drinking etc.;
- a photocopy of descriptions of television programmes featuring the police taken from a television guide;
- a word search puzzle with words relating to different kinds of television programmes.

It is noticeable that the English group produced very diverse products (see, for example, Appendices 1.3 and 1.4). It is also important to note that there was no teacher intervention and media other than information technology (IT) were used.

It would be very tempting for teachers to set up the materials exchange project with structured guidelines for the students (this after all is a useful basis for many other teaching and learning activities). This would block one of the major project objectives, though, namely that the pupils experience a sense of cultural awareness through having to make choices and difficult decisions.

The use of IT and particularly the internet already facilitates quick and easy communication between classrooms but there can also be limitations: there may be a limited range of options available and there is noticeable lack of physicality (the sound of the children's voices on tape, hand-written scripts, hand-drawn pictures, the paper and card used – the photo-documentary for example used a complicated folded format for its text where each section unfolded from the next).

Final production of materials

Perhaps the most important factor here is that students are given a sufficiently long period of time to explore ideas and create their materials. In both French and English classrooms, students had several days when they were involved. They also spent some time gathering materials outside the classroom. The French boys' group, for example, photocopied material from five different cartoon sources and brought these to the lesson (*Mickey, Tuniques Bleues, Lucky Luke, Asterix* and *Gaston la Gaffe*). Comments from the English group in interviews also give some flavour of the students' perception of their involvement: 'First of all we went round all the groups and asked them what their little bit of the project was about and then we adapted the questions to what would be good about it and then put them in sections about all the different things . . . we thought we'd have "Did you enjoy your project?" first' (student producing questionnaire); 'We thought about doing jokes first of all, but we didn't know enough. Then we thought about doing a play and we couldn't think of enough things to do, so then we came up with a series of sketches about situations where police were needed' (student producing audio-tapes).

Students seemed to need a period of interim indecision and false starts in order to find their own voice. Intra-group discussions at this stage were highly valuable since this was the moment when students questioned what is culturally important and what are good modes of presentation.

As well as preparing the text, we also needed to produce explanatory help-sheets in the target language, as mentioned above.

Reflexivity

A key development in the preparatory stage is that students can become aware of a deeper level of significance of things within in their own culture, and in this way prepare themselves for understanding another culture. Throughout the time spent with the French and English students, I interviewed individual students (the six in France and 12 of the 27 in England) eliciting their views on the experience of the project and asking for explanations of different aspects of the texts. These views were then used to create the accompanying help-sheets. Comments from the interviews also give some indication of growing reflexivity and awareness.

The French girls had taken a relatively sophisticated view of law and order by portraying the police as instigators of disorder: 'On a voulu faire une caricature . . . c'est pour faire le contraire . . . c'est un dessin humoristique . . . c'est pour dire qu'ils arrivent en retard toujours les policiers, ils sont jamais là quand il faut . . . c'est le contraire, le désordre' (we wanted to do a caricature to show the opposite, it's a humorous drawing . . . to show that the police always arrive too late, they're never there when you need them . . . it's the opposite, lack of order – my translation).

The French boys were able to explain the symbolic value of many of the features of the cartoons: the iconic figures, the play on words, the fact that the policeman was a symbol for the law: 'le symbole de la loi . . . la loi, c'est le policier'.

In the English classroom there was an even higher level of reflexivity. Thus, one student was able to empathise with a possible reaction from the French pupils to English school uniform and to accommodate a multiple perspective herself:

Researcher: What do you think the French might think about school uniform?

Student: They wouldn't like it because they're used to wearing the clothes they want to wear and don't have to wear one set of clothes every day.

Researcher: Do you think they might think it looks really strange?

Student: Everyone looking the same, yes. Only the heads are different really. I think they'd find it strange. Not peculiar, but all like soldiers really.

Researcher: Yes. How do you think you might be able to explain the reason for it?

Student: So that we all look smart and belong to one school.

Another student reflected on ways of presenting ideas and what the process of materials preparation had meant to her: 'I was going to do a demonstration on something like animal rights but I thought that would be too controversial . . . it would be difficult to do a sketch because if you're trying to teach someone a point and they've got divided opinions then you can't really get through the message clearly . . . it [doing the project] actually made me think a lot more about how the law is practised in England and all the different roles a policeman would have. Before I was just thinking basically of a policeman going out and patrolling the streets but now that I've thought about it I can see a lot more situations.'

Receiving the Materials

I was with both sets of students when they received the packages from their partner classrooms. Activities in the English classroom were generally more successful than those in France for several reasons: all the class had participated (in France the other 25 students had not been involved); the students were already familiar with cultural awareness activities; and the teacher allowed discussion in the mother tongue (in France, much of the lesson was in the target language).

In the two follow-up lessons that I observed in England the following activities took place:

Lesson 1 (70 minutes)
- A discussion of the French materials in groups (these were the same 'production' groups formed earlier) with comments written down and presented.
- A class discussion on several different points relating to law and order. For example, how would you register protest if you had to come into school to do an extra three hours of Religious Education on a Saturday morning? How do the French protest? (an instance of this was part of the French boys' cartoon text). How do people protest about animal rights and what different views of the rights of animals exist in France and England?
- Groups wrote down five words to describe the police and then presented these (given in Appendix 1.5)
- A discussion of the groups of five words produced by the French students.

Lesson 2 (35 minutes)
- Distribution of a typed list of school rules from the French school and possible reasons for rules. Students were asked to link up rules and reasons.

- A discussion of rules in the students' own school and a comparison of the two schools.
- Introduction provided by the teacher on how a school in France operates.
- Playing the French students' audio-taped answers to the question-naire (Appendix 1.3).

In both lessons, awareness was raised of differences in attitudes in France and England towards law and order when this was embodied by the police, particularly in terms of being respected or not. The five-words technique was noted as being helpful here. One student commented: 'I liked talking about the words they came up with. When we suggested the words, I felt it was expressing other people's opinions [from the group] not just yours.'

The English students also became aware of the more pervasive presence of cartoons in France and their popularity, whereas in England comics or cartoons were not popular for their age-group.

Students thus gained some cultural information about France; they were able to observe both intercultural and intracultural differences in attitudes and began to recognise possible differences in modes of presentation.

In the lesson in France (50 minutes):

- the six students talked about their texts;
- the English texts were distributed and discussed;
- the question of school rules in general was discussed: their origin and rationale and possible alternatives;
- the video-text was played (Appendix 1.4) and the teacher asked questions and gave information on traffic offences in the UK.

In the individual session (50 minutes) with the six students that I ran myself, we had a wide-ranging discussion of the materials and related issues including school uniform and homework diaries. Students particularly liked the audio-tape with sketches because of its lively presentation style: 'c'est vivant, quoi . . . ils mettent le ton' (it's really lively . . . they create the mood – my translation). The students also prepared answers to the questionnaire [Appendix 1.3] and we taped them saying the questions and answers. Issues that were of particular interest were the strictness of the school system as shown in the texts about school rules: 'It is very strict. C'est nul' (It's rubbish); 'C'est trop strict' (It's too strict)'; 'On se croirait à l'armée' (You'd think you were in the army). The lack of privacy of homework diaries was also deplored: 'Tout le monde peut le regarder . . . on a même pas le droit de marquer ce qu'on veut dedans. C'est nul' (Everyone can look at it. You haven't even the right to mark what you want in it. It's rubbish).

The French pupils here then felt that the freedom that they enjoyed in their own classrooms was superior and that the imposition of law and order in the English classroom was unacceptable. On the whole then there was less intercultural understanding demonstrated.

The unfamiliarity of the exercise and the more fragmented nature of the class experience may have contributed to the lower level of engagement of the French students at the 'receiving' stage of the project. Nevertheless there was a high level of commitment in creating the materials and interest voiced by the six group members: 'C'est bien'; 'C'est intéressant'; 'C'est marrant' (it's good; it's interesting; it's fun).

Amongst the English students, clear benefits were identified by the pupils themselves both in producing and receiving materials: 'It's good. We feel they're relying on your information. You're explaining what goes on in your country'; 'It's really different and interesting and you find out about different cultures'; 'In textbooks it's second hand but this is straight from the children'.

Although this intercultural project had initially been set up with a primary focus on the reception of authentic ethnographic materials from another culture, it appeared in fact that it was in the production stage that the most valuable experiences took place. Certainly in an interview with one of the project students four years later, it was the production of the materials that she remembered as significant.

Evaluation and Future Developments

Three major areas of difficulty emerged during the trial which present areas for future development:

- the role of the teacher as ethnographer and facilitator;
- the use of the mother tongue in a foreign language lesson;
- handling inaccuracies in language and information.

The teacher plays a different role in this project, compared to the usual role where he or she takes the major decisions regarding structures and activities. Support and training for the teacher can be useful because of this. Not only does the teacher facilitate rather than directly teach but also ethnographic skills are required in decoding both the home and foreign cultures. Future developments planned for the project include special teacher training in the area of intercultural understanding. Also, because of the higher demands in terms of lateral thinking and empathy on the part of both the teacher and students, it is likely that this kind of project will be most effective as a later activity if teachers are planning a cultural awareness programme of learning.

The use of the mother tongue in a foreign language classroom may be a more difficult problem to overcome in that many national curricula insist on a high level of target language use, consistent with current communicative approaches. In our trial we were lucky that the teacher saw the benefits of using the mother tongue and had sufficient autonomy in her institution to be able to follow an alternative route.

The question of inaccuracies in student texts is another area to be considered. These can be handled in different ways. Clearly where there are spelling or grammatical mistakes these can be corrected before packages are sent off, especially where texts are word-processed. Where students' 'vision' of a topic contains inaccurate information or an unusual interpretation (the music hall flavour of the video text scene at the police station for example – Appendix 1.4), then it may be useful for the teachers in the two countries to provide their own help-sheets for each other, pointing out anomalies. It is also possible to envisage pupils' perceptions of reality themselves becoming discussion points.

There remains though the question of the transferability of this project in terms of its suitability for other schools and other age-groups. It is useful to select year-groups where some time can be taken out from any strict curriculum programme. The 14-year-old age-group seemed a good choice since they had no major examination pressure at the time of the project. For teachers in Europe, the European Union COMENIUS programme may be able to support such a project, and the help of other members of staff (including other disciplines with an interest in intercultural understanding, such as the Humanities) can also act as valuable sources of support. The pupil interviews proved an invaluable source of information in accessing pupils' own constructs of law and order so it will be helpful to consider ways of replicating these, perhaps using a foreign language assistant or arranging for interviews via e-mail. Later exchanges between pupils via fax, telephone or e-mail could also provide further developmental possibilities.

In general, though, despite potentially problematic areas our project was enthusiastically received and appeared to bring about some development in cultural awareness. One considerable advantage is that much can be achieved using resources that are already available (as can been seen from the examples provided). In this way students can build from the foundations of what they know, try to defamiliarise these resources in considering their partner audience, and thus prepare themselves for a further level of intercultural engagement with the foreign culture.

Appendix 1.1 The French Students' Five Words Associated with 'Law and Order'

Student 1	la discipline	Student 4	le respect
	la hierarchie		les jugements
	la police		les effractions
	la prison		les poursuites
	la justice		la prison
Student 2	la justice	Student 5	la justice
	la police		légal
	la discipline		la police
	les tribuneaux		le procès
Student 3	la prison	Student 6	la prison
	la justice		la constitution
	la police		la police
	les malfaiteurs		légal
			la justice

Appendix 1.2 The French Students' Caricature of Traffic Chaos

Appendix 1.3   The English Students' Questionnaire (with Some French Students' Answers in Italics)

- Did you enjoy our project?
  Yes, it was very interesting

- Which was your favourite cassette?
  The cassette which explained English laws

- What did you learn from the cassettes?
  1 *About police: first we learned all the different laws people have to respect and for each law, one example, which was very useful*
  2 *About St Augustine's rules: We think these laws are very strict and not funny at all*
  3 *About the video: It was very funny to learn the strict laws this way*

- What is your opinion of our school rules?
  We think it's old-fashioned and very strict

- Which school rules are the same as yours?
  No swearing; no chewing; no running; no fighting

- Do you agree with our school rules?
  Not at all

- At our school do we have homework diaries?
  We can choose the diary we want. We can decorate it as much as we want

- What do you think of our school uniform?
  We don't like it. We think it's old-fashioned

- What colour are our pullovers?
  They're maroon

- Is driving through a red light a crime in Britain?

- What side of the road do British drivers drive on?

- What is the speed limit on British motorways?

- Did you enjoy the scripts for the role plays?

- Which script do you prefer?

- What was your overall opinion of our project?

Appendix 1.4 Transcription of the English Students' Video of a Traffic Offence Sketch

Murray [in car]: I wonder if this baby can do eighty-five. Won't do it again. Try it though. Going quite fast. I'm hungry. I'll go to McDonald's.

Policeman: Hello, hello, hello, hello. What have we here then? Parked on double yellow lines I see.

Murray: Sir, sir.

Policeman: Is this your car then?

Murray: No.

Policeman: It is, isn't it? You've parked on double yellow lines. You've been through a red light and you're speeding. What have you got to say to that?

Murray: Ehm . . .

Policeman: Right. What's your name?

Murray: Murray.

Policeman: Murray . . .?

Murray: Murray Wood.

Policeman: Where do you live then?

Murray: 32, Manor Road

Policeman: Right. We're going to have to take you down to the station. The officers here will be there to take down details. [On the mobile phone] I'm bringing him in boys. Be ready!

[Puts handcuffs on Murray and takes him to the police-station]

Sergeant: Hello, what have we here then!

Policeman: We've got a young joy-rider, child prodigy. Thinks he's the real bees' knees.

Sergeant [*to Murray*]:	Take a seat.
Murray:	Sir.
Policeman:	So where were you on the night of the 21st?
Sergeant:	The 21st!
Murray:	I don't know. I'm not speaking till I've got a fag.

[*Murray smokes*]

Murray:	I was in the car.
Sergeant:	And . . .?
Murray:	Speeding, going through a red light. I was joy-riding.
Sergeant:	Ooh! We have you now, you dirty swine!
Policeman:	You dirty swine!
Murray:	What's going to happen to me?
Policeman:	We're going to lock you up.
Sergeant:	And throw away the key!
Policeman:	And throw away the key!
Sergeant:	The key!
Murray [*slumps forward again*]:	Oh!
Sergeant:	And you could end up in jail
Policeman:	In jail!
Sergeant:	In jail!
Murray:	In jail! But what about my mum! She'll kill me!

[*Sergeant laughs*]

Appendix 1.5 The English Students' Five Words to Describe the Police

Group 1	helpful control brave discriminated against	**Group 4**	conservative respected effective smart
Group 2	punishment strict caring thoughtful	**Group 5**	respected scary fit effective fast
Group 3	crooked/bent restrained smart efficient glorified	**Group 6**	suspicious respectful [respected] faithful loyal dedicated

Note

1. More detailed descriptions of the Anglo-French project can be found in Morgan and Cain, 2000 and of the Anglo-Austrian project in Morgan and Penz, 1998.

References

Braham, C. (1995) Desired ideal or current reality. Unpublished MA dissertation: University of Bath.

Cain, A. (1990) French secondary school students' perception of foreign cultures. *Language Learning Journal* 2, 48–52.

Cuff, E. and Sharrock, W. (1985) Meetings. In T. van Dijk (ed.) *Handbook of Discourse Analysis: Volume 3 Discourse and Dialogue*. London: Academic Press.

DfEE (1995) *Modern Foreign Languages in the National Curriculum*. London: HMSO.

Jones, B. (1995) *Exploring Otherness: An Approach to Cultural Awareness*. London: Centre for Information on Language Teaching and Research.

Morgan, C. (1995) Cultural awareness and the National Curriculum. *Language Learning Journal* 12, 9–12.

Morgan, C. (1996a) Creative writing in the foreign language classroom. In L. Thompson (ed.) *The Teaching of Poetry: European Perspectives*. London: Cassell.

Morgan, C. (1996b) The interview as a measure of cross-cultural competence. *Language, Culture and Curriculum* 9 (3), 225–242.

Morgan, C. and Cain, A. (2000) *Foreign Language and Culture: Teaching from a Dialogic Perspective*. Clevedon: Multilingual Matters.

Morgan, C. and Penz, H. (1998) Dialogic foreign language learning. In J. Ciglar-Zaniz, D. Kalogjera and J. Jemersic (eds) *Cross-Cultural Challenges: Dialogues in Action.* Zagreb: British Council.

Swarbrick, A. (ed.) (1994) *Teaching Modern Languages.* London: Routledge in association with the Open University.

Tomalin, B. and Stempelski, S. (1993) *Cultural Awareness.* Oxford: Oxford University Press.

Ur, P. (1996) *A Course in Language Teaching: Practice and Theory.* Cambridge: Cambridge University Press.

Chapter 2

Teaching Intercultural Communicative Competence through Literature

EVA BURWITZ-MELZER

Students in a secondary school read a story which introduced them to an unfamiliar experience and they were asked through a range of techniques to respond to the story from different perspectives and to identify and understand aspects of a foreign culture in the story. The assessment of their understanding was carried out against specific criteria. The chapter shows how a literary text can be used to develop an understanding of otherness.

Introduction

For several reasons, fictional texts are suitable for developing intercultural communicative competence in pupils of all ages. Not only do they invite their readers to view subjectively a nation or an ethnic group by portraying specific values, prejudices and stereotypes, but they also offer their audience the chance to exchange their culturally restricted points of view together with the hero or heroine of the narrative, or with the narrator telling the story. Fictional texts guide their readers through the reading process focusing their attention not only on actions and characters (Rosenblatt, 1981; Bredella, 1996). The 'efferent reading' of fictional texts, a special way of reading fictional texts 'aesthetically' (Rosenblatt, 1981; Bredella, 1996), enables and strengthens the readers' interaction with the text, their predicting abilities, their emotional responses, as well as their forming and re-forming of hypotheses during the reading process, all of which are necessary to fill the text with meaning. These ideas, based on concepts of literary receptionist theory, imply that teachers work with a story or poem in class not only on a cognitive but also on an affective level, offering analytical and creative tasks to arrive at a deeper understanding of the text. Often creative tasks lend themselves to a blend of literary and intercultural objectives, leaving enough space and an 'anxiety-free' zone for the learners in which they can experiment with different perspectives and culturally different points of view as well as compare their own culture to the culture in the text.

The following case study deals with a sequence of four English lessons which were videotaped in the ninth grade of a German secondary modern branch (*Hauptschule*) of a comprehensive school (*Gesamtschule*) with 14/15-year-old pupils. The school has about 1,300 pupils and is situated in a small industrial town on the outskirts of Frankfurt am Main. In this class there are eleven boys and fourteen girls aged 14 or 15. Though the school has about 30% non-German pupils, there was only one non-German pupil in this particular class.

The subject of the lessons is the short story 'The Circuit' by Francisco Jimenez, a story about a family of Mexican migrant workers who are illegally staying in the United States. The lessons will be described briefly, emphasising the teacher's methods, the various tasks and the pupils' performances, some of which will be rendered and analysed in full detail to demonstrate the actual intercultural potential of story and tasks.

The Intercultural Objectives for This Unit

Writers on the subject have found it difficult to define intercultural objectives for the foreign language classroom clearly and unambiguously, though numerous attempts in this direction have been published. In 1990 Knapp and Knapp-Potthoff published one of the first lists of intercultural objectives, which led to a vivid discussion about which has priority, linguistic and discourse competence or sociolinguistic aims and political awareness (Edmondson & House, 1998; Hu, 1999). The most important and comprehensive model is, however, the catalogue of objectives referring to the assessment and evaluation of pupils' intercultural communicative competence (Byram, 1997). Based on a model of foreign language teaching that provides pupils with linguistic, sociolinguistic and discourse competences, Byram suggests that the learner should become an intercultural speaker instead of aiming at a near-native capacity (Byram, 1997; Byram & Cain, 1998; Kramsch, 1998) and arrives at a catalogue of objectives that includes skills, attitudes, knowledge and educational factors in teaching intercultural competence. Yet, his model is an all-encompassing one that cannot easily fit into most European national or school curricula. Singling out some of its parts, however, would deprive the model of its consistency.

Other attempts to assess intercultural learning aim at the description of special methods of teaching intercultural communication, like, for example, ethnographic projects (Byram & Cain, 1998; Barro, Jordan & Roberts, 1998), lessons based on informative texts or other authentic material (Tomalin & Stempleski, 1993) and lessons based on the teaching of literature (Bredella, 1997a; Schewe, 1998; Schinschke, 1995). In most cases, however, the formulation of objectives remains somewhat vague (Bredella, 1997b; Nünning, 1997; Seletzky, 1996), leaving teachers at a loss as to what to expect from their learners, how to structure their lessons and how to assess their pupils' achievements. The following intercultural objectives for literature-based EFL (English as a foreign language) lessons have been tested during my empirical work, which involved fifteen case studies of classes 6 to 10 in twelve German secondary schools. The objectives aim at a combination of abstract criteria – as can be found in publications like Byram (1997: 57) – with objectively observable behaviour. Thus, a teacher can verify and assess the learners' attempts to solve various tasks. In most classes, a meta-phase at the end of a teaching unit allows learners to look back on and discuss their own progress and their learning process in the field of intercultural learning. As far as possible, my definitions of objectives include observable behaviour, i.e. learners' actions, answers, texts, etc. It cannot be avoided that these intercultural objectives often overlap with educational or linguistic ones, which is, however, irrelevant here. The catalogue shown in Table 2.1 contains two lists linking definitions to observable behaviour.

The Text

For the videotaped lessons, the short story 'The Circuit', by Francisco Jimenez, was used. It is a story about a large family of Mexican migrant workers who are illegally moving from one harvest site in the American South to the next one. All their belongings fit into a ramshackle car, the huge pot in which all family meals are cooked being strapped on top of it. In the first person narrative, Panchito, the second eldest child of the family, describes his life between swiftly changing harvest sites and equally rapidly changing schools. It is a new kind of experience for him as a non-native speaker in American schools, surrounded by children who are strangers and reject him, that a kind teacher not only offers him help in class with his English but also starts teaching him to play the trumpet. If it were not for his situation, Panchito would have a lot to look forward to in school, but he fears the day when he will have to leave again. In the end, he returns from school full of plans and expectations only to see his family round the car packed to leave once again.

Table 2.1   Objectives and observed behaviour

Objects: the learners . . .	Observed behaviour: the learners . . .
1. can identify and recognise elements from foreign cultures in the literary text	name these elements and relate them to various cultures; they also discuss their decisions
2. can identify a conflict/misunderstanding/dichotomy between cultures in the literary text	name and explain the conflict/misunderstanding/dichotomy and its (culturally determined) causes
3. understand the fictional characters in the literary text	talk about the fictional characters, their living conditions, their situation and their problems, taking into consideration their different cultural origin, if necessary
4. express their own feelings about the fictional characters	• identify their own feelings towards the fictional characters in the text • reflect upon their own feelings towards these characters or their understanding or lack of understanding of the characters and their actions and decisions • reflect upon their own empathy with the fictional characters
5. identify national stereotypes, culturally based prejudice and overgeneralisations in the text	name these stereotypes, culturally based prejudices and overgeneralisations and explain them
6. compare their own culturally determined opinions and attitudes towards the text and its fictional characters with that of other learners in their class; if the learners are of different cultural origins, they take this fact into consideration	compare their differing opinions and attitudes about the text and the characters, looking for culturally determined reasons ('You as a Turk have a problem with the behaviour of this girl, while for me her behaviour seems absolutely normal. But . . .'); they discuss their differing attitudes

Table 2.1   (*continued*)

Objects: the learners . . .	Observed behaviour: the learners . . .
7. write their own short fictional texts/ scenes/title or adaptations according to the creative task that was proposed	according to the task, the learners • write their own short prose texts • suggest a title for the literary text • write a poem • write a new scene, etc. taking the model text and its characters with their specific culturally determined behaviour into consideration
8. use different perspectives while writing the new texts, scenes, etc.; they can • use their own cultural perspective, which looks at the text and its characters 'from the outside' • coordinate their own perspectives with that of a fictional character in the model text, thus arriving at both an insider's and an outsider's point of view • take over the perspective of a character belonging to a different culture, thus sharing his/her view 'from inside'	for the various creative tasks the learners choose • suitable personal pronouns and verbs • emotions and actions for their fictional characters that correspond with their emotions and actions in the model text • a suitable sociolect or dialect, if necessary • suitable proxemic and non-verbal behaviour • a suitable situation • a suitable location • a suitable background • a suitable (historical) period • suitable costumes
9. discuss the texts, scenes, titles, etc. written by the class taking into account cultural differences between the model text, their own texts and their own cultural origin	comment • on their own texts in relation to the model text • on texts by other pupils and the model text • on differences, especially culturally determined differences, between their own and the other pupils' achievements

The Lessons

The first lesson (20 minutes, not videotaped)

As a warm-up, the pupils were given a multiple-exposure photograph of a worker's hands sorting screws into boxes. They talked about the topic 'work, cheap labour, cheap labour in countries of the Third World, child labour'. Then the short story was handed out in a slightly abridged form with a glossary of unknown English and Mexican Spanish words. The story had no title and the ending was left out; also the pages were not numbered, leaving the learners the task to find out their proper order.

The second lesson (90 minutes, videotaped)

The learners had to give reasons for the order they had chosen for the pages. The teacher asked for key words in the text to help them with their decisions. This led to a discussion about the story, though on a rather superficial level, concerning the content and the characters depicted in the story.

The next task was to suggest an ending for the story. The pupils had to write down short endings of two or three sentences. The endings were discussed in class before the proper ending was handed out. After having read it, the pupils were to decide on a title for the short story. This task was designed as partner work. The titles they suggested were written on the board. The following discussion of the titles also included the original title ('The Circuit'). Implications and advantages of various titles were discussed. As homework, pupils were asked to write a new scene to finish the story. They were given the beginning of this scene and were asked to complete it with a partner in approximately five sentences. Two alternatives were proposed, one asking the learners to put themselves into the roles of Panchito's mother and father, the other one to imagine a discussion between Panchito and his older brother:

Task 1:   The family moves on to their next job. They sit in the car. Mother and father start quarrelling about Panchito. Work with a partner. Write down what they say to each other. Do you think they talk loudly?

Task 2:   The family moves on. They all sit in the car. Panchito is very sad and disappointed. His brother who has to work more tries to make him feel better. They start quarrelling. Work with a partner. Write down what they say to each other. Do you think they talk loudly?

The third lesson (45 minutes, not videotaped)

The pupils were asked to work on their scenes with their partners. They corrected their mistakes with the help of dictionaries and prepared the performances of their scenes in class.

The fourth lesson (90 minutes, videotaped)

The pupils read their scenes to the class since they decided they did not want to perform in front of the video camera without a script. The performances were discussed according to a list of criteria (tone, dramatic expression, content, probability/realism of the scene, etc.) agreed upon before the performances. The whole unit was concluded by a discussion about the story and its interest for an English class in Germany.

The Pupils' Achievements

The new endings of the story

These are the four endings that were suggested by most pupils (written task):

(A) Panchito's father has a heart attack. Panchito and Roberto can't go to school any more; they have to earn money for the whole family now.
(B) As Panchito gets off the bus, he tells his parents about school and his new teacher. At first he is afraid what his parents will say, but later he is really proud of himself.
(C) Panchito's family stays in town so that he can go to school for a longer time. His father and Roberto look for better jobs. Panchito can go on learning to play the trumpet; he even joins the school orchestra.
(D) When Panchito gets off the bus, his family has moved on without him. Panchito stays in town on his own. He tries to make a living with odd jobs and stays in school.

According to the catalogue of intercultural objectives, pupils had to fulfil the following tasks (these numbers refer to the list of objectives in Table 2.1): (7) write an ending to the story taking the model text and its fictional characters into consideration; to fulfil this complex task, pupils also had to keep in mind the requirements of some other objectives such as (2) to identify a conflict and its culturally determined causes, and (3) to understand the fictional characters in the text taking into consideration their different cultural origins. Linguistic and literary objectives are not considered in this context.

Ending A is successful insofar as the structure of the story and the principal cultural conflict have been recognised and worked into the solution (objectives 7, 2 and 3 have been achieved). This solution even shows a good feeling for the typical climactic end of a short story.

Ending B offers a somewhat unrealistic 'happy ending' that does not really take into account the cultural conflicts of the story (objectives 7 and 3 have been achieved however). The reference to Panchito's feelings, however, shows a successful shifting of perspective and a lot of empathy with the boy.

Ending C also offers a 'happy ending', neglecting the family's trial for survival and the cultural conflict of the original story (objectives 7 and 3 have been achieved however).

Ending D does not take into consideration the culturally determined behaviour of the fictional characters. A Mexican family like the one portrayed in the story would probably not abandon their second eldest child just because he wants to follow a school career. The ending, however, expresses a favourable attitude to Panchito's wish to finish his school career and to learn to play the trumpet (objectives 7 and 3 have been achieved). Yet, like *ending A*, it shows the wish to end the story with a surprising climax rather than a happy ending.

In the discussion about the various suggestions for endings, many pupils expressed scepticism and disapproval of endings B and C, rejecting them as 'improbable' and 'unrealistic' or being like a 'fairy tale'. *Ending A* was generally considered as unrealistic but, surprisingly, pupils approved of this solution of the fictional conflict, whereas *ending D* was strongly debated. The actual ending of the story (that shows Panchito moving on with his family) was later discussed in class, while its severe consequences on Panchito, like the end of his school career, the loss of his new friends, etc., were outlined in detail.

Title of the short story (oral task)

The following titles were suggested by the pupils:

(A)   The new school
(B)   The life of a migrant family in the USA
(C)   The life of a Mexican family in the USA
(D)   The new beginning
(E)   A new life
(F)   From work to work
(G)   The new friend
(H)   Losing a friend
(I)   My new life in the USA

All titles containing the word 'new' emphasise Panchito's new and satisfying experiences at school, setting them off against the drab and monotonous background of his family's annual tour through the American South and their daily routine work. These titles do echo large parts of the action and the main conflict of the story, yet they neglect the unhappy ending of Panchito's school life and his family's ongoing search for work. Though the titles emphasise Panchito's happier experiences, leaving out important and unhappy events in his life, the task may be considered as fulfilled (objectives 7 and 3 achieved). The title 'Losing a friend' focuses on Panchito's loss of his teacher, thus stressing the unhappy ending of the story. The title echoes the pupils' empathy with the fictional character (objectives 7, 2 and 3 achieved). 'The life of a migrant Mexican family in the USA' is a very convincing title which takes into account all important factors of the story. Yet, it sounds like the title of a newspaper article or a piece of non-fiction writing and demonstrates the lack of experience with literature of these pupils (objectives 7, 2 and 3 achieved however).

The suggestion 'From work to work' echoes the cyclical structure of the short story. Implicitly, this title refers to the ending, focusing on the fate of the immigrant family looking for work rather than on Panchito's situation and schooling (objectives 7, 2 and 3 achieved). During the discussion in class, after they had been told the actual title of the story, pupils were surprised how close this group had come to the original title 'The Circuit'.

The suggested title 'My new life in the USA' is evidence of some pupils' problems with the task. The narrative perspective of the short story is reflected in the title, since the group chose to focus their attention on Panchito's view. Apart from the perspective, however, the title suggests that Panchito begins a totally new life in the US – a statement that is not in accordance with the story. With this solution, the objectives have only partially been fulfilled (7 and 8a achieved, 2 and 3 not fully achieved). The text, its main conflict and the fictional characters have not been fully understood and worked out properly for the title. Yet, as is often the case with mistakes, the title was the one most vividly talked about in class. This helped to re-interpret the story again and to compare different views of Panchito's fate.

New scenes written by the pupils (written task, partner work)

Of twelve pieces of partner work, the following three were chosen as representative. Whereas spelling errors were corrected, idiomatic and grammatical mistakes remain uncorrected to show the learners' language proficiency (and deficiencies). To fulfil the task, learners had to cope with objectives 7 and 8 (i.e. write a new scene and use various perspectives) while objectives 1, 2, 3, 4 and 5 were needed implicitly.

1. The parents

Mother: I think we should have stayed so that Panchito could have gone to school!

Father: In my opinion, it's OK that he works, because he wasted much important time at school.

Mother: Wouldn't you agree that it's better that he has a good education so that he can have a better life than us in the future?

Father: I see what you mean, but we can't live from school; we can only live from money!

Mother: Without any good education, you can't earn much money.

Father: But you wasted much time when you go to school; in this time you could work.

Mother: We will see what the future will bring.

Only one group of learners chose to write a scene in which Panchito's parents were the protagonists. Responsible for this choice are, first of all, the learners' strong empathic feelings for Panchito and his problems, and, of course, the fact that the reader does not learn many details about the parents in the story; they remain blurred and somewhat 'flat' characters.

The seven 'moves' of the short dialogue contain only few grammatical and idiomatic mistakes. The task has been solved in a rather successful way since the pupils manage to take over the parents' perspective. They use appropriate personal pronouns and verbs to express the actions and emotions of the fictional characters. Panchito's father is introduced as a pragmatic man and head of the family who does not approve of his son's wish for a proper schooling but regards him as an important helping hand to sustain the family. Panchito's mother, by contrast, hopes for a proper education for her son while secretly planning a better life for him. The discussion between the parents reflects arguments which the pupils probably know from 'real-life' discussions at home where they are in a similar situation since they are about to embark on their own working life. Yet, they use the arguments in a way that is suitable for the fictitious characters, their gender and their culturally determined roles. The central conflict of the short story (i.e. the cheap labour of illegal immigrants that does not allow for a permanent home or for qualification for better jobs) is adequately echoed by the dialogue in the scene. Realistically, the opposition between father and mother is not solved, and Panchito's mother postpones the discussion to a later date with a remark typical of her ('We will see – Que sera'). Though the content of the dialogue reflects the conflict of the story, the sociolect in the dialogue is not appropriate for the fictional characters; some of their phrases were obviously found in a dictionary. But then, a proper treatment of sociolect is certainly beyond the abilities of a class like this, which has no experience with English literary texts and probably little experience with literary texts in the mother tongue.

2. Panchito and Roberto

Roberto: Panchito, why are you so sad? Be glad, you are at home.

Panchito: I am not happy to come home now where Mama and Papa go away from the cotton field, I have lost a good friend.

Roberto: A good friend?

Panchito: Yes, his name is Mr. Lema and he is a teacher.

Roberto: A teacher? Why a teacher?

Panchito: He was so nice to me and he teached me English.

Robert: English, you don't need English. At home we speak Mexican. Furthermore can I be your friend and when you have problems come to me.

Again, we have seven 'moves' in a short dialogue which contains some grammatical and idiomatic mistakes. The task has been solved quite successfully, this time focusing on the conversation between the two brothers. The personal pronouns indicate that both perspectives have been adopted.

Above all, this dialogue is concerned with the boys' emotions. The pupils have tried to illustrate Panchito's feelings when sitting in the car, his hopes for staying at school once again shattered. Roberto and his opinion about their constant moves is revealed in some depth, too, showing the creative potential of this group of learners that goes beyond this fictional character's rather superficial treatment in the story. Panchito is portrayed as sad about the loss of his friendship with his teacher, who has taught him the foreign language that is so important for the boy and, in fact, his family, too. These sentences are, first of all, proof of the learners' awareness about the importance of learning English and foreign languages in general, but they also capture the notion of learning a language to integrate into a society one has entered by immigration. Both ideas not only reflect the awareness of the central immigration conflict of the short story but also a budding intercultural awareness that could and, in fact, did lead to fruitful discussions in class. Panchito's problem has been fully understood by this group of pupils, though they don't mention his loss of the trumpet lessons.

Roberto's part of the dialogue shows some insight into the sociological role of the family in Mexico. Being the elder brother, he is an important source of labour, responsible for the financial support of the family. His last sentences combine the empathy of a brother with paternal authority. The pupils stress Roberto's view of the family as the only and most important pivot for himself and his brothers and sisters. Questions like integration into American society, school education and personal success or friendships are insignificant when compared to the role of family life. Panchito's wishes, his ambition and his first attempts to break with these unwritten rules are simply brushed aside by his elder brother's authority. Again, we see how the fictional characters in this short scene are modelled according to the pupils' culturally determined views, giving Roberto a 'typically Mexican' attitude that clashes with his younger brother's striving for individual goals. Here again is a good starting-point for discussion, leading to a comparison of views about the Mexican, American and, of course, German attitude towards family (all other cultures and ethnic groups represented in class should, of course, be included, too), personal success and freedom to strive for one's own goals. The short scene can be considered as a successful attempt to take over a foreign perspective, an insider's view, achieving intercultural objectives 7 and 8 as well as 1, 2, 3, 4 and 5.

3. Roberto and Panchito

Roberto: Come on, boy, your situation is better than my situation. I want to go to school, but I must work.

Panchito: I don't like school so much because I have sometimes problems with other pupils. But I like Mr. Lema.

Roberto: That's not the problem. You mustn't be afraid of problems at school.

Panchito: You don't understand. I liked to go to school and learnt much but the languages are difficult for me.

Roberto: You can be happy that you can learn the languages. I've no chance!

Panchito: You are right. I'll think about it!

Roberto: We must talk with our parents, that we stay and have a real own home. That's also the right thing for the other kids.

There are seven 'moves' in this short dialogue, too, containing grammatical and idiomatic mistakes, however. The task has been fulfilled quite successfully from the point of view of both Roberto and Panchito while also taking into account the plot of the short story. In contrast to the outline and characteristics of Roberto in the preceding scene, this Roberto develops into the main character of the scene, showing a lot of sympathy with Panchito's sadness about his loss of learning opportunities and of a kind teacher. He actually envies Panchito his modest schooling.

Panchito tells him about his positive experiences with his last teacher, also mentioning his problems with the other children in his class. He admits having been rather shy in class because of his language deficiencies. Here the pupils touch the subject of language proficiency as an important factor for successful integration, a point that lends itself to further discussion in class. Roberto seems to know about the importance of language learning: he deplores his deficiencies in this respect, which will diminish his chances for a professional career in the United States. Roberto even goes so far as to make some plans for the future: he wants to change their annual migration and talk to their parents about a 'real' home, a home that need not be packed into a car and moved from field to field to earn some money.

The authors of this scene have not only understood the most important issues of the short story, the migration problem, Roberto's and Panchito's lack of proper learning opportunities and the language barrier, but they also attempt to find a solution that might satisfy all members of the family. With the idea of family hierarchy in mind, it is Roberto who suggests talking to their father about the issue. A proper home, though only vaguely hinted at in the scene, seems to be the basis for an improvement of Panchito's and Roberto's life. Not only does this scene present ample opportunity to discuss intercultural problems with the class, but it also shows that the authors have successfully taken over the perspectives of the two Mexican boys, thereby proving the achievement of the intercultural objectives mentioned above, i.e. 7 and 8 as well as 1, 2, 3, 4 and 5.

By reading the fictional text written in a foreign language, by forming hypotheses about it, by searching for an ending that corresponds with the characters and the plot, and, finally, by re-writing scenes for the text or adding scenes to it, pupils in EFL classrooms internalise the text – it becomes part of them. Fragments of values and opinions they hold from their own cultural experience seep into their discussions and written contributions, thereby creating a 'Zwischenwelt' (a kind of 'in-between world'), a kind of third or 'inter-' culture, or simply an anxiety-free zone where foreign cultures can be freely discussed and explored. The unit has shown how the encounter with foreign fictional texts may be valuable even for less experienced learners who are reluctant to read but are eager to share their own experiences and opinions, which are often taken from their own bi- or multicultural background. The learning objectives suggest how to assess the learners' achievements, as the examples have shown, which is a challenge that can be met by many teachers in many countries with differing curricular backgrounds.

References

Barro, A., S. Jordan and C. Roberts. (1998) Cultural practice in everyday life: The language learner as ethnographer. In M. Byram and M. Fleming (eds) *Language Learning in Intercultural Perspective: Approaches through Drama and Ethnography.* Cambridge: Cambridge University Press.

Bredella, L. (1996) Warum literarische Texte im Fremdsprachenunterricht? Die anthropologische und pädagogische Bedeutung des ästhetischen Lesens. In W. Börner and K. Vogel (eds) *Texte im Fremdsprachenerwerb: Verstehen und Produzieren.* Tübingen: Narr.

Bredella, L. (1997a) Interkulturelles Verstehen im Fremdsprachenunterricht: *Do the Right Thing* von Spike Lee. In G. Jarfe (ed.) *Literaturdidaktik – konkret: Theorie und Praxis des fremdsprachlichen Literaturunterrichts.* Heidelberg: Universitätsverlag Winter.

Bredella, L. (1997b) Minderheitenliterartur und interkulturelles Lernen: Maxine Hong Kingston's *The Woman Warrior. Der Fremdsprachliche Unterricht/Englisch* 3, 26–31.

Byram, M. (1997) *Teaching and Assessing Intercultural Communicative Competence.* Clevedon: Multilingual Matters.

Byram, M. and Cain, A. (1998) Civilisation/Cultural Studies: An experiment in French and English schools. In M. Byram and M. Fleming (eds) *Language Learning in Intercultural Perspective: Approaches through Drama and Ethnography.* Cambridge: Cambridge University Press.

Edmondson, W. and House, J. (1998) Interkulturelles Lernen: Ein überflüssiger Begriff. *Zeitschrift für Fremdsprachenforschung* 9 (2), 161–188.

Hu, A. (1999) Interkulturelles Lernen: Eine Auseinandersetzung mit der Kritik an einem umstrittenen Konzept. *Zeitschrift für Fremdsprachenforschung* 10 (2), 277–303.

Jiménez, F. (1993) The Circuit. In A. Mazer (ed.) *America Street: A Multicultural Anthology of Stories*. New York: Persea Books.

Knapp, K. and Knapp-Potthoff, A. (1990) Interkulturelle Kommunikation. *Zeitschrift für Fremdsprachenforschung* 1, 62–93.

Kramsch, C. (1998) The privilege of the intercultural speaker. In M. Byram and M. Fleming (eds) *Language Learning in Intercultural Perspective: Approaches through Drama and Ethnography*. Cambridge: Cambridge University Press.

Nünning, A. (1997) Perspektivenübernahme und Perspektivenkoordinierung: Prozessorientierte Schulung des Textverstehens und der Textproduktion bei der Behandlung von John Fowles' *The Collector*. In G. Jarfe (ed.) *Literaturdidaktik – konkret, Theorie und Praxis des fremdsprachlichen Literaturunterrichts*. Heidelberg: Universitätsverlag Winter.

Rosenblatt, L. (1981) On the aesthetic as the basic model of the reading process. In H.R. Garvin (ed.) *Theories of Reading, Looking and Listening*. Lewisburg: Bucknell University Press.

Schewe, M. (1998) Culture through literature through drama. In M. Byram and M. Fleming (eds) *Language Learning in Intercultural Perspective: Approaches through Drama and Ethnography*. Cambridge: Cambridge University Press.

Schinschke, A. (1995) *Literarische Texte im interkulturellen Lernprozeß: Zur Verbindung von Literatur und Landeskunde im Fremdsprachenunterricht Französisch*. Tübingen: Narr.

Seletzky, M. (1996) A process-oriented and learner-centered approach to the teaching of 'Landeskunde' in the German-Language Classroom. In H. Christ and M. Legutke (eds) *Fremde Texte Verstehen: Festschrift für Lothar Bredella zum 60. Geburtstag*. Tübingen: G. Narr.

Tomalin, B. and Stempleski, S. (1993) *Cultural Awareness*. London: Oxford University Press

Chapter 3
'Up the Hills of Identity'
ELENA TARASHEVA AND LEAH DAVCHEVA

In the lessons described here, students are invited to think about aspects of their own cultural inheritance, the stories they have read in childhood, the myths which are part of the national heritage. The authors suggest how this approach in the foreign language classroom helps students to gain a deeper awareness of what they have taken for granted in their own world.

Introduction

In this chapter we attempt to describe and reflect on a teaching and learning experience central to which is a culture-oriented lesson. As the title suggests, it takes the students on an imaginary quest up the hills of cultural identity – but it also means that it was an uphill struggle for us to prepare the journey.

Initially, the lesson was designed to acquaint British students aged 12–16 with Bulgaria, but we have also adapted it for Bulgarian secondary schools. The pedagogical challenge we faced in the Bulgarian context was equally worthwhile and proved even more demanding. In this chapter we focus on the variant for the Bulgarian pupils. Through presenting it for discussion we would like to suggest an approach to culture and language learning which explores the origins of cultural values rooted in one's native culture.

Teaching One's Own Culture

Teaching about one's own culture, like the theoretical endeavour to lift the Globe with a lever, depends critically on the choice of a starting point: if one proceeds from too close, the sweep of force is suspended; if, alternatively, the levering bar is left too far, the object escapes the tool.

The lesson that was originally designed for the British pupils provided a natural distance from the topic and thus gave a good view of the subject. The teacher's task was mainly to help achieve depth and enable the pupils to draw their own conclusions. The lesson for the Bulgarian learners, on the other hand, meant providing critical distance before reaching the stage of making any conclusions at all.

It was also crucial to find an entry point to Bulgarian culture which could serve as a conceptual focus and lend itself to the process of unpeeling layers of personal experience, representations, core values, ideas and imaginings. The search for such a productive and unifying notion led to the discovery of the 'mountain': the mountain in its role of a cultural construct exemplifying the multiplicity of Bulgarian culture. The perception of this concept as representative of Bulgarian-ness, on the one hand, and the variety of viewpoints about its aspects in Bulgarian society, on the other, promised to give British pupils a multi-faceted picture. The very same representativeness, however, obstructed the vision of the Bulgarian pupils for something they deemed obvious. Understanding familiar concepts as a part of one's identity, we believe, does not come automatically but needs to be carefully worked out. Structured learning about the processes that shape identity helps develop a critical cultural personality.

Why the Mountain?

Mountains overarch Bulgarian culture, both physically and symbolically. Their place in the Bulgarian national, historic and regional cultures is pervasive – the view from the window, the place where people earn their living, the sight of fun and recreation, wildlife and the increasing tourist invasion, the myths and legends that people grow up with, the numerous battles fought for a variety of causes, the shelter to refugees from every oppressor who sets foot in the country. It is not by chance that mountains rise high in the opening line of the national anthem and their woods sing the chorus in most popular songs and poems.

Representations of the mountains abound and the Bulgarian public is lavishly treated to them. Children, in particular, learn about them at school, see them on television, read tales set in the mountains.

Representations of the mountain in Bulgarian children's books are plenty. We assume that they play a subtle role in shaping the perceptions of their readers. That is why we chose stories and illustrations in children's books to be the main focus of our lesson. We felt they would encourage our learners to reflect on the evolving image of the mountain, while drawing upon existing schemata and building new ones. In addition, reflecting on books' formative influence brings home to the pupils the idea that identity does not grow of its own accord; it is shaped and fashioned, even when – perhaps most of all – one is least aware of it.

Preliminary research into the text and pictures in Bulgarian books for children revealed that the mountain appears in the following representations:

- the home and shelter of wild animals, birds and plants;
- the setting of stories where humans interact with nature in various ways; mostly, the characters are put on trial;
- a place for sports and recreation, challenge and effort;
- the setting of traditional legends, inhabited by various mythical creatures.

Illustrations range from the realistic to the metaphorical. Some show rocks and dales in a true-to-life fashion, in others peaks are drawn as spreading angel's wings or mournful sages. They easily lend themselves to unravelling the nature of metaphors, and further on, to the critical reading of the denoted image.

Theoretical Concepts

The following key pedagogical constructs have fashioned our approach to the classroom:

- critical native cultural awareness;
- the intercultural speaker;
- a sense of national identity.

Critical cultural awareness

Critical cultural awareness with respect to one's own country is nowadays seen as one of the major aims of language and culture learning. In accordance with Byram and Risager (1999) we interpret it as the ability on the part of the learner to reflect upon his or her own culture and how it appears to outsiders. The approach we have chosen to illustrate leads, we believe, towards an understanding of the various meanings of the mountain as a place and as a concept. It challenges the common understanding of what it means to teach culture as it makes no attempt at informative geographical descriptions. What it does is assist the learners to think back to their childhood and reflect on their experiences from the position of a more mature perception.

The intercultural speaker

Again in agreement with Byram and Risager (1999) we have accepted the concept of 'intercultural speaker'. Our lesson aims to develop this one aspect of the skill, which suspends ready judgements of one's own culture and explores it through the eyes of another. This develops critical awareness of self and own values, as well as an ability to see other people's views. Learning not to assume that familiar phenomena in one's own culture are necessarily understood in the same way by others involves the exploitation of a range of analytical approaches and we hope our lesson sets the beginnings of it.

National identity

Learning a foreign language inevitably makes reference to national identity. Therefore we strive to provide our learners with the means to analyse, understand and mediate one of the main aspects of national identity, concerned with the meaning of places. The lesson develops its logic and rationale on the grounds and geographical territory of Bulgarian culture.

Learning Materials

The lesson is based on a set of pictures from four well-known children's stories, all set in the mountains. We chose several illustrations, combining in varying degrees metaphorical and realistic elements.

The first one illustrates a story, *Deer and Fawn*, about a dispute between the oldest deer in the herd and a young fawn over which route to choose to escape from some hunters. The fawn is right that the shortcut suggested by the deer is not safe, but the herd obeys the old leader and falls victim to the hunters. The illustration shows beautiful deer on the run to the distant snow-topped mountain in the background, and the grotesque figure of a hunter, with gun pointed at the deer and accompanied by his vicious dog: two dark figures lurking by a tree in the foreground.

The second story, *Old Woman Tsotsolana,* is an epistolary tale of a group of children going to the mountain and their elderly aunt who refuses to climb up the hill. After several attempts to persuade, coax or cajole her, the children finally trick her by lying that an evil dog is behind her. The illustration shows a rather challenging cliff with a bunch of smiling, healthy children at the top and the dowdy lady puffing up chased by a puppy.

В красивата стара гора на една да-
лечна планина живеело стадо елени и
сърни.
   Предвождал ги един стар, престар
елен - много преживял и много препа-
тил. Той знаел всички пътеки из плани-
ната и всички места, където ловците
залагали капани и копаели трапове, за
да залавят в тях живи сърни.
   Един ден ловци обградили стадото.
Уплашените сърни и малките сърнета
хукнали да се спасяват. Водел ги опит-
ният елен.
   Успели да избягат и еленът ги повел
по една тайна пътека навътре в плани-
ната. Не щеш ли, пред водача запъхтя-
но изтичало малко сърне:

Figure 3.1   Illustration from *Deer and Fawn*.

A borderline case between metaphor and realism is presented in the third story, *The Dragon*. It is a legend about a breed of dragons, who inhabit the mountain and protect people from evil forces. The illustration shows a very man-like – except for the wings – dragon, who is flying away into the mountain with his beautiful human bride. Although the creatures are mythical, the illustrator has chosen to represent them as quite human. The environment in particular – a village huddled in the foot of the mountain and the sun-lit peaks – seems true to life.

The fourth tale, *White Story*, besides bearing the highest degree of symbolism in the presentation, is the most contemporary one. It is about a boy who goes skiing in the mountain, leaving his cat behind. This makes the cat angry, and it teams up with some animals and the local weather man to punish the boy for being a bad friend. In the end, it turns out that the animals and the weather man have been testing the cat to see how far it would go causing the boy to suffer. The book abounds in pictures where the mountain features in a number of metaphorical images: an angel, an old man, the gaping mouth of a monster, etc. From the wealth of illustrations we chose two. The first one shows an image of the mountain with its peaks depicted as wizards towering over the animals who plan the tricks for the boy; the second presents the mountain as a monster whose toothy mouth has swallowed the boy while the animals disguised as ghosts dance around.

Figure 3.2   Illustration from *Old Woman Tsotsolana*.

Figure 3.3   Illustration from *The Dragon*.

Figure 3.4 Illustration from *White Story*.

Figure 3.5 Illustration from *White Story*.

Aim and Objectives of the Lesson

The overall aim of the lesson is to enable learners to look for and discover cultural messages in images that have become so deeply embedded in the process of socialisation that they are not easily recognisable as tools for shaping values and beliefs.

To achieve this aim we set out to develop a number of culture learning skills, particularly those leading towards the reading of visual images and critical observation: the ability to question the familiar and adopt a critical distance from what has always looked natural in order to break down the complexity of the whole and put it together again.

Procedure

Warm up

The teacher introduces the topic of the mountain. She may or may not bring up the subject of it as a symbol and a source of emotions. Such a presentation is potentially a double-edged weapon: if given, the teacher may be in danger of leading pupils to associations not existing in their minds and depriving them of the pleasure of their own discovery; if not given, less motivated classes may miss the point and remain at a superficial reading of the concept. A golden middle should be easy to strike, based on knowing one's class and the methods they are used to.

Mind maps of the mountain

The teacher splits the class into groups of four or five and asks them to produce a mind map of what the mountain means for them. If the pupils have not worked with mind maps, the teacher may need to explain and give an example with another concept. The mind maps are best done on A1 sheets and kept for reference at the end of the lesson.

Short presentations from the groups

Each group reports on what ideas of the mountain they have included in their mind map and how these interrelate. With a committed class a wealth of images can emerge and the previously uniform notion of the mountain gradually loses its wholeness. A point in the lesson is reached when the students begin to realise that the concept is not as easily obvious as it seems and it can be approached from a variety of perspectives.

The role of children's books in developing these ideas

The teacher introduces the idea that the stories and illustrations in children's books can combine powerfully to build one's awareness of the image of the mountain. This should be done very briefly so as not to pre-empt the discussion.

Eliciting the stories

The teacher projects the illustrations from the stories on overhead transparencies (OHTs) and elicits the stories from the class. If the pupils do not know or can't remember them, the teacher helps them with the story line. Getting the details of the stories is important. Without them the discussion is left floating in vague generalisations. This is the point where linguistic input is required as the pictures and the familiar stories force a fairly accurate rendition of the details. At this stage, doing the lesson in a foreign language proves extremely useful, allowing the pupils to revisit familiar images and tales from a new perspective.

Critical reading of the pictures

In their groups the pupils consider the illustrations to the stories. Each group has a different picture. Firstly the pupils answer a set of descriptive questions, e.g.

- What and who can you see in the pictures?
- What is the setting?
- What are the characters doing?
- What is happening?

The second group of questions is more interpretative in nature. Their aim is to lead the students towards an understanding that pictures are not 'transparent windows on the world', but constructed representations of it. The students are asked to observe carefully and drawing upon their own experience to interpret and identify what they see. They want to think about how the illustrations represent reality, how they, each in its own distinct way, categorise and classify the events in the story and send out a number of coherent messages. The questions can be like:

- What is the position of the characters in the picture? Are they in the foreground or in the background? What does this tell you of the artist's view of their relationship to the mountain?

- How is the mountain represented in the picture? Is it in the foreground or the background? What do you think is the artist's view of it?
- What is the focus of the picture?
- What can you say about the colours in the picture?
- Would you interpret the pictures differently if any of the images were changed?

A third group of questions may focus on the overall impact that each of the illustrations has on the students:

- What is the effect of the picture(s)? Harmony? Tension? Conflict?
- What sort of things can the mountain represent?
- Is it a metaphor for or a symbol of anything?

Each group concentrates on the description and analysis of their picture(s) and prepares a short presentation of their answers and internal discussion. It is essential that groups have enough time for discussing opinions and putting them on paper. The variety of perspectives, as before, is the asset of this activity. Pupils need to recognise and acknowledge the difference in perceptions and attitudes.

Group presentations

While each group presents their answers, the teacher projects the pictures for the whole class to see. To ensure that pupils listen to each other, the teacher may decide on different while-listening tasks. Questions to the presenters are welcome.

Recapitulation

After the presentation stage has been completed, the teacher invites the students to remember that the pictures they have been looking at come from children's books. She asks them to think about what children learn about the mountain as they read the stories and look at the pictures. On the basis of their descriptions the pupils discuss the issue as a whole class.

Overview of Techniques

Below we outline some of the techniques which have proved to work well for the purposes of the lesson.

Achieving critical distance

As the depth and wisdom of the conclusions crucially depended on providing the necessary critical distance, we used a combination of methods to achieve it. Firstly, we explained to the pupils that a version of this lesson had been prepared as one of a series of lessons to be taught to British children. In a way, this got them seeing the subject matter through the eyes of peers from another culture. Secondly, the medium of English, apart from helping adopt a different perspective, required translation of stories familiar from childhood, which necessarily involved a critical reflection on the plot and characters and also transposing concepts and perceptions otherwise taken for granted. Thirdly, a degree of analytic capability was achieved due to the pupils' desire to be viewed as people who have 'risen' above childhood. The analytical tasks required – and the pupils were willing – to adopt a bird's eye view and reflect on what *a child* would make of the images and stories.

Encouraging close work with text and pictures

It is often the case that students are not motivated enough to describe in great detail something as obvious as illustrations in children's books. In the case of this lesson, however, failing to elicit details means students coming up with sweeping generalisations instead of proper conclusions. To ensure the greatest amount of details, we arranged a multi-staged discussion and descriptive analysis of the pictures and the stories. Firstly, the pupils were asked to tell the stories by looking at the pictures. Secondly, the three sets of questions allowed an in-depth critical reading of the pictures. Thirdly, group work provided the opportunity to compare with peers and pool ideas.

Varying the channel

Matching textual and pictorial messages provided the necessary richness of impressions, as well as the variety of perspective to the same object. None of the illustrations followed the story slavishly and the mismatch was enriching and thought-provoking, thus encouraging the pupils to take their own perspective. It fed into the lesson to be learned – that such simple material could lead to profound and important conclusions.

Structuring reflection

It is often the case that reflection is left to take care of itself. However, with younger learners and with topics that appear obvious, staging the reflection phase in our experience proved worthwhile. With the abundance of material thus amassed during the lesson, reflection was initiated in class and left to the pupils to expand in their own time. Spending time on this, as well as listening to other students' opinions, was a good point to start. On the other hand, forced conclusions preclude getting deeper into one's own perceptions, so one treads on very delicate ground there, searching for a delicate balance.

Feedback

Our main source of feedback is rooted in the students' answers to the question: 'What do you think you learned from this lesson?' We offer a sample of how 15-year-old students perceived their learning achievements on one of the occasions of teaching this lesson. The headings below summarise the opinions that recur most often.

The lesson had strong impact on the students' thinking

I learned some new stories but actually I learned how to succeed in finding a way to put my thoughts down, how to learn and think as a team and to combine the members' opinions.

I love this kind of lesson because it makes us think, that's the main thing.

I like the idea of the mind-map – a new learning experience for me.

The lesson created a context for the students to revisit their childhood and see it from a different perspective

I had the opportunity to go back to my childhood and to think about the things that were around me when I was forming my view of the world and the things that have influenced my values.

This lesson helped me do one thing – remember something that I thought I had lost for good.

Children's stories took on a great deal of new meaning

Although we discussed stories which were told to us years ago, I learned a lot of new things about human relations, about the influence of nature over people. Maybe as a child I wasn't able to realise these things.

Old fairy tales are a magnificent way to learn something new. They are not for children only. The most important thing was that we spent the time discussing, learning things in a different way.

I learned how difficult it is to write stories for children. Adults, who write the stories, have a totally different type of thinking.

The mountain emerged as a newly discovered familiar notion

We learned different concepts about the mountain and how it is presented to children in tales, what information is given by the pictures and the text around them.

I had never thought what the mountain means to me before. Now with the tales and the pictures I learned a lot of things.

The lesson suggested that there is more than one view of reality

What I learned from this lesson is that there are different perceptions about things. So much depends on the age of the person who's reading the story. When you are a kid you see miracles and unknown creatures. When you grow up you already know what exists and what not, so you are able to look at the story in a different way.

I learned from this lesson that each man, each one of my class is a small world. We all see things in a different way and everyone finds something beautiful for herself in the mountain.

You can see how magnificent and gorgeous ordinary things can be.

Conclusion

Exploring concepts and images of one's own culture can be a productive activity. It touches upon the subtle mechanisms of forming identity. The discovery of hidden resources in familiar concepts serves as a good starting point for the development of self-awareness. Pupils, in our experience, welcome the opportunity and prove able to plunge below the surface and reach depths of understanding.

The task of exploring the familiar demands of the teacher to provide a suitable topic and appropriate methodology, motivating the pupils to take a step back and de-centre. Group work and analytical tasks teach the lesson of seeing multiplicity of interpretations of what appears a monolithic image.

Re-visiting childhood is a good opportunity to discover the roots of identity and reflect from a different perspective. Tales inspire the imagination but also, by virtue of the opportunities to be interpreted differently, can trigger off critical thinking about one's own identity.

Acknowledgements

The authors would like to thank the following for permission to reproduce copyright material:

Figure 3.1: Ivailo Ivanchev and Fiut Publishing House, Sofia. From *Bulgarian Folk Tales* (1993).

Figure 3.2: Ivan Anastasov and Bulgarski Hudojnik Publishers. From *Patilansko Tsarstvo* (1968).

Figure 3.3: Victor Paunov and Panorama Publishers, Sofia. From *Vampires, Centaurs and Dragons* (1998).

Figures 3.4 and 3.5: Danail Raikov and Otechestvo Publishers, Sofia. From *Byala Prikazka [White Story]* (1977).

Reference

Byram, M. and Risager, K. (1999) *Language Teachers, Politics and Cultures.* Clevedon: Multilingual Matters.

Chapter 4

Visual Codes and Modes of Presentation of Television News Broadcasts

MARIA METODIEVA GENOVA

Cultural studies is often associated with media studies and this chapter describes how learners were introduced to modes of analysing the media, in particular new broadcasts. The analysis was not focused only on one country, however, but by comparative study of news broadcasts in Britain and Bulgaria, learners acquired a critical understanding of both.

Introduction

In this chapter I describe some work on British and Bulgarian television news broadcasts that convinced me of the usefulness of teaching cultural studies in the classroom through television – especially when combined with the choices and control offered by video recordings. In the beginning I myself was a little sceptical about the whole idea – mainly because of coursebook writers always reminding us to be on the alert for the 'journalese' used, or for arcane cultural references. These factors, without teletext, can make a text impenetrable for learners of English, even highly proficient ones. However, my work in the field and teaching experience helped me to look at things from quite a different angle. I have to give credit to my students whose interest in television actually inspired me and eventually aided the process of trialling my ideas.

As a teacher I firmly believe in the importance and usefulness of studying the media at school. To begin with in Bulgaria, for example, the access to newspapers, radio or television is easier in many ways than access to literary works. Secondly, there are a great number of ways to incorporate or supplement the textbook with such materials. Thirdly, I have noticed from experience that often students discussing media are not only more motivated to participate; they also feel more confident when dealing with areas within their interests (radio and television).

It is generally acknowledged that today's children tend to read less than children ten or twenty years ago, preferring to obtain information through radio, television or the computer. Some journalists, parents and teachers claim that society ought to defend children from the 'destructive power' of the media and television in particular. I myself think that we as teachers can use students' affinity for television as a powerful tool ensuring that television has a positive and constructive influence on them. In fact I will concentrate on this aspect of television in my work, trying to prove my thesis with some practical ideas and classroom activities.

How can we use television? What do children and students gain from television? Whether we want or not, we have to admit the media are a dominant part of our lives. We ought to recognise this reality and enable students to become active viewers, not simply passive consumers. We ought to ask students to speak of the impact of television on them, how it changes their lives, how it affects their understanding of the world. Through involving the students in different productive activities, such as comparing/contrasting tasks or discussions, we ought to be able to facilitate experiential learning. That is surely one of the main ideas behind cultural studies – to teach different cultural and life skills and create life-long learners.

Context

The learners involved in the project were 17/18-year-old learners of English in their last year at a language school with intensive classes in English. A language school in the Bulgarian educational context means a five-year course of intensive studying of a foreign language and literature. In their first year the students have approximately 24 classes per week in the given foreign language. The four major skills are taught together with grammar. In the successive years of their schooling the students have about eight to ten classes per week. They are acquainted with the most outstanding British and American writers as well. Very often the Bulgarian teachers of English are assisted in their work by qualified teachers who are also native English speakers. Towards the end of the course a student is supposed to have a good command of English and communicate without difficulties.

The linguistic competence of the students who participated in my project ranged from upper-intermediate to advanced level. Although the project was designed mainly for language schools it could be used successfully in schools with intensive courses in English as well. Later I tried to use a simplified version of the project with beginners, aged 14–15. Their linguistic competence ranged from lower intermediate to intermediate. The tasks set, however, differ to some extent and there was not a pre-teaching session on specific vocabulary.

The Project

The aim of the project is for the learners to become literate in the language of media used in the national (i.e. Bulgarian) and the British television news broadcasts in a series of three lessons, each one focusing on a specific task and graded in difficulty (see Appendix 4.1 for lesson plans). Teachers, however, might choose to teach just one of the suggested lessons (Appendix 4.2). Taken as a whole, these lessons aim at raising the students' awareness of another culture than their own. Their objective is to teach students to 'read' the screen and the messages it sends by means of comparing and contrasting – two of the main cultural studies skills. First this is done with the elements of presentation, then the visual modes of presentation, and finally the visual codes used in the national and British news bulletins. With respect to the aims of the teaching, the students should learn to understand how the elements, codes and modes of presentation work on the screen, thus learning more about the routine conventions of camera work and other media characteristics.

I have also adapted the project for the level of beginners (Appendix 4.3). Here, it aims at raising the students' awareness of their own culture, as well as other cultures, i.e. to show them other points of view. Its objective is to show students how they can start 'reading the screen' and find similarities and differences first between different national channels and then between a British and a national programme.

Theoretical Frame

To understand television better, one has to study it. This could be partially done at school through recognising the different techniques used for the production of a broadcast – reading and interpreting the messages sent to us as viewers, comparing different programmes and similar introductory tasks. For all these we need some special terminology and explanation concerning the following: elements and modes of presentation, codes of presentation and techniques of shooting.

Although it might sound too academic to begin with terminology, there are sound pedagogical reasons for this strategy. Firstly, it is for the sake of clarity and better understanding of the procedures and all the activities given further in the lesson plans on the part of teachers. Secondly, to be able to 'decode' messages and interpret them, students should be taught some basic media terminology either in a separate lesson or through the lesson itself. This is actually Stage One from the lesson plans, without which it is impossible to do the activities.

As the title suggests, we are interested in different visual codes and modes of presentation. How can these be defined?

Elements and modes of presentation of television

I have used Hartley's classification of media terms and definitions (see below), which is pretty exhaustive. However, it is not obligatory or advisable to give students all those terms but only the basic ones or the ones the teacher will find useful. If the students come to a term they do not know, the teacher is there to help them using the already mentioned classification. Of use can be the *Collins Cobuild Key Words in the Media Dictionary* by Bill Mascull as well. In case the terms turn out to be insufficient to cover the variety of elements and visual codes and modes of presentation, both the teacher and the students might try to adopt some terms of their own, giving their reasons for that. This in itself can be quite a challenging exercise because it will make students think on their feet.

Elements of presentation:

- *the newsreader*: the dominant figure on the screen that frames the topic and provides a link between the other elements;
- *the correspondent/commentator*, who sets the topic in context and explains its significance;
- *the film report* which presents images and actuality.

(Hartley, 1993: 107)

Modes of presentation:

Verbal

- the institutional voice;
- the accessed voice.

Visual

- *talking head*: the newsreader/correspondent, who is differentiated by the addition of both graphics and nomination;
- *graphics*: including animation, computer display etc., with a voice-over supplying the commentary or used behind the talking head;

- *still-photograph*: head full-frame with a voice-over;
- *nomination*: the caption or verbal introduction with literally named participants in the news (either reporters or interviewed individuals nominated by a caption suggesting usually name, position, and place of report);
- *actuality*: the so-called backbone of television news in the film report:
  - film with *voice-over*: the reporter does not appear on screen;
  - the *stake-out*: the reporter addresses his or her commentary direct to camera;
  - the *vox-pop*: the interviewee is seen talking full-frame to an unseen reporter outside the camera-shot.

(Hartley, 1993: 108)

Codes operating in television news

These might be summarised as:

- *visual codes*:
  - *codes of composition*: codes which govern the way a picture is framed, coloured and lit;
  - *codes of movement*: they govern movement within the frame of both camera and subject: 'the pan' (moving from an apparently insignificant object to the real subject of report); 'the zoom' (shooting an object from a distance or immediate proximity); 'the hand-held camera';
  - *codes of sequence*: they have to do with editing: how quickly shots are changed, what images are juxtaposed etc.;
- *verbal codes*: derived from conventional speech, narrative and journalism
- *absent codes*: television devices are music, studio debate, and dramatic reconstruction of events.

(Hartley, 1993:180)

Techniques in shooting/camera work

These might be summarised as:

- *establishing shot*: at the beginning of a programme;
- *extreme close-up* (*ecu*): shot showing the head;
- *close-up* (*cu*): shot showing the head and shoulders;

- *medium close-up (mcu)*: shot showing from the waist up;
- *two-shot*: shooting two people simultaneously;
- *field/reverse field shot*: successive movement from one to another subject shot in profile.

(Masterman, 1985)

Practical Application: Suggestions and Examples

How can the theoretical frame suggested above be actually applied in practice, familiarising students with some key terms?

This may be done by means of a warm-up exercise of up to fifteen minutes before the substance of each lesson. Another option is a separate lesson on terminology, which might not be taken seriously by the students or might be too boring. If the lesson plan for beginners is going to be used, then no terminology is taught in the warm-up session.

Let us start from the easiest task and take the elements of presentation, for example. The best idea here is to start with a brainstorming exercise, asking students to identify the people that appear on the screen from personal experience. They come up with a list of words and the teacher acts at first as monitor, then as a facilitator, helping them with clues, and finally, if necessary, as an instructor – explaining and giving examples on the video. Once the students have a clear idea of 'who is who' and 'what his/her role on television is', they can start the other activities.

We then move to the next stage, the second lesson, which is a bit more challenging because it deals with different visual modes of presentation, i.e. some special vocabulary such as 'nomination', 'voice-over', 'stake-out' or 'vox-pop'. It is advisable that the teacher starts with an explanation based on the national news, using different video techniques. Then he/she might give the students a task while watching a very short excerpt to distinguish between these techniques. He/she might go further and play a longer excerpt – two or three minutes – and ask students to count the different visual modes of presentation, working in small groups and then discussing their results as a class.

Finally we come to the third stage – lesson three, the most complicated one. Here the students need some terms describing the codes operating in television news, as well as different techniques of shooting and some of the vocabulary on visual modes of presentation, which have already been covered.

The teacher should again start with a brief explanation of the camera techniques by means of the video. The students have similar tasks to recognise these techniques while watching stills. After that, in small groups, they follow a very short excerpt and try to use their knowledge to describe the shots.

To make the students' task easier in the next stages of the lesson, the teacher gives an example of how they should work to 'read' the messages sent from the television screen. I can make this more explicit with the following examples focusing on the opening shots of the BBC1 and ITV news.

Establishing close-up shot (ITV):

A quick change of shots – in just about 10 seconds – from establishing close-up through close-up to medium shot of the face of a clock. The effect is immediate – Big Ben is chiming the time, second after second. Do not forget to follow us (ITV) at 5.40 p.m.

Establishing very long shot (ELS) (BBC1):

In the foreground are seen the codes of geography, while in the background the studio itself.

A very long shot of the two newsreaders.

The studio is symbolically divided into two by a transparent panel-board on which a heraldic symbol is seen.

The very long shot suggests the ideas of the complexity of broadcasting: a whole crew is operating behind the glass window. The two-shot and the panel-board imply the division of work in the newsroom. The panel-board itself implies that something important will be 'pinned' there.

Full-face field/reverse field medium close-ups (BBC1):
(framed stills in the background)

Both newsreaders address the audience directly from the screen, shown up to the waist. The switch from one to the other demonstrates the similar roles they are playing – bearers of truth. They have authority vested in them by the television channel they represent. Besides, using two talking heads, instead of one, increases this authority and is a better guarantee for 'telling the truth'.

A similar analysis of the codes operating at the opening of the Bulgarian news bulletin and that of BBC1 could be done.

BBC1 uses a very long establishing shot accompanied by magnificent and complicated computer graphics. The studio is brightly lit, so that the viewer can even see what is going on behind the glass windows. The immediate effect is of space and size, suggesting that while we see one or two people directly, a whole squadron of professionals is also involved in producing and broadcasting the news.

The picture is quite different in the Bulgarian news bulletin. The predominant colours are dark; usually the background of the studio is dark, whereas the newsreader is brightly lit. There is not a hint of the crew working behind, and the effect is just the opposite – the figure on the screen personifies the whole crew, although the audience is aware he/she is just a voice. The quality of the computer graphics used and the absence of a transparent panel-board for the headlines speak for themselves. In my opinion this is not because of lack of knowledge or some cultural differences. Rather, the reason might be of an economic nature – the poor financial state of the Bulgarian television as a government institution as a direct result of the present political situation in the country.

Although on the whole the British crew may follow a number of routine conventions when broadcasting the news, they are more flexible in the change of modes and visual codes of television and more open to experimenting and piloting new ideas. There is a desire to add a personal touch to an already existing convention, to create something, not merely imitate.

The above are just suggestions of how teachers might interpret a still shot. The idea is to encourage the students to think about what is behind the pictures they see, why they are shot that way, what effect they have on the viewers, and what attracts the attention. Only then may they start analysing the methods used by the different channels. They are in no way judging the truthfulness of the events or their importance as such. However, without a proper comparison and contrast between the modes/ elements of presentation or the visual codes of the different television programmes, and especially suggestions as to why some are used while others are not, the lessons should not come under the heading 'cultural studies'.

In this context, what I suggest here is to ask the students to prepare a list of the most effective methods of presenting the news, to describe the programmes' distinguishing features, and to compare and contrast the programmes studied, but avoiding any easy or glib generalisations.

As an illustrative example, the conclusions my students reached when given the above tasks, analysing the elements and modes of presentation, are as follows:

- the key figure on the Bulgarian screen is the newsreader, while on the British screen the reporter seems primary and the newsreader secondary;

- the main sources of information for the British and the Bulgarian bulletins are almost the same, with very slight difference in the order of appearance: film-reports and interviews on the spot, graphics with voice-over and talking head;
- regardless of nationality, social, political, economic and cultural differences, the two television news programmes use approximately the same visual modes of presentation.

Similarities:

- the wide usage of graphics, especially symbols denoting the programme;
- the presence of newsreader, reporter and correspondent;
- favourite area – interviews;
- the use of music (denoting a programme).

Differences:

- one talking head in the Bulgarian news bulletin;
- the stake-out, the live link-up, the still-photograph are entirely missing from the Bulgarian news;
- the reporter/correspondent in the Bulgarian news is almost always nominated only by caption and not by the newsreader;
- credit is given to the work of the cameraman in the Bulgarian news, nominated by caption beneath the reporter's name;
- the reporter is always known by name only and not by face; he/she never appears in person in front of the camera in Bulgarian bulletins.

To summarise, the key points in evaluating the project include the following:

Advantages:

- Realistic objectives – raising students' awareness of other cultures
- Adequate range of classroom procedures
- Authentic texts
- Relevant to their life experience
- Stimulating thinking and creativity
- Possible to develop to a higher level
- Not a conventional type of lesson/ not routine work

Disadvantages:

- The need to establish basic theory and terminology

- Needs planning and preparation in advance – video recording of different news bulletins
- Technical problems: facilities, available room, inappropriate or spare time
- Need to convince doubting colleagues/students/parents *et al.*

Appendix 4.1   Plans for Three Lessons on Television News Broadcasts

Lesson 1

Aim:	To make students literate in the 'language' of television To raise their awareness of cultural differences
Rationale:	To enable students to 'read' the screen To distinguish between the key figures on the screen and their roles
Level:	Advanced students
Timing:	45 minutes
Materials:	Pre-recorded videotape of news (national and British ones); video-recorder; questionnaire on board/flip chart; clippings from British newspapers with different kinds of news (international, regional news, sports news, the weather forecast)
Method:	Lead-in:

1. General introduction to the Media with the help of the questionnaire (10 minutes):
   Which is your favourite channel?
   Which is your favourite programme?
   Your parents' favourite one?
   Do you watch the news? If YES, why? If NO, why?
   Tick the ones you agree with:

   ☐ Easier/lazier way to learn
   ☐ Learn more/the hottest news through picture and sound
   ☐ Cheaper than newspapers
   ☐ Interested in politics
   ☐ Will help my preparation for university
   ☐ Other reasons (specify)

2. Brainstorming exercise (5 minutes):

Ask the following question:

What words can be used to define the people on and behind the screen?

The students give their suggestions and make a list of the most appropriate ones. The teacher might help if necessary, giving clues in the form of questions. For example: 'What do you call a person who . . .?'. Then they define what the roles of these people are.

Stage One: The students work either individually or in pairs. A couple of short excerpts from the British news are played with the sound off. The students have to guess 'who is who' on the screen and 'what are their roles'. Then they give reason for their decisions. Finally the teacher plays the excerpts with their sound on and students check their answers. (10 minutes)

Stage Two: The students work in groups of four. The teacher plays some excerpts from the national news and asks them to take notes about the key figures on/behind the screen. After that they have to compare them with those from the British news. The students report their findings and discuss similarities and differences. (10 minutes)

Stage Three: Role play. The students work in groups of four. Each group is given some clippings and they have to produce a short news bulletin assigning themselves roles. Each student takes a definite role, for example, that of the newsreader, the sportscaster or the weathercaster. Their task is to act out the 'television news', choosing what actually to report. A group or two does this in front of the class. (10 minutes)

Follow-up: Project work assigned as a homework task. The students work in pairs or small groups. They have to choose a channel and follow the news bulletins at different times at the weekend and compare them having in mind the elements of presentation.

Lesson 2

Aim:	To make students literate in the 'language' of television To raise students' awareness of cultural differences
Rationale:	To analyse and compare visual modes of presentation in television news bulletins
Level:	Advanced learners
Timing:	45 minutes
Materials:	Pre-recorded videotape of news (British and national ones); video-recorder; handouts with basic terms and explanations
Method:	1. The students report back their project work in groups. (5 minutes)
	2. The teacher starts with an explanation of some special terms, i.e. visual modes of presentation/nomination, still photo, vox-pop, stake-out, etc. It is advisable to support it with examples from the national news, using different video techniques. The students are given handouts with the basic terms and techniques of shooting to help them in their work. Then the teacher might give the students a task while watching a very short excerpt to distinguish between these. He/she might go further and play a longer excerpt (2–3 minutes) and ask them to count the different visual modes of presentation. The students work in small groups and then discuss their results as a class. (15 minutes)
Stage One:	The students are divided into groups of four or five. The teacher plays an excerpt from the national news (not longer than 5 minutes) and asks them to analyse the images on the screen. The students take down notes and then, using the handouts, check their answers and discuss in their group their findings. (10 minutes)
Stage Two:	The students choose a speaker who reports back to the class just one technique. The groups take turns reporting back till all visual modes of presentation are mentioned. (10 minutes)

Stage Three: The students work in groups. Their task is to compare the beginning of the national and the British news and take down notes having in mind the different elements and modes of presentation. The excerpts should not be longer than a minute. Then they report back to the class. (5 minutes)

Lesson 3

Aim: To raise students' awareness of cultural differences
To respond and analyse the visual messages of television news

Rationale: To interpret and understand how visual codes work on the screen

Level: Advanced students

Timing: 45 minutes

Materials: Pre-recorded videotape of news (British and national ones); video-recorder; a short script of national news

Method: Explanation of terminology. Here the students need some terms describing the codes operating in television news, as well as different techniques of shooting and some of the vocabulary on visual modes of presentation. The teacher starts with a brief revision of the techniques of shooting with camera by means of the video, and then introduces some new vocabulary such as 'zoom', 'pan', 'frame light', etc. by using the national news. The students have the task to recognise them while watching some more stills. (10–12 minutes)

Stage One: The students work in groups of four or five. To make the students' task easier in the next stages of the lesson, the teacher gives an example of how they should work to 'read' the messages sent from the television screen. He/she gives his/her reasons using the opening of the news on one of the television channels. In small groups the students follow a very short excerpt from the opening of the national news on another channel. Their task is to answer the following questions:

1. *Recognise who is the producer? Any symbols?*
2. *What information do you get? How do you get it?*
3. *Do you recognise any techniques discussed?*
(8 minutes)

Stage Two: The students discuss their answers in their group and choose a speaker to report back. One of the groups reports back, the other checks their answers. (5 minutes)

Stage Three: The students watch a selected passage from the pre-recorded video of the British news (2–3 minutes long). In groups the students discuss the same questions as in Stage One. A class discussion follows on the similarities and differences between the two television programmes. (7–8 minutes)

Stage Four: 1. The students are given copies of the beginning of the script of the Bulgarian (national) news – about 2–3 minutes. In groups they design a plan of how to shoot it and prepare a short presentation. (5 minutes)
2. Students' presentations. (2 minutes per group)
3. Students watch the original news excerpt and compare.

Appendix 4.2   Plan for Single Lesson on Television News Broadcasts

Aim: To become literate in the language of media, i.e. to respond to the visual messages of television

Rationale: To understand how visual codes work on the screen, i.e. to learn about some routine conventions of camera work

Level: Advanced learners

Timing: One lesson of 90 minutes

Materials: Pre-recorded videotape of two news broadcasts of different British channels and one Bulgarian, video-recorder; television-set; copies of part of the script from the Bulgarian news (not longer than 5 minutes); OHP and transparencies (optional) or flip-chart board; blackboard

Method:

Part One: The first part of the lesson is devoted to a general intro-
              duction of media: types of media, people involved, types
              of audiences, types of programmes, etc. This is done in
              the form of asking questions and eliciting answers from
              the students. Explanation is possible when needed. All
              the questions lead to open discussion of the impact of
              television on our lives (habits, behaviour, upbringing
              etc.). (20 minutes)

              Explanation of terminology/selected visual codes, especi-
              ally codes of movement of camera, is done either orally
              or playing video and pausing at selected shots. For clarity
              put the terms on the board. (10 minutes)

Part Two: Students are divided into groups of five (4×5) and asked
              the questions:
              Recognise who is the producer? Any symbols?
              What information you get? How do you get it?
                 (expected answer – through camera work)
              Do you recognize any techniques discussed? Use terms.

              Students watch a selected passage from the pre-recorded
              video of one British news broadcast (preferably the begin-
              ning, about 2–3 minutes long). In groups the students
              discuss the questions and note down codes. (10 minutes)

              Class discussion. (5 minutes)

              Students watch a selected passage from the pre-
              recorded video of the other British news broadcast (2–3
              minutes long). In groups they discuss the same ques-
              tions and note down codes. Then compare them with
              the codes of the other bulletin. (5 minutes)

              Class discussion. (5 minutes)

              Students are given copies of the beginning of the script
              of the Bulgarian news (less than 5 minutes). In groups
              they design a plan how to shoot it. They prepare a short
              presentation. (15 minutes)

              Students' presentations, (2 minutes per group)
              Students watch the original news excerpt and compare
              with their version. (5 minutes)

Appendix 4.3　Plan for Beginners' Lesson on Television News Broadcasts

Aim:　　　　　To raise students' awareness of cultural differences through television news bulletins

Rationale:　　To teach the students 'to read' some visual messages

Level:　　　　Beginners

Timing:　　　45 minutes

Materials:　　Pre-recorded videotape of news (British and national); Video-recorder; questionnaire on board or flip-chart

Stage One:　　Warming-up in the form of a questionnaire. (10 minutes)

1. *How often do you watch television?*
   - ☐ Every day
   - ☐ Every other day
   - ☐ Twice a week
   - ☐ More

2. *How many hours a day do you watch television?*
   - ☐ One – two hours
   - ☐ Three – four hours
   - ☐ More

3. *Which is your favourite channel?*

4. *Which is your favourite programme?*

5. *Which is your parents' favourite programme?*

6. *Would you like to watch the television news? If YES, why? If NO, tick the following:*
   - ☐ Time not convenient
   - ☐ Do not like politics
   - ☐ Do not understand politics
   - ☐ Not interested at all

Stage Two:　　1. The teacher asks the question:
   How can you recognize the news is on television?
   Suggestions: specific time; music; symbols; familiar faces and voices
2. In pairs or small groups the students put down questions they would like to ask about the British news.

They read them and the best ones are written down on the board. For example:

What time? How long? How often? Are sports news and weather forecasts included? etc.

3. In their groups the students answer the list of questions having in mind the national news.
(15 minutes)

Stage Three: The students work in groups of 4 – 5. The teacher asks the questions:

Which are the main participants in the news?
How do you know?
What information are you given?

1. The students watch an excerpt from the national news and then one from the British news. While watching they have to answer the above questions. The students take down notes, then discuss them in their groups and report back.

2. The students are asked to compare the two pieces of news.
(15 minutes)

FOLLOW-UP: As a homework assignment the students are given the task to follow the news on two different national channels or at different times and note if there are any differences between them.

References

Hartley, John (1993) *Understanding News*. London: Routledge.
Masterman, Len (1985) *Teaching Media*. London: Routledge.

Chapter 5
An Approach to Implementing a Cultural Studies Syllabus

ISKRA GEORGIEVA

Teachers often feel unsure about a cultural studies syllabus because they think they do not have sufficient knowledge or experience of other countries. This chapter shows that it is more important to concentrate on skills than knowledge and on encouraging learners to analyse the familiar cultural world around them as a basis for intercultural comparison and reflection.

The Cultural Studies Syllabus: The Teacher Trainer's Perspective

This chapter is a description of and reflection on a series of lessons designed and taught in response to a seminar held in Varna in October 1998. At this seminar the cultural studies syllabus was presented to a group of interested teachers from the English medium and some vocational schools where English is taught intensively. The brainstorm on potential problems that teachers could foresee revealed that most teachers lacked the confidence to try and introduce a 'cultural dimension' into their teaching of the language. The underlying reason was that they felt they didn't have enough knowledge and materials about British culture. As a teacher trainer for the area I saw the necessity to develop a series of lessons which emphasise the high value that the syllabus places on skills rather than knowledge, on the ability to seek out relevant information, present it in appropriate ways and interpret it, rather than memorise facts (as has often been the case). These were designed as generic lessons – ones that would lend themselves to being easily adapted to different contexts, topics and levels of language proficiency. I wanted to persuade my colleagues that there is enough material for cultural studies 'on our own doorstep' and above all to demonstrate how theory works in practice. I invited the teachers who participated in the seminar to observe me teaching two of the lessons in order to challenge and encourage them to make the crucial step from theory to practice. They were also encouraged to use the classroom observation sheet format provided by the authors of the syllabus to evaluate my lessons. This was an opportunity for the teachers to test the tool which they were subsequently going to use for evaluating their own and their partner's cultural studies lessons. Completed observation sheets would also give me valuable feedback about the lessons, my teaching and my students' performance. The lessons were recorded on videotape to be used later for teacher training purposes. This, in brief, was the context in which the idea for these lessons was conceived.

The Cultural Studies Syllabus: The Teacher's Perspective

The teaching context was 10th class students, aged 17–18, studying at the English Medium School in Varna, Bulgaria. The school is selective and competitive. The students have had one year of intensive English language study of 21 lessons (each 40 minutes) per week and two years of six lessons of English per week. In the 10th class they also have six lessons of English per week, three of which focus on English literature. Their language level is fairly advanced.

The lessons I designed were based on students' essays on the topic: 'Given the chance to pick from one to three items to be put in a time capsule to be opened in a thousand years, what would you choose to represent the way of life on the Earth in the last decade of twentieth century? Give reasons.' The lessons aimed at developing the four cultural studies skills (critical reading, comparing and contrasting, ethnography and research as defined in the syllabus) in an integrated way with the main focus on comparing and contrasting.

Procedure

After correcting and marking the essays I returned them to the students with the usual feedback on language, content and organisation. Then the students conducted a kind of survey in order to compile a list of all the items chosen in their essays and ranked them according to how frequently each one was chosen. They also interviewed their parents with the same question (see essay title) and ranked the answers in the same way. In the process the students developed their ethnographic skills and the skill of grouping items into categories – each class chose their own way of collecting the data and presenting it. Two volunteers put together the information from all the four classes, so we had data from about one hundred student respondents and from roughly twice as many parent respondents (see Table 5.1). On these two lists I based a fluency-oriented lesson which consisted of two sessions of 40 minutes. In drawing up the lesson plan, I followed the observation sheet format so that my perspective could be easily compared with that of the observers (see Table 5.2).

Table 5.1   Survey data

	Parents' list			*Students' list*	
1.	computer	36	1.	computer	43
2.	book	33	2.	book	29
	• not specified	26		• not specified	10
	• encyclopedia	4		• encyclopedia	6
	• History of the World	1		• History of the World	5
	• Bible	2		• The Red Book	5
				• on psychology	1
				• on ethnography	1
3.	photo (not specified)	11	3.	photo	14
				• not specified	9
				• Demi Moore	1
				• street fashion	1
				• rich and poor person	1
				• people (not specified)	1
				• landscape	1
4.	video tape (not specified)	11	4.	video tape	13
				• content not specified	12
				• the war in Bosnia	1
5.	CD	11	5.	CD	10
6.	car	10	6.	television set	9
7.	plant	9	7.	weapon	9
8.	television set	7	8.	plant	7
9.	weapon	6	9.	car	6
10.	medicine plant	5	10.	drugs	11
11.	ball	4	11.	ball	5
12.	drugs	3	12.	newspaper	5
13.	mobile phone	2	13.	food	5
14.	money	2	14.	money	4

Table 5.1 (*continued*)

Parents' list		Students' list	
15. pine tree	1	15. cigar	4
16. stone	1	16. condom	3
17. cat	1	17. piece of the Berlin Wall	3
18. Ms Lewinski	1	18. painting	3
19. cross	1	19. human being	2
20. syringe	1	20. leaf of a tree	2
21. human being	1	21. coke	2
22. surgical instruments	1	22. sheet of paper	2
23. handful of soil	1	23. human DNA	2
24. Madonna	1	24. newly invented medicine	2
25. leaf of tree	1	25. love letter	1
26. ex-communist	1	26. apple	1
27. coke	1	27. Madonna	1
28. sheet of paper	1	28. Dolly the sheep	1
29. condom	1	29. Clinton's cigar	1
30. newspaper	1	30. F-18	
31. food	1	31. ex-communist	1
32. microwave oven	1	32. blue flag	1
33. gold	1	33. piece of barbed wire	1
34. recipe	1	34. HIV-positive person	1
35. a piece of Berlin wall	1	35. mobile phone	1
36. epigrams of Radoi Ralin	1	36. VCR	1
37. icon	1	37. virus	1
38. my own self	1	38. air	1
39. my dog	1	39. plastic container	1
40. my Grandma	1	40. world map	1
41. information on AIDS	1	41. audio cassette	1
42. information on cloning	1	42. gold	1
43. my sister	1	43. model space shuttle	1
44. frozen sperm and ovum	1	44. poster of Leonardo di Caprio	1
45. robot	1	45. astronaut's suit	1
46. painting	1	46. picture of an alien	1
47. DNA sample	1		
48. space shuttle model	1		

Table 5.2   Lesson plan

No	Stage and timing	Purpose (objectives)	Classroom management	Comments
1.	Prediction 1 Predict the five most common objects chosen by students. Give reasons. (5 minutes)	To raise awareness of existing stereotypes about own culture.	Individually, in pairs; voting – results on blackboard.	Top three items easy to guess; items 3 and 4 expected to provoke discussion.
2.	Prediction 2 Teacher dictates a list of items. Students put them into the following categories – items chosen by: • students • parents • both • neither (10 minutes)	To reveal stereotypes about own culture and other culture.	Pairs, groups of four, report to the class.	The prediction is meant to provoke discussion which may bring to the surface assumptions and beliefs about own and other culture.
3.	Students are given two lists of ranked items – students' ranking and parents' ranking. They guess which is which and give reasons. Teacher provides the answers, students check their predictions. (5 minutes)	To question stereotypes.	Pair work, feedback by show of hands.	
4.	Interpreting the meaning of some of the items from both lists. (20 minutes)	To develop skills for decoding images.	Whole class – teacher-led discussion.	Students also have the opportunity to practise communicative functions: expressing opinions, probability, possibility, (dis)agreement, etc

Table 5.2 *(continued)*

No Stage and timing	Purpose (objectives)	Classroom management	Comments
5. Comments on similarities and differences between the two lists. (25 minutes)	To develop skills for: comparing and contrasting, recognising age-specific attitudes.	Whole class – teacher-led discussion.	Remind students to use linking words: both, similarly, likewise, while, whereas, unlike, etc.
6. Home assignment: report the results of the survey in a newspaper article. Illustrate it in the most appropriate way – graph, bar chart, pie chart, etc. (optional but recommended).	To develop skill for distinguishing between fact and opinion, representing and interpreting graphical representation of statistical data.		Refer students to previously done work on comparison and contrast paragraphs.

Commentary

Here are my stage-by-stage comments on the lesson illustrated with parts of the transcript, quotations from students' essays and articles, as well as sample diagrams.

Stage 1

As I expected, the first three items were guessed by everybody, but for items 3 and 4 there was a wide range of suggestions: a CD, a television set, a weapon, money, drugs, etc. The following short extract reveals an interesting process – how a student's mind is groping to express an abstract idea through a concrete image.

Student: World famine.
Teacher: Pardon?
Student: World famine.

Teacher:	World famine? How can you . . . represent world famine?
Student:	Starvation.
Teacher:	Yes. Starvation. This is a *problem*. We are talking about *objects* and *items*, so you have to think of an object which will . . .
Student:	Maybe . . .
Teacher:	. . . represent . . .
Student:	. . . videotape with . . . evidence.

The extract clearly shows the necessity to train students to translate abstract ideas into concrete images and vice versa.

Stage 2

This is the list of items that I dictated: *a bottle of scent, a syringe, a Bible, a ball, a cross, a newspaper, a diary (an ordinary person's diary), a piece of the Berlin Wall, virtual reality equipment, a love letter, Madonna, Dolly the sheep, gold, a sample of DNA, an icon, a blue flag (the United Nations Organization flag), morning dew, a piece of barbed wire, a plastic container.* The 'false' items that I had added were *a bottle of scent, a diary, virtual reality equipment* and *morning dew.*

Here are the answers that some students gave:

Daniella

Students' choice:	*a ball, a diary, virtual reality equipment, a love letter, Dolly the sheep* and *a sample of DNA.*
Parents' choice:	*a syringe, a Bible, a piece of the Berlin Wall, gold, an icon* and *a blue flag.*
Both:	*a cross, a newspaper, Madonna.*
Neither:	*a bottle of scent, morning dew, a piece of barbed wire* and *a plastic container.*

Kiril

Students' choice:	*a syringe, a ball, a diary* and *virtual reality equipment.*
Parents' choice:	*a bottle of scent, a Bible, a cross, a newspaper, Dolly the sheep* and *an icon.*
Both:	*gold, a piece of the Berlin Wall.*
Neither:	*a love letter, Madonna, a sample of DNA, a blue flag, morning dew, a piece of barbed wire* and *a plastic container.*

Zhenya

Students' choice: *virtual reality equipment, a diary, a blue flag, a syringe.*
Parents' choice: *a piece of the Berlin Wall, a love letter* and *gold.*
Both: *a bottle of scent, a newspaper, Dolly the sheep* and *an icon.*
Neither: *a Bible, a ball, a cross, morning dew, a piece of barbed wire*
                        and *a plastic container.*

The students were right in their guess that *morning dew* was a distractor but wrong in their judgement that *barbed wire* and *plastic container* were also distractors. Obviously at first sight these objects carried no meaning for them. This is the comment that Zhenya gave on the choices of categories Both and Neither:

> The bottle of scent has something to do with Nature because most of the scents are associated with flowers and that's why maybe both students and parents, the . . . both generations chose this item. The other – newspaper . . . because it represents not only our culture and our language but also the political and social . . . side of our society. And Dolly the sheep because . . . it became very popular. This is a kind of scientific progress . . . I put the icon also here . . . although . . . religion is not the same thing as it was years before. Probably some students may associate it with computers – click the icon . . .

> And the last column. The Bible. I think it's something like old-fashioned thing, maybe nobody now cares about it. . . . And a ball. . . . the ball isn't a kind of symbol of our generation. It became popular many years before our time, it's not interesting. That's what I think. . . . The cross is the same as the Bible. Barbed wire . . . Maybe it's . . . It might be a symbol of war but I don't think anybody . . . (Pause)

> Teacher: Anybody in the future will . . . be able to interpret that symbol?

As can be seen from this comment, while giving reasons for each choice students have already begun to interpret the images.

Stage 3

The students were unanimous in identifying the two lists – which comprises the students' choices (right column) and which the choices of their parents (left column). As items which most clearly indicate whose choice they are, students pointed out a poster of Leonardo di Caprio, drugs, a photo of Demi Moore.

Stage 4

I used the following questions in order to elicit interpretations and steer the discussion: What surprised you? What is the message that this object is meant to carry? What are the feelings that an item would evoke? What are the messages that the item will convey to the future generations? What are the associations that it evokes in you as a contemporary? *Barbed wire*, for example, evoked in the students the following associations: 'hostility', 'war', 'terror', 'violence', 'separation between people, it stands on their way to each other . . .'.

Here is a short dialogue between me and a student:

Teacher: Now let's look from the perspective . . . of people who live in the thirtieth century. Look back one thousand years earlier. . . . Is there an image that would not make sense to you? . . . Or you find difficult to understand?

Student: An apple.

Teacher: An apple. Any interpretations offered for an apple? . . . Apple?

Student: It may represent the environment.

Teacher: Environment. Environment, not yet irretrievably damaged. . . . Fertility, the fruitfulness of Nature . . .

At the beginning I also participated in developing the interpretations, thus implicitly giving the students examples of what they were expected to do and also suggesting to them ideas which they could include in their articles if they chose to. Here is one more example:

Student: A piece of the Berlin Wall . . . because it separated East from West Germany and . . . and in that way, people who lived in different countries, yet were one nation.

Teacher: So it has become a symbol, in a way, of the changes, all those changes that followed.

Stage 5

This stage was a more immediate preparation for the written task 'Write an article, reporting and interpreting the findings of the survey'. We looked at the items in three groups: the top five (which were the same and therefore students practised generating sentences about similarities), the single items and the group in between. The single items were the most original and the most difficult to interpret. We also discussed how the students' expectations (elicited in stages 1 and 2) compare with the real results and in what way the differences have changed the students' image of their parents' generation. This is what one student said:

> Well, for example, I was impressed that the CD is number five, in the top five, because I . . . I thought that parents are not that much interested in music, especially if we are talking about music on CDs. It's ... well, it's characteristic of our generation but I wasn't aware that it was also of my parents' generation.

We also looked at the findings of the survey from two other points of view: the range of aspects of contemporary life that the two lists cover and whether the objects listed give a predominantly positive, negative or balanced picture of life today. The first task demanded that students identify categories and group items accordingly. The following areas were identified: science and technology, politics, entertainment, social life, sports, nature and environment, religion, history. As to the second task, after receiving a few examples illustrating the bright and dark sides of life, the students decided that on the whole the survey gave a balanced picture of contemporary life. Some items, such as a History of the World, provoked an interesting discussion because of their inherently contradictory nature.

Stage 6

As a home assignment the students wrote an article based on the findings of the survey. Some students used the data from their class only, others used the 'integrated' list of items. The aim of this task was to make the students review once again the ideas discussed as well as to reinforce work already done on organising comparison and contrast in writing. In setting the task I emphasised that students were expected not only to give facts but also to interpret what state or tendency these facts imply or indicate. In addition, they had to be as objective as possible and interpret but not judge!

Here are some extracts from the articles that the students wrote:

> . . . The survey reveals that the choices of students and parents are very much alike. Both youngsters and grown-ups aim to show the advance in technology. That is why the most common item on both lists is the computer. Surprisingly, not only teenagers but also their parents consider that items like CD or a television set are worth being sent. It seems adults enjoy sitting in front of the television or spending their time listening to music as much as their children . . .

. . . It is quite amazing that six out of twenty-three children have chosen weapons while only one out of forty-one parents wants to put a weapon in the time capsule. This fact shows how cruel and dangerous the contemporary world is. Perhaps a lot of the students have experienced some kind of violence whereas their parents have lived in a more peaceful and secure world. . . .

. . . The students are more creative and clever in finding the items corresponding to their ideas but what would happen if they participate in the same survey ten years from now? . . .

. . . Students are more aware of the danger caused by the most widely spread diseases during the last decade of twentieth century – AIDS and cancer. . . .

. . . The results of the survey contradict to a certain extent the common expectation that each generation lives in a world of its own. . . .

Phrases like 'surprisingly' and 'it is quite amazing' show that the students did indeed find out unexpected things about their own generation and that of their parents.

Presenting the statistical data through a diagram was optional but a lot of students volunteered to do it with varying degree of success (see Figures 5.1 and 5.2). I saw this as a good opportunity for applying an interdisciplinary approach in learning – the students practised skills from different areas of study, including computer science.

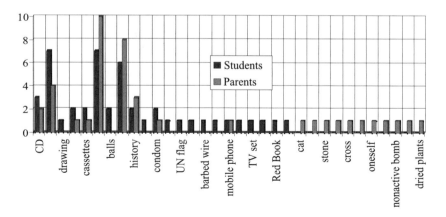

Figure 5.1 Bar chart of time capsule survey.

PARENTS (100% = 44 items)

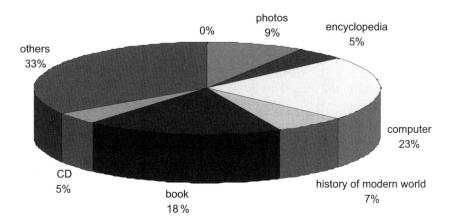

STUDENTS (100% = 54 items)

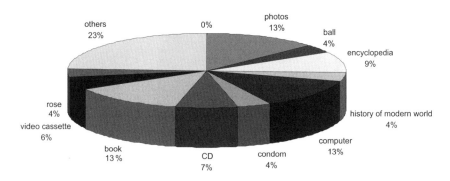

Figure 5.2   Pie charts of time capsule survey.

I am also tempted to offer as an illustration one short essay and some extracts from a few others:

The last ten years of the twentieth century could be described with a single word – contrast. It is a time of great progress and deep stagna-tion, brilliant knowledge and total ignorance, startling cruelty and touching humanity. As a symbol of this contrast I would put in the time capsule a drawing made by a child and a piece of barbed wire.

In a thousand years all the achievements of science, considered nowadays as 'extremely sophisticated' and 'revolutionary new discoveries' would seem primitive. That is why I will not try to impress the people of the future with any of them. Though these people will not think and see things like we do, they would be able to understand a drawing in bright colours, made by a child, on which there are happy people from all races holding hands, flowers, a rainbow and planes and rockets in the sky. It would symbolise the good side of life today – technical progress and love among people, who help each other.

On the other hand, the piece of barbed wire would symbolize the terrible and frightening side of life in the last decade of twentieth century. It would show the wars still going on, in contrast with the happy children of all races holding hands, the screams of children dying of hunger, in contrast with the children making fine drawings. It would be a symbol of all the cruelty that turns many places on Earth into a living hell.

Hopefully, in a thousand years people will be able to understand our mistakes, to keep the good aspects of today's life and throw away the bad ones. Thus they will make this planet a better place to live in and they would be much happier than we are.

A lot of other students also chose two contrasting objects, such as a rose and a weapon. Unlike the majority of students who gave priority to the computer, there were the precious few who wrote things like:

. . . I think that people a thousand years from now would be more advanced and a computer would not be so interesting. More interesting, in my opinion, would be objects of artistic value, representing our way of thinking, our values and morals . . .

Some students, like the one quoted below, found different ingenious ways of presenting concepts through an object:

The first thing which I will put in the capsule is the book by the French writer Antoine de Saint Exupery – 'The Little Prince'. In this book are hidden the secrets of the most important feelings for people – love, friendship, loneliness and grief. These feelings are explained in a very simple way, so everybody would be able to understand them. I think that every contemporary has read this book and it is very important that the future generations should read it too.

Evaluation

To sum up, the skills that the students practised during this lesson and the preceding one were collecting, presenting and interpreting statistical data in different formats, differentiating between fact and opinion, decoding images. Through the discussion that took place I wanted to raise students' awareness of certain assumptions and stereotypes about the two generations – about their generation and their parents' generation. Some of the students were quite surprised that their parents' answers were not dramatically different from theirs, which led to the conclusion that the so-called 'generation gap' is not that deep after all, in other words that they have a lot of common ground to share. On the other hand, some images were interpreted in different ways within the student group. *Icon* was one of the ambiguous images. It was meant to represent religion by the person who suggested it but there were interpretations connected with computers. Other such items were a *hamburger* and *a Coke*. The person who suggested hamburger and Coke as types of fast food meant them to be an expression of our hectic life. 'Our life is hectic, we drive fast cars and eat fast food and we enjoy it!' Another interpretation of the same two items was that the quality of life has deteriorated and we eat junk food. This shows that even within one culture, community or any group with its own identity, objects and phenomena may be ambiguous and carry different meaning for different individuals.

Most students supported their conclusions with relevant facts and gave objective, unprejudiced interpretations. There was only one student who after severely criticising the parents for lack of imagination, sensitivity and awareness of the major problems of the day, finished his article with the following angry exclamation: 'It is high time for adults to wake up and do something!'

While planning the lesson I found it extremely helpful to refer to the package of cultural studies materials produced by a team of Bulgarian teachers and especially a list of the characteristics of a good cultural learning activity. Here are some of these characteristics which provided useful guidance for me in planning my lessons: A good cultural learning activity should:

- enable learners to describe, analyse and reflect on specific features of language and culture;

- have tolerance built into the process of learning;
- involve learners in solving a problem and coming to a conclusion;
- involve learners in working together in teams;
- involve learners in risk-taking;
- utilise Bulgarian culture as a resource;
- increase awareness of how concepts can vary depending on one's culture;
- allow learners to rehearse in class the communication and cultural skills they will need in the world outside.

This last feature is crucial and it partly gives the answer to the question: how does the lesson outlined above relate to the cultural studies syllabus?

The connection has been present implicitly all through my account of the lesson. However, to make it more explicit I would like to give the following suggestion for transferring the idea to a real cultural studies project. If the teacher finds a colleague from another country/culture willing to participate with his/her students, then the two groups of students may follow the procedure outlined above and develop an exciting and potentially very enlightening project. Here is a sample project plan:

(1) Both groups of students (representing C1 and C2) write essays on the same topic. (The one that I have used is just an example of a wide range of topics suitable for the purpose.)
(2) After the essays have been marked by the respective teachers, the students from each group process the factual information from their essays and present it in condensed form through a table or diagram.
(3) The two groups exchange via e-mail sample essays and the statistical data that they have compiled.
(4) Students from each group write a report comparing the statistical data, which the two groups have produced.
(5) The two groups exchange reports.
(6) If appropriate, publicity may be given to the products of the project (essays, reports, tables of comparison, etc.) either locally or through an international forum such as Cultural Horizons. The prospect of their work being published will strongly motivate the students to edit until they produce a polished version.
(7) Teachers and students together evaluate the effectiveness of the project.

My anticipation is that such a project will provide a framework for the students to transfer and apply the skills which they 'rehearsed' during this lesson to another context in the world outside the classroom, e.g. instead of looking for age-specific differences, to recognise culture-specific, regional or global attitudes and issues.

I hope that this material will help teachers to spot opportunities that arise naturally in the process of their language teaching and encourage them to give the latter a 'cultural dimension'.

Chapter 6

'Family Life' and 'Regional Identity': Comparative Studies While Learning French

SYLVIA DUFFY AND JANET MAYES

Students in upper secondary education learning French as a foreign language were offered a course which introduced them to a number of themes in French social life. In this chapter the project as a whole is described and then two themes are described in detail to show the techniques for encouraging students to work with ethnographic materials and to learn how to conduct ethnographic data collection for themselves.

Introduction

In this chapter we will give a brief overview of the Cultural Studies for Advanced Language Learners project, which was developed in the School of Education at Durham University by a team of teachers and researchers (Byram & Morgan *et al.*, 1994). We will outline the context of the course we developed in terms of the learners themselves and indicate how it was integrated into different teaching programmes at the time of its implementation. The aims of the project itself and the rationale for the topics chosen will be followed by detailed accounts of the teaching of two topics, the Family and Regional Identity, together with samples of materials, plans and work from the students themselves. There will also be some suggestions for suitable assessment activities based on our experience.

The Project

The project lasted for two years and involved five teachers of French at upper secondary level and two researchers. During the first year the teachers familiarised themselves with the theoretical background to the teaching of culture and intercultural competencies and devised a teaching programme for the first year of the two-year Advanced level French syllabus. Each teacher then took responsibility for one of the five topics and collected suitable teaching materials. It is possible to teach non-literary topics which relate to contemporary French society in place of the more traditional literary texts at Advanced level and the five institutions concerned offered this possibility. In the second year of the project the five topics were taught by the teachers concerned, and at the end of the year some assessment activities were carried out in the School of Education with the students concerned and also within the institutions themselves.

Prior learning

Upper secondary students normally begin their Advanced level French course after five years' prior learning, during which language is taught for the purposes of practical communication following the prescriptions of the National Curriculum. The learner is presumed to be a visitor to a French-speaking country, or host to a native speaker. Topics and setting for the last two years of the course, which culminates in an examination (GCSE), are closely prescribed and are intended to concern the experiences and interests of the average British 16-year-old. In contrast, in the upper secondary school, three or more subjects are chosen for intensive study over two years, as a preparation for university entrance level. The student who opts may specialise further at university/tertiary level, or may choose other areas of study.

Advanced level French

The content and scope of Advanced level studies are much broader than those for the GCSE. Students are expected, at the end of two years, to be able to express themselves orally and in writing on a range of general and social issues and give and seek both information and opinions. Teachers are free to choose from a range of textbooks and supplementary materials, and collect or devise materials themselves in the course of teaching four linguistic skills. In addition, there is a choice of prescribed literary texts or non-literary topics which entail a more detailed study of an aspect of French life. Assessment in the course of the latter is by examination essay, coursework or oral presentation.

The aims of the Advanced level French syllabuses include the concept of cultural awareness in that they state that the study of French should:

- encourage first-hand contact with the culture and civilisation;
- foster an interest in the views of French-speaking people;
- develop awareness of the various aspects of a society in which the language is spoken.

However, despite these stated aims, the assessment objectives are almost entirely defined in linguistic terms. (Recently, candidates have been awarded a small proportion of marks for the knowledge displayed in the context of a prepared topic.) For these reasons it was decided at the beginning of the project that the intercultural competencies to be taught during the course should, as far as possible, harmonise with the linguistic aims in order to provide a coherent cultural learning experience in the context of an appropriate language learning course. In some cases, where teachers were in sole charge of their group, they integrated the teaching of general linguistic skills into the course. In other cases, where classes were shared, it was not always possible to exploit the materials to the extent the teachers would have preferred.

Aims of the project

In teaching intercultural competencies we aimed to encourage attitudes of curiosity and openness towards France and French speakers, and also speakers of other languages. We hoped that a better understanding of the socialisation experienced by young French people would encourage feelings of empathy and enable English students to understand what it was like to be French.

However, these attitudes involved an understanding of 'otherness' which would be based on knowledge. In the first place this knowledge would involve a more objective perspective on the students' own culture. Instead of assuming it to be the norm, they would be encouraged at each stage to view it as specific to time and place and subject to various influences. Each topic involved the acquisition of knowledge which, consciously or unconsciously, would be acquired by a young French person during their socialisation. Linguistic knowledge would include an understanding of the link between language and culture. New skills would involve techniques of participant observation and ethnographic enquiry, together with mediation between different points of view.

The five topics

After consideration of a number of topics which would offer the possibility of developing intercultural competencies and take into account progression in terms of linguistic skills and difficulty of concepts, it was decided to teach five topics: the Family, Education, the World of Work, Regional Identity, and Power and Politics. The first and fourth of these will be described in some detail in this chapter.

These topics give some indication of how cultural learning can be introduced using relatively simple language and concepts and how students progress towards using a wider range of resources and develop critical cultural awareness. The study of the Family at the beginning of the course allowed for the revision of lexis and syntax already familiar to the students at the same time as they were introduced to the primary socialisation of young French people. Education and the World of Work offered a logical progression from the first topic and carried the added advantage that they could be resourced from coursebooks already available as well as from authentic materials, which were obtained from various sources, including French colleagues. The topic of Regional Identity was chosen from other social identities (based on age, gender or ethnicity), both because it allowed access to French history (collective memory) and geography (collective space), and because it fitted into most examination syllabuses. Power and Politics allowed students to consider questions of personal influence and introduced them to basic knowledge about local and national government.

Sources of materials

Each teacher was responsible for planning one unit and collecting materials, which would then be duplicated or shared between the group. In the first place, video material was held to be particularly important, because it offered direct visual access to the culture, stimulating interest among the students. Extracts were taken from material produced by the BBC and independent companies, as well as material produced in France. Some audio material which accompanied Advanced level course books was found to be suitable for cultural as well as linguistic learning. Tapes were produced with the help of French assistants and by the teachers themselves, in the course of ethnographic enquiries during visits to France. There was a wide variety of documentary material, which included extracts from coursebooks, articles from the French press, statistical information, and materials obtained from tourist offices, schools and friends in France. In literary style, there were short stories, extracts from autobiographical accounts, poems and songs. Were the experience to be repeated, material would also be obtained through the internet and e-mail.

Methodology

In cases where the topics could be completely integrated into the Advanced level course, teachers used the normal techniques for presenting and practising new vocabulary and structures. As these are already familiar they will not be detailed here. There were also some new approaches used to encourage effective cultural learning and these are outlined below.

At the beginning of each unit strategies were employed which encouraged students to see their own culture through the eyes of young French people. In the early units interviews were carried out, live and on tape, with language assistants, i.e. French native speakers teaching 'conversation classes' in English schools, on the subject of home or school life. For example 'time lines' were drawn by assistants and students to highlight occasions when the family might gather during the year (Appendix 6.1). These might also be obtained through partner schools by electronic means. Simple written questionnaires were devised to enable students to carry out surveys among their families or friends, thus enabling them to look more carefully at aspects of their culture which they had previously taken for granted.

In order to sensitise students to different styles of verbal and non-verbal communication, such as rules of politeness and the establishment of hierarchy, they learnt techniques of participant observation. Ideally these techniques would be practised in the context of a fieldwork visit or an exchange. These were not possible at the time, but the use of film or video showing events of everyday life allowed for practice in a French context (see Chapter 9 of this volume).

Students were also taught how to carry out an ethnographic interview, by designing a schedule and learning how to listen for key information and ask supplementary questions. Subsequently the taped interviews themselves were used to extract points of interest. The opportunity to analyse a number of different responses helped them to avoid generalisations based on limited information.

In oral work role play was used to gain insights into areas of conflict within French society. For example, different views could be expressed by members of the same family on the importance of tradition, by young people discussing a strike or a demonstration, or deciding whether or not to leave their home region. French and English experiences could be brought together and compared. Sometimes a third student mediated between two conflicting points of view in order to propose a solution acceptable to both sides. Suggestion for assessments involving these and other activities will be found later in the chapter, in the sections which outline the teaching of the first and fourth units of the course.

Unit 1: The Family

The unit of work focusing on family life formed the first section of the project; it therefore aimed to introduce students to the study of French society and culture and to elements of intercultural competence in a context which, as well as being a prime focus in any study of a society, need not be too conceptually or linguistically daunting for 16 year olds just embarking on Advanced level study.

Coursebooks designed for use at this level frequently focus on the teenage experience of relationships and family life, encouraging comment and reflection on parent–child and girl–boy relationships, marriage, cohabitation and divorce. Such material tends to assume and emphasise the universality of such experiences in Western society rather than looking at specifically French attitudes and values. We chose instead to examine aspects of everyday family life which might highlight its significance to young people in France and their parents; these include family gatherings, meals, and family occasions, especially weddings. Audio and video recordings, interviews and discussion with native speakers (mainly language assistants), articles and authentic documents, statistical information and short literary extracts all helped students to build up some knowledge and understanding of a French teenager's experience of family life.

When students encountered this material, the initial focus was on comprehension and language development, which was integrated throughout; however, there was also an emphasis on acquiring cultural knowledge which quickly enabled them to make comparisons with their own experience. The realisation that their own norms and assumptions were cultural constructs was reinforced by encountering an outsider's perspective on their own experience. Role play and imaginative writing asked students to go a step further towards empathy, using the knowledge and language they had developed to take on the role of a French person or mediate on their behalf in a cultural conflict or misunderstanding.

Family gatherings: Timelines and interviews

Family gatherings, their frequency, the type of activity and the number of family members involved give some indication of the significance of the extended family. This was analysed using timelines produced by a group of French teenagers taking part in an exchange visit. They were asked to produce a calendar of family occasions, noting briefly when they occurred, who attended and what happened (Appendix 6.1). Small groups of students each analysed a different timeline, guided by a few questions, and reported back in French to the class. Spontaneous comparisons with their own experience was developed by the production of their own timelines; the limited geographical mobility of many families in northeast England meant that many of them had extended family networks living close by, but few seemed to meet as frequently or celebrate as often as their French counterparts. The theme was developed using extracts selected from extended and open-ended interviews recorded for the project with French native speakers living locally, mainly language assistants.

At this early stage of the course, the most useful or significant sections of the material were selected and isolated for the students, with questions combining comprehension with cultural learning. This material also introduced a French perspective on local practices: for example Ghislain expressed his astonishment that the English family he lived with so rarely gathered together or even sat down to eat together.

Chacun prenait son repas à l'heure qu'il voulait, mais il n'y avait aucun moment dans la journée où la famille pouvait se réunir, et ça m'avait frappé parce que, en France, le repas, le repas du soir notamment, permet à la famille de se retrouver et de discuter . . .

[Everybody ate at whatever time they liked, but there was no point during the day when the family could meet, and that struck me because, in France, the evening meal especially allows the family to meet up and talk . . .]

Food and family life: French perspectives on north-east England

Similar techniques were used to learn about the conduct and composition of meals, starting with simple, oral accounts by students of their own meals: what they normally eat, time and duration of meals, where and with whom meals are eaten. These were compared with parallel accounts by French people: live by the assistant (taped for future use) and commercial audio recordings from a unit of work on food. A video of a French father and daughter preparing and eating a meal encouraged students to observe the non-verbal conventions associated with setting the table and serving and eating food. Recorded interviews with language assistants both commenting on family life in France and giving their impressions of and reactions to English meals encouraged some level of critical self-awareness and provoked mixed reactions, as in the case of Laure's comments:

Et par exemple, là où j'étais, les enfants, quand il y avait autre chose que les sandwiches, ils en voulaient pas. Et je trouvais que quelquefois j'avais envie de dire, 'Oh vous ne pouvez pas, leur faire manger des crudités ou des choses comme ça?'

[And for example where I was, when there was something different from sandwiches, the children did not want it. And I sometimes felt that I wanted to say, 'Oh, can't you give them vegetables and things like that to eat?'.]

Students were quick to comment on the stereotyping of English family life by French assistants, who had encountered families who rarely ate together and ate potatoes at every meal. This experience can be used to foster an awareness that stereotyping and emphasis on difference are an initial stage in intercultural learning, but one which does not take full account of the range and variety that exist within any culture. Their own initially somewhat stereotypical view of the French family meal provides a useful starting point against which they can subsequently place supplementary reading of, for example, articles on the erosion of the traditional meal by convenience foods.

Creative writing and role-play

Speaking and writing in role provides a straightforward mechanism for encouraging students to step outside their own cultural context and identify with the practices of French people. It also encourages them to make freer use of language already developed in a structured way (in this work, for example, the expression of comparison, frequency and quantity). It offers opportunities for more formal assessment of cultural knowledge and their ability to respond imaginatively to situations presented in a French context. After work of the kind outlined above, followed by completion and discussion of a simple written summary in tabular form, to support and check on students' learning to date, they were asked to write a letter in French in one of two roles: either as an English au pair working in France, writing to a French friend about their experiences of and reactions to the place of meals and family gatherings in family life, or as a French au pair or student staying with an English family, writing home about their experience of and reactions to family life and meals. Even the least able students at this level can produce a simple, factual account based on prior reading and listening. Paul, writing in role as a French teenager staying with an English family, wrote:

Au repas du midi toute la famille mange à la place différente. Les frères mangent au collège, la sœur mange à sa école (un sandwich et une boîte de coca cola) et la mère et le père ils mangent au travail.

[For the midday meal the whole family eats somewhere different. The brothers eat at school, the sister eats at her school (a sandwich and a can of coca cola) and the mother and father eat at work.]

Je trouve que la nourriture que les anglais mangent est très bizarre aussi. Ils ne mangent pas beaucoup de pain et un peu des légumes. Les enfants mangent les gâteaux et beaucoup de chocolat – ce n'est pas bon pour la santé! Je ne pourrais pas vivre en Angleterre en permanence!

[I think the food the English eat is very strange too. They don't eat much bread and vegetables only a little. The children eat cakes and a lot of chocolate – it's not good for your health! I couldn't live in England permanently.]

More able students are capable of entering creatively into their chosen role and incorporating prior learning into an imaginative response to the situation presented. Peter wrote in role as an English teenager staying with a French family:

Les repas du soir sont très importants ici. Le repas permet à toute la famille de se retrouver et de discuter de la journée. Ça commence tous les jours à 7h et finit entre 8h et 8h30. Le repas dure entre une heure et une heure et demie parce qu'il y a beaucoup de discussion – on se parle beaucoup. Je le trouve très utile parce que je peux améliorer mon Français (j'espère!). J'aime le repas du soir ici parce que c'est très agréable et aussi je pense que c'est important pour les liens de famille . . .

[The evening meals are very important here. The meal allows the whole family to meet and talk about the day. It begins every day at 7.00 and finishes between 8.00 and 8.30. The meal lasts for an hour or an hour and a half because there is a lot of discussion – we talk to each other a lot. I think it's very useful because I can improve my French (I hope!). I like the evening meal because it's very pleasant and also because I think it's very important for family relationships . . .]

Chez moi nous mangeons vers 5h30 et le repas peut durer moins de vingt minutes ... il y a un plat principal seulement alors qu'il y a trois ou quatre plats en France. . . . Le regime en France est plus équilibré, ce qui est très bien pour moi parce que je mange plus de crudités et plus de fruits et moins de chocolat aussi.

[At my home we eat about 5.30 and the meal may last less than 20 minutes . . . there's only one main course whereas there are three or four courses in France. . . . The diet is more balanced in France. Which is very good for me because I eat vegetables and more fruit and less chocolate too.]

J'aime les repas du soir en France et quand je rentrerai en Angleterre j'espère changer l'attitude de ma famille. Je crois que nous devrions donner plus d'importance aux repas en famille . . .

[I like the evening meals in France and when I return to England, I hope I can change the attitude of my family. I think we should give more importance to family meals.]

This work was marked using a modified version of the mark scheme used in the A level examination to assess a short written response to a printed or recorded text: half the marks were awarded for quality of language; the other half for cultural learning and imaginative response. Students who showed knowledge and understanding of key points addressed in the unit achieved moderate marks, while high marks were awarded to those who entered imaginatively into the chosen role and demonstrated some ability to adopt a different frame of reference.

Role-play situations also offer the possibility of one participant being asked to mediate between two sets of cultural conventions or explain differing expectations. Students were asked to work in pairs, and were given a short time in class to think about the situation outlined on their role-play card (Appendix 6.2), but were not given a copy of their partner's card, so did not know in advance what attitudes or arguments their partner would express. They were free to develop the situation in whatever way they chose, with the 'English' partner resolving the problem with tact or refusing to compromise, and the 'French' host successfully explaining the problem and achieving a happy outcome for everyone or becoming exasperated with the guest's lack of awareness. Students were encouraged to improvise initially, working simultaneously in pairs with the opportunity to pause and reflect or ask for help; they then recorded conversations, without script or written notes. Some adopted the roles of model intercultural learners, showing understanding of each other's expectations and achieving a harmonious outcome; others delighted in playing the awkward English guest who embodies all the worst stereotypes, but in so doing ably demonstrated their awareness of the conventions they were flouting. These conversations were assessed using a similar approach to the one outlined above, with the usual marks for accuracy, fluency, pronunciation and range of linguistic structures, and a content mark based on the level of cultural knowledge demonstrated (perhaps with a simple checklist of aspects studied which might be incorporated into the conversation) and the student's ability to identify convincingly with a French viewpoint.

Weddings: Documentation and legal requirements

Weddings were chosen as an example of a family occasion which would show how a French family might celebrate an important event, and approaches similar to those outlined above were again used, with written and audiotaped personal accounts and short literary extracts leading into imaginative writing and role-play. Weddings, however, also allowed us to introduce some awareness of the state's interest in family life, using documents to present the necessary steps in planning a wedding in France. Published material introduced basic information; the example of an English woman explaining English traditions to her French fiancé served to clarify the situation in Britain, contrast it with French expectations, and provide an outsider's commentary on an English wedding. Students also saw examples of the documents required by couples planning to marry, with their medical emphasis on fitness for childbearing. Students' lively reactions to this material sparked heated debate. Students also watched a video of a French civil ceremony, considering both its visual aspects and the expectations embodied in the wording, with its overt emphasis on the rearing of children. Small group clarification and discussion of the procedures and underlying values was followed by writing in role (as a guest at a French wedding) and role-play discussion between a young English man and his French future father-in-law as to where and how the wedding should be celebrated. This, like the earlier example, provided clear indications of the knowledge students had acquired and their ability to enter into a French frame of reference, either by showing understanding of a French point of view or by playing a French role. The latter also offered students the opportunity to comment on their own culture from the outside.

Changing patterns: Social trends and statistics

Government publications provided statistics indicative of social trends: material illustrating changing patterns in France and Britain was selected for comprehension, discussion and analysis. Some ability to describe and comment on statistical data is often required at Advanced level, so the necessary language can here be practised and used in conjunction with cultural learning. We used material drawn from *La population française de A à Z* and *Social Trends*; now, this type of information is more readily available on the internet. At this relatively early stage in students' cultural learning, salient information was presented selectively. For example, tables showing percentages of men and women living together outside marriage were analysed in terms of age-groups, geographical distribution in urban and rural areas, and trends over a ten-year period. Figures on marriage, divorce, and size and composition of households were similarly discussed, leading to more formal writing on changing patterns of family life in France and Britain.

Work on the family took place over a period of about six weeks and occupied two 70-minute lessons each week; in total, it took about fifteen hours of class time and about nine hours of homework. Much of the initial reading and listening was completed at home, as was almost all the written work, leaving class time available for clarification and exploration of the material through questioning, structured discussion and role play, alongside language development, preparation of tasks and feedback. Much assessment, especially of oral work, was ongoing, as described above; a formal end of topic assessment used a mixed skills approach, testing students' listening and reading skills by comprehension questions on material closely related to earlier work, then using the same material as the basis for a written response which served to assess both their language skills and their intercultural learning.

Many of the students who took part in this work had little experience of life or travel outside their home region and fierce local loyalties. Although students' knowledge and understanding of French culture on completion of this first unit of work were still relatively unsophisticated, they had begun to learn how to look at French life through French people's own accounts and enactments of it, and stepped back from their own habits to see them through an outsider's eyes.

Unit 4: Regional Identity: Brittany

In many respects, the materials and methods used to teach this unit were not dissimilar from those which are normally used to teach such a topic. Geographic and economic features were covered, as well as a minimum of historical knowledge. The conventional interpretation of 'culture', in this case Breton folklore, language, customs and traditions, was studied, with the help of photographs, film and tourist literature. However, it was intended that the teaching of intercultural competences would allow the students to approach the topic from a different perspective, that of people with whom they could identify. For this purpose, a number of new techniques were incorporated into the teaching programme. In the first place, students would become aware of the concept of regional identity as part of the individual's social identity. Subsequently, they would be taught to become participant observers, either in real life or through the medium of film. They would use material gathered by the teacher in the form of ethnographic interviews and then learn how to conduct an ethnographic enquiry themselves. They would also use literature, both autobiography and fiction, in order to engage with the life experiences of others.

The concept of regional identity

Before beginning the study of Brittany, students explored the concept of regional identity in their own environment, the north-east of England, with the help of a questionnaire designed by the teacher (Appendix 6.3). Each student was given ten response sheets to accompany the question-naire and was asked to interview family and friends. Although this activity was carried out in English, the subsequent classroom activity, in which the information was collated and the report written by the students themselves, was in French. By reflecting on their own identity and by examining these responses, students were able to understand some conflicts and contradictions within their own culture. In addition, they were prepared for the fact that, although generalisations would be made about Brittany and Bretons, they would have to guard against over-simplifications in their own approach to the topic.

Film and participant observation

The introduction to the region was carried out with the help of a video produced by the Brittany Tourist Office, which was watched with the help of a worksheet. Students were helped to discuss the 'clichés' in terms of their significance for Bretons and French people generally. It would also prepare them for subsequent consideration of the way in which the 'Heritage Industry', both in Britain and elsewhere, exploits and trivialises regional cultural identity. Another film extract, which showed modern village life, including groups of people interacting at a social event, was used to provide some basic training in participant observation. Instead of answering questions simply based on the soundtrack, students were firstly asked to watch and comment on the behaviour of the particpants in the film, looking at a range of behaviours including non-verbal interaction (Appendix 6.4). They were then able to contrast the scene with social gathering in their own culture, describe it and make comparisons

Ethnographic Interviews

When teachers are able to choose a region to study on the basis of the fact that they have French friends in the area or that they visit it in the course of a holiday, it is possible to carry out ethnographic interviews on a wide range of topics which can later be used in the classroom. In this case the concept of regional identity was explored with the interviewees with the help of a simple interview schedule. Questions were deliberatly open-ended and points of interest were explored from the perspective of each of the individuals concerned. This was in no sense a survey, where answers would be compared in order to produce a result. It was an opportunity for individuals to describe their own experiences and to give their views. For example, interviews covered various aspects of regional identity, depending on the individual concerned: Ronan, a 17-year-old of Breton origin, living in St Nazaire and spending his holidays with his Breton grandparents; Richard, a student working as a *surveillant* in a secondary school near Rennes; a school teacher who had chosen to remain in Brittany; and a retired lady who was Breton 'by adoption', having arrived as a young woman and married a local man.

The subsequent use of the interview material varied according to the individual teacher or the group being taught. When students encountered audio tapes of such interviews for the first time, they were daunted by the quantity of material and needed the support of vocabulary and carefully worded questions. They worked in small groups, helping each other to extract the necessary information. Later they worked independently, producing summaries of sections of the interview or short transcriptions, with the help of the counter marker. They were then able to compare, discuss and make their own records of the accounts, integrating this personal knowledge with other sources of information, such as autobiography, short stories and statistical data. Finally, with the aid of the teacher, students were able to draw up their own interview schedules in preparation for a French Day at the university (Appendix 6.5), when they had the opportunity to interview a number of native speakers on the subject of regional identity. In ideal circumstances, such interviews would have been carried out in the context of fieldwork or a visit. It would also be possible to use videoconferencing or electronic communication to carry out a similar activity.

Assessment took the form of written homework and examination, and discussion in the form of role-play. The intercultural dimension was assessed on the basis of the individual's ability to identify with different expressions of regional identity in a French context, showing both knowledge and empathy. The written or oral work was also marked on the usual linguistic qualities, which accordingly attracted lower weightings. Subjects included discussions or a letter on the decision to remain in the region or go to find work in Paris, the use of Breton cultural traditions to promote tourism, the siting of a hotel complex and golf club on the

Breton coast, the teaching of Breton in primary schools and the practice of acquiring second homes, which remained unoccupied most of the year.

In conclusion, it was felt that the intercultural approach had enhanced students' understanding of, not only Brittany and Breton identity, but also the concept of cultural identity on a regional and national basis. In particular, this approach had encouraged the ability of the learners to empathise with the experiences of others, in itself one of the main aims of the project.

Appendix 6.1 Example of a 16-year-old French Boy's Timeline

31 décembre: Réveillon du jour de l'an avec la famille de ma mère et ma belle soeur. Nous dansons toute la nuit jusqu'au petit matin.

6 janvier: Nous fêtons l'Epiphanie à Abbeville. Nous mangeons la galette des Rois avec mes parents.

16 février: L'anniversaire de ma cousine (à Sassetot, chez ma cousine). Toute la famille est présente.

20 mars: L'anniversaire de ma belle sœur (à Fosses, chez sa mère). Il y a mes parents, mon frère et la famille de ma belle sœur.

15 juin: Mariage de mon frère (à Fosses). Tout le monde est là, on danse jusqu'au matin.

5 juillet: Anniversaire de mon grand-oncle aux Grandes Dalles avec la famille de ma mère.

7 juillet: Anniversire d'un ami. Il fait un barbecue avec 100 personnes.

14 juillet: Fête Nationale à Fosses, avec mes parents et toute la famille de ma belle-sœur.

23 juillet: Nous fêtons tous les ans l'anniversaire de mon cousin aux Grandes Dalles.

17 aout: Anniversaire de ma marraine aux Grandes Dalles.

26 aout: Anniversaire de Jean Michel (un copain). On fait la fête toute la nuit avec tout le monde (à Fosses)

10 septembre: Anniversaire de mon père (à Abbeville)

26 septembre: Anniversaire de ma mère (à Abbeville)

10 décembre: Anniversaire de mon frère (à Fosses)

25 décembre: Soit nous allons au restaurant avec toute la famille, soit on va chez quelqu'un de la famille pour faire la fête toute la nuit.

Appendix 6.2   Role-play Cards Used to Assess Cultural Learning and Mediation Skills on Topic of Family Meals

Jeu de rôle, A: Vous êtes un jeune Anglais. Vous passez deux semaines chez votre correspondant français dans le cadre d'un échange scolaire.

Normalement vous mangez chez votre correspondant le soir, mais ce soir vos amis anglais ont prévu d'aller au cinéma et de manger un sandwich au café avant la séance; vous voulez y aller aussi. Donc, vous ne voulez pas rentrer à la maison avec votre correspondant après les cours.

Il est midi, et vous êtes au collège. Expliquez vos projets pour la soirée à votre correspondant.

Il aura peut-être des doutes... à vous de décider ce que vous allez faire.

Jeu de rôle, B: Vous êtes un jeune Français, et votre correspondant Anglais passe deux semaines chez vous dans le cadre d'un échange scolaire.

Aujourd'hui, c'est l'anniversaire de votre grand'mère, et elle vient manger chez vous ce soir. Elle est impatiente de faire la connaissance de votre correspondant aussi. Votre mère prépare un bon dîner pour toute la famille.

Il est midi, et vous êtes au collège; votre correspondant vient vous parler de ses projets pour la soirée. A vous de réagir à ce qu'il propose et de chercher une solution.

Appendix 6.3   Questionnaire: Le Nord-Est

(1) Quels sont les départements de cette région?

(2) Qu'est-ce qui caractérise le plus notre région?
     A mettre dans l'ordre 1–5
     A – ses paysages   B – ses industries   C – sa langue (dialecte)
     D – sa cuisine   E – ses sports traditionnels

(3) Est-ce qu'il y a une autre chose caractéristique?

(4) Par rapport aux autres régions, considérez-vous que la nôtre est:
     A – plutôt favorisée? B – plutôt défavorisée?

(5) Lisez-vous A – un journal régional B – un journal national C les deux?

(6) A la télévision, quelles sont, pour vous, les plus importantes?
     A – les actualités nationales?   B – les actualités régionales?

(7) Savez-vous nommer 3 chansons traditionelles de la région?
3 plats typiques de la région?

(8) Le geordie:
A Vous le comprenez, mais vous ne le parlez pas
B Vous le comprenez et vous le parlez
C Ni l'un ni l'autre

(9) Comment les gens de cette région sont-ils différents des gens du sud?

(10) Vous considérez-vous attaché(e) à:
A mettre dans l'ordre 1–3:
A – votre ville   B – votre région   C – votre pays

Merci d'avoir répondu à ce questionnaire

Appendix 6.4   Participant Observation Exercise

The following questions were asked about a video of the Breton village of Guerlescain. This could have been conducted in French. English was used to allow a greater variety of response.

Dancing

(1) What kind of music is being played? Is it similar to any you know?
(2) What kind of dancing is being done? Is it similar to any you know?
(3) What is the occasion? Who is there?
(4) How are the spectators behaving? What are they doing?
(5) Describe the dances.
(6) How can you tell the 'maire' is someone special?
(7) What kind of instruments are being played? Is this usual?

Pub/Café

(1) How does the narrator describe the people going to the pub/café?
(2) Who is drinking?
(3) Who is serving?
(4) What age-groups are represented in the clientele?
(5) What different groups are there in the pub/café, and what are they doing?
(6) Does this look particularly French to you? If so, why?

Appendix 6.5   Schema de Questions pour un Entretien

Introduction

Nous voudrions vous parler de vos origines en France et de vos opinions sur l'influence des régions

Première section: Origines

- Pourriez-vous nous dire où vous êtes né(e) et où vous avez été élevé(e)?

Points à poursuivre:

- la région;
- village, ville, grande ville;
- combien de temps elle/il y est resté(e);
- est-ce que ses parents étaient du même endroit;
- sinon, d'où.

Deuxième section: Identité

Quand vous êtes en Angleterre, vous sentez-vous français(e)? Pourriez-vous le décrire?

Points à poursuivre:

- dans quelles situations il/elle se sent plus français(e);
- s'il/elle rencontre d'autres Français, est-ce qu'ils se distinguent par leur région d'origine;
- dans quelles situations il/elle oublie qu'il/elle est français(e);
- demander toujours des exemples et des détails.

Troisième section: Identité Régionale

Nous voudrions savoir plus sur votre région d'origine. Si vous aviez à décrire les caractéristiques principaux pour un Anglais, que diriez-vous?

Points à poursuivre:

- la même question, mais en décrivant la région à un(e) autre Français(e);
- demander des exemples des caractéristiques donnés.

Reference

Byram, M., Morgan, C. *et al.* (1994) *Teaching-and-Learning Language-and-Culture.* Clevedon: Multilingual Matters.

Chapter 7

'It Must Be Cultural Because I Don't Do It': Cultural Awareness in Initial TESOL Teacher Education

MARY WILLIAMS

> *Teachers who will introduce their students to new cultural values and beliefs as part of the development of intercultural competence themselves need to experience and reflect on what this means in practice. This chapter describes how teachers participated in a short training course and experienced some of the techniques which they could use. The chapter thus contains ideas which teachers can use as well as suggesting approaches to teacher training.*

Introduction

The quotation in the title was a response from a student to the first activity of the cultural awareness session described in this chapter. The student was one of a group of teacher trainees learning to teach English to speakers of other languages (TESOL) in England. Their initial teacher education course begins with a twelve-week distance learning foundation course (language awareness, phonology and an introduction to the classroom teaching of English to speakers of other languages). This is followed by a four-week direct contact phase which includes this cultural awareness session. Finally, during a further eight-week distance phase, they produce an extended essay on a TESOL-related subject of their choice. Students are normally graduates with a wide age range from 21 to retirement age. There are often one or two students for whom English is not their first language, but in the group of nine students recorded for this chapter, all spoke English as their first language and had British nationality, although several had spent extended periods abroad, for example in Kuwait and Brazil.

Rationale

Seminars in the four-week direct contact phase as far as possible are based on the 'loop input principle' (Woodward, 1991). This principle for language teacher education uses an activity frame (e.g. mêlée) for the content of a language teacher education syllabus, for example an aspect of vocabulary teaching. This model has two advantages. Firstly, the trainees experience activities 'hands-on' rather than listening to a lecture. They are more able to discuss and negotiate input, take an active role and integrate this knowledge and experience with existing knowledge. Secondly, as participants in these activities, they have temporarily taken on the roles of language learners and have thus experienced as class members procedures which they will organise as teachers. Usually for these activities, content remains teacher education content; however, the activities below can be used as they stand either with language learners or teacher trainees. I have used most of them also with learners at various levels.

An important aim for my use of cultural awareness activities with learners has been the defusing of cultural tensions within the group. In England we teach multilingual, multicultural classes of learners of English and divisions are sometimes perceptible between different groups of learners (NB this applies to groups of learners, not the teacher education group whose session is described here). The use of cultural awareness activities brings culture out into the open. Students may have attributed behaviour to personality traits and have entered a cycle of 'self-fulfilling prophecy' (Schmuck & Schmuck, 1975: 25) where their expect-ations, for example, of a lack of response from another student perceived as reticent, are reinforced and may be transmitted to the other person. Self-concept and acceptance of the other, two vital ingredients of group cohesiveness, can be affected. The use of cultural awareness activities on the other hand means learning about each other, which is 'the most important factor promoting intermember acceptance' (Ehrman & Dörnyei, 1998: 142).

Such activities enable learners to do some 'social perspective taking' (Johnson & Johnson, 1995: 105), that is, understand other perspectives, which also contributes to inclusion. The outcomes of the activities may thus promote affiliation; the modes of interaction (mêlée, variation of pairs, groups) and student co-operation may promote diffuse friendship patterns, another component of group cohesion. The activities can enhance group dynamics; good group dynamics can facilitate the questioning of assumptions and may lead to attitude change.

Trainees as much as learners may need to question assumptions which can affect their interaction with members of the group from different cultures. Many are about to leave England to teach in another culture and will need to develop awareness and sensitivity inside and outside the classroom. While on the course, they are teaching multinational groups and need to be aware not only of their own interaction with students but of student–student interaction in order to lead these mixed nationality groups successfully. The aims of this culture teaching are therefore conceived principally in terms of an affectively oriented approach concerned with attitudes (Jaeger, 1995) or '*savoir-être*' and '*savoir apprendre*' (Byram, 1995).

Description of the Session

The activities in Table 7.1 have a variety of interaction so that trainees experience 'culture' through various mediums and discuss it in different modes of interaction. Timing is conservative; the learner-centred and group phases may take more time, though I used these activities in a two-hour session with some input about aspects of culture and about using cultural activities with learners. There is a progression from a first activity which builds a definition of culture, to an activity which focuses on body language, to later activities which look at cultural values and concerns.

Word association

This starter activity is a pen and paper word association activity where students write down the first word they associate with each of four words spoken by the teacher. They then in pairs decide whether their associations are cultural.

Objectives

• To enable the students to construct their own working definition of culture in order to differentiate between cultural, personal, and general associations.
• To raise awareness of some (mainly national) cultural specificity.
• To raise awareness of links for vocabulary organisation and retrieval (learners).

Table 7.1   Activities used in the session

Activities	Level	Skill	Thinking task	Interaction
1. Word association (10 mins)	Any from pre-intermediate up	Speaking; vocabulary links	Classifying	Individual and pair work
2. Meeting of cultures role play (25 mins)	Intermediate up	Speaking (or remaining dumb!); body language	Reflecting on experience	Mêlée
3. Culture bump (critical incident) (15 mins)	Intermediate up	Reading; speaking	Evaluating responses	Pair work
4. Evaluative adjectives (25 mins)	Intermediate up	Discussion	Identifying perceptions	Group work
5. Behaviour and values (video) (15 mins)	Intermediate up	Viewing; speaking	Analysing behaviour	Whole group work (or group work first)
6. Written genres (10 mins)	Upper intermediate up	Reading; speaking	Comparing and contrasting	Pair work

Procedure

(1) Teacher instructions: 'I'm going to say four words and get you to think of the first word that comes into your head. Write it down please. Then you'll talk to your neighbour, so be careful about the words you put down – they've got to be words you can tell at least one person.'

(2) Teacher says four words, leaving time between each for the students to write down a word: *breakfast, sport, animal* and *Sunday.*

(3) Teacher instructions: 'Decide whether the words are cultural or personal – or they may be general'.

(4) Pair work.

(5) Whole group work focusing mainly on the cultural association.

(adapted from 'Connotations' in Tomalin & Stempleski, 1993: 125)

Outcomes

Here are some examples of associations generated by the group of teacher trainees:

Breakfast: cornflakes, bran flakes, cereal
Sport: football, squash, snooker, basketball, boxing
Animal: cat, dog, rabbit
Sunday: Archers (a British radio serial), rest, church

This first activity is a 'make your own definition of culture' activity. Students classify words as cultural associations rather than personal or general ones. In my experience, students have never asked for a definition of culture at this point. The (mainly concrete) associations they find (objects, practices) are a good departure point before moving on to abstract features of culture. The quote in the title of this paper – 'It must be cultural because I don't do it' – came from a feedback session for this activity and is an example of the type of realisation about culture that may emerge from this activity. Students may say, for instance, that they wrote 'bacon and eggs' though they never eat it for breakfast. In this particular session in pair work, a student said of her word *football* that: 'I hate football but it's something I just see all the time wherever I go'. This type of association may make students aware of the stereotypes that they hold for their own culture (we tend to think of stereotypes for other cultures) and of the social nature of behaviour and values. Associations can be seen as both universal and national-cultural, e.g. *football* where practices related to football may vary from country to country. Examples of general associations are *lunch* or *meal* for *breakfast*. A student from Hong Kong provided *congee (breakfast), ping pong* and *panda*.

This exchange of associations also led on to a discussion of specific words which are difficult to translate into other languages and which may represent important concepts for a particular culture, for example:

'Jogo de cintura' (Brazilian Portuguese) is typically Brazilian, it means 'play with the waist', you know Brazilians can samba, 'jogo de cintura' means how to get on in life, get round things, be very flexible.

If you present a compliment, you have to go and say 'maashallah' (Arabic) which means 'God protect you' because the idea is that you can inadvertently put the evil eye on someone by admiring something.

Meeting of cultures role play

In this role-play activity, students divide into two groups: representatives of a different culture and researchers investigating communication patterns. The groups intermingle, with each student contacting two or three members of the other group. The representatives enact communication features different from those normal in their culture and the researchers attempt to identify these.

Objectives

- To enable students to focus either as researcher or culture representative on body language which may vary between cultures. Another possible cultural variation, communication between sexes, is also a feature of this role play.
- To enable students to reflect about body language in their own culture and in another/other culture(s) through the use of a few features of a fictional culture. For learners, comparison is with the target language culture.

Procedure

(1) Teacher instructions: 'I want to play a cultural awareness game: a mêlée game where half of you are going to be representatives of a different culture and half are going to be "researchers" trying to find out how people communicate in that culture. The "researchers" need to talk to two or three representatives of the other culture to find out as much as they can about norms of communication in this culture. You can talk about anything you like but "researchers" should observe how the people from the other culture are communicating'. Teacher divides the group (counting off 1, 2 round the class), checking that there are sufficient males and females in each group to ensure that 'researchers' are likely to encounter both. Cue cards (see Appendix 7.1) are handed out to culture representatives first. They must not show them to the 'researchers' and should memorise the instructions.

(2) Mêlée: students stand up and mill around, talking to two or three different people according to the instructions on the cue cards.

(3) Whole group discussion with teacher eliciting: 'How did you feel? What were the first impressions of the other culture ("researchers")? Did the "researchers" discover the communication "rules" of this culture?'

(inspired by Shirts, 1966)

Outcomes

Two quotations from students:

In this culture (referring to her Kuwaiti husband's culture), kisses between the genders are exclusively reserved for husband, wife, mother and son, like that. Especially male friends of mine that predate our relationship, when you haven't seen them for ages, you want to give them a little peck on the cheek – how are you? And that kills him every time because he can't see it in any other way than outrageous. I try to see his side, he tries to see my side, but they just don't meet. (Student 1)

(about men holding hands in another culture) You think, oh my God what's going on? That's weird, but for them it's natural. I think it's actually quite nice to actually have the chance to realise that what you accept as the norm isn't for others. (Student 2)

There was a discussion of personal experiences both during the role play and from their experience (as above for Student 1) focusing on aspects of body language. The 'researchers' discovered most of the communication 'rules' of the other culture and students commented on norms in their cultures and in other cultures (as above – Student 2).

Culture bump

In this activity, students read a short account of a cultural 'incident' (or 'culture bump') (Archer 1986), that is, a situation where someone from another culture finds him/herself in a strange or uncomfortable situation when interacting with someone from a different culture. The account is followed by two multiple choice questions offering interpretations of the behaviour of the two people involved. Students discuss in pairs and in whole group the factors underlying this behaviour.

Objective

- To cause students to think about possible reasons for behaviour in a classroom context.

Procedure

(1) Teacher instructions: 'We're going to continue the culture bump theme but with a teacher–student relationship this time. I've got a

cultural incident here (see hand-out in Appendix 7.2). What I want you to do is read the situation. There are multiple choice questions here (pointing to hand-out) but you can choose more than one answer. Discuss this in pairs.'

(2) Pair work.

(3) Whole group discussion of answers and of appropriate teacher (and student) response.

(adapted from Tomalin & Stempleski, 1984)

Outcomes

Interpretations of the behaviour expressed in the answers to the multiple choice questions provoked discussion. Students recognised that more than one answer to the questions was necessary, that there were various interpretations of the behaviour described, including individual and contextual reasons as well as cultural ones. The appropriate teacher response was also seen to be dependent on more specific contextual information, e.g. type of class, the length of the student explanation. Discussion of appropriate teacher response produced the following: 'Make sure you lay out your stall and that people know where you're coming from instead of just moving the goal posts'. This was a recommendation for the teacher to make her expectations of classroom behaviour explicit.

Evaluative adjectives

This activity uses brief descriptions of behaviour, for example a bus-stop queue, accompanied by a few adjectives/expressions, e.g. 'proof of discipline', reflecting perceptions of that behaviour. Students are invited in groups to choose adjectives/expressions given or write their own to express cultural perceptions in their own or another culture.

Objectives

- To raise awareness of relative perceptions and evaluations from the perspectives of different cultures.
- To raise awareness of both variety and change within national cultures.
- To generate evaluative phrases to describe behaviour in a culture or cultures (learners).

Procedure

(1) Teacher instructions: 'The next one (see hand-out in Appendix 7.3) is about how perceptions are relative to different cultures, for instance, people are queuing at a bus-stop. This shows that they are very disciplined, that it's like military discipline. This is how other cultures may see queuing up in England so think of how you perceive particular behaviour. Can you think of another culture where perceptions of this behaviour might be different?'
(2) Group work (groups of about four).
(3) Whole group discussion.
(adapted from Sercu, 1995: 138)

Outcomes

In group work and whole group work, students relate personal experiences: for instance, arriving on time and finding hosts not ready. This particular personal account stimulated discussion of relative perceptions of punctuality and lateness. The following discussion about drink-driving also took place:

> Now it's become like a social mores you're a social leper if you drink and drive whereas before the law was tightened up it was really the threat of the stick if you did drink and drive but now . . . (Student 1)

> People have changed their attitudes. People don't like to admit now (that they drink and drive). It's not because of the fear any more. (Student 2)

In this description of changes in attitudes in their own culture, the students showed an awareness of the dynamic nature of cultural values and the influence of the law and social pressures.

Behaviour and values (video)

For this activity, video is used as a stimulus not only to describe communication between two people of different cultures but also to interpret their behaviour in terms of cultural values. The video chosen (BBC, 1991) is an appraisal interview within a financial organisation in the USA but other videos could be used to show interaction between people of different cultures.

Objective

• To consider how interaction (verbal and non-verbal) may be related to cultural values.

Procedure

(1) Teacher introduction to the video extract used: 'We're going to look at the language used here, the body language and cultural values. The woman on the left is white American, the woman on the right is Chinese American, both in California working for a big bank. The woman on the left is doing an end of the year appraisal. What can we observe about their communication? Remember what we have discussed about body language and verbal communication. Can we explain their communication in cultural terms?

(2) Viewing.

(3) Whole group discussion.

Outcomes

Discussion looked at different verbal and non-verbal features of communication, e.g. eye contact, which might be attributable to different traditions and norms in the subcultures of ethnic groups within the USA. However, students also discussed the difficulty of distinguishing ethnic cultural factors from factors that might be attributable to the culture of the organisation, of the possibility of a 'blame culture' within the company.

Written genres

This activity is a comparison of two texts which are similar in type (here two examples of newspaper advice columns) but which come from different cultures.

Objectives

• To identify cultural concerns in their own culture and another culture through comparison of two texts similar in type.

• To improve reading comprehension skills by analysing two texts with a similar function (e.g. advice column) to raise awareness of formal and content schemata (learners).

Procedure

(1) Teacher instructions: 'We're going to look at written genres. Here is one text from an English magazine and another from a Malaysian newspaper (see Appendix 7.4). What is the genre here and do the two texts represent different concerns within the different cultures?'

(2) Pair work.
(3) Whole group discussion.

Outcomes

The Malaysian text was associated by the students with 'traditional beliefs' whereas they saw the English text as a more recent concern in English culture:

Teacher: Is this (home improvements) a concern that's important in our culture?

Student: Yes, it's become a religion, it's an obsession. Instead of going to church on a Sunday you go to the DIY store. The Englishman's home is his castle.

This quotation shows that the student is able to take a critical, evaluative position in relation to a phenomenon in contemporary English culture rather than accepting practices and related concerns in her own culture as the norm. Concerns and debates may vary between cultures; the concerns of source or target cultures may be reflected in language coursebook topics so that it is important for trainees (and learners) to be aware that they may be culture-specific.

Evaluation of the Module

Student evaluation (see Appendix 7.5 for the questionnaire) produced positive results, though it should be borne in mind that this was only a small group of nine students. The mean for statements *b*, *c* and *d* (see Appendix 7.5: *b* and *c* were reversed for analysis) was 3.8 on a scale of 1 to 5 with 5 as 'strongly agree'. This shows some measure of student recognition that these objectives had been attained. The mean for statement *a* ('I have thought more about my own culture') was 3.5, slightly lower than for the other three; perceptions of other cultures may be more salient than of one's own culture or this may reflect a predominant focus on other cultures in the session. Of three students who used the midpoint for two or more statements, two had lived in three or more countries and spoke three or more languages in a range of situations. These students may have acquired through their experience a high level of intercultural competence so that the session would not have further raised their awareness.

More important evidence for the effectiveness of the session is the fact that students often choose to explore this area further in an extended essay and also the quality of discussion in the session. The reports of discussion after each activity under Outcomes show evidence of the types of reflection described in the thinking tasks column in the table of activities. Affective reactions (e.g. 'I hate football') or personal anecdotes may emerge with objective comments as discussion establishes a forum of tolerance for student opinion. Group dynamics both promote and benefit from the dialogue for learning. Analogising with the use of metaphor (lay out a stall, move the goalposts) is important for it shows student reflection about key issues. There is some evidence here of the promotion of awareness through both individual thinking and group discussion.

Development

There are two directions for session development with trainees. Firstly, further thinking about cognitive and affective processes and classroom relevance could be elicited through the use of a student reflection sheet (see Appendix 7.6). This would be in line with our implementation of the reflective teacher education model which involves student teachers in reflection about their teaching and learning.

Secondly, there could be more integration between the cultural awareness session and lessons taught by the trainees with student teachers using cultural awareness activities in their lessons and bringing more accounts of interaction in their lessons to the cultural awareness session.

The consciousness-raising aim remains the same for these developments. Through reflection about language awareness activities, Wright and Bolitho (1993: 299) aim to enable teacher trainees to become 'autonomous and robust explorers of language'. Through cultural activities such as these, it is hoped that both language teacher trainees and learners will become sensitive and autonomous explorers of culture.

Appendix 7.1   Meeting of Cultures Role Play – Cue Cards

Researcher:

You are researching cultures different from your own and are about to meet a group of people from a different culture. You are interested in the 'rules' governing communication in different cultures.

In the next ten minutes, try to speak to two or three representatives of the culture to find out as much as you can about communication in their culture.

You should be friendly and welcoming in order to make them feel relaxed and comfortable.

Representative of a different culture:

You want to help the researchers who are interested in your culture but:

- you can only say yes or no to a person of the opposite sex but you can speak normally to someone of the same sex;
- you can have no physical contact with them;
- you have to stay about half a metre away from them;
- you do not engage eye contact when the researcher is speaking but you can while you are speaking.

Adapted from Shirts (1966).

Appendix 7.2   Culture Bump

Read the following situation and choose the best answers to the questions. You can choose more than one answer.

A British teacher was teaching a class of learners of English from different countries. The lesson had started about ten minutes before and she was preparing students for a learner-centred activity by explaining the purpose of the task.

One of the students had allowed the usual amount of time to come to class but had waited for a bus for a long time and arrived after hurrying from the bus stop.

He knocked on the door and then entered and started to tell the teacher what had happened to make him late.

The teacher cut him short, telling him where to sit.

The student decided that the teacher did not appreciate the effort he had made to come to class on time.

The teacher decided that she would make a new rule, excluding latecomers till the break.

(1) Why did the student start to tell the story about the bus?

    (a) He thought everyone would be interested.

    (b) He wanted the teacher to know the reason for his late arrival.

    (c) In his experience of classrooms, students usually give reasons to the teacher.

    (d) He wanted to interrupt the teacher.

(2) Why did the teacher stop him telling his story?

    (a) She did not want to be interrupted (at that point in the lesson).

    (b) She thought he spoke too much in class generally.

    (c) In her experience of classrooms, latecomers usually come in without speaking.

    (d) She was not interested in his story.

Inspired by Tomalin and Stempleski (1993).

Appendix 7.3   Evaluative Adjectives

Read the following descriptions of behaviour. Does one of the adjectives or evaluative phrases under each description correspond to your evaluation? If so, circle it. If not, use the blank space provided to insert your evaluation. While you are evaluating the behaviour, discuss the following questions:

- Is your opinion influenced by cultural norms?
- Can you think of another culture where perceptions might be different from yours?
- How might the behaviour be perceived and what is the culture?

(1)   People are queuing at a bus stop

     proof of discipline   military   ....

(2)   Maria asks her friend Gaby to go and pick up theatre tickets for tonight. Gaby says she can't go because she is very busy.

     direct   unkind   ....

(3)   Several people eating together in a restaurant all pay separately

right, proper   petty-minded   ....

(4)   You are invited to dinner at 8 o'clock. You arrive at 8.20.

on time   too late   ....

(5)   A mother drives her child to school. She drops him/her off right in front of the school door. The other cars wait until the child has gathered together all her/his things. A little further on there is a waiting area.

spontaneous   lacking consideration   careful   ....

(6)   In a built-up area you're only allowed to drive at 30km/h. At the moment there are no people in the street. A car is driving at 30 km/h.

silly   responsible   ....

(7)   A second car comes from behind, hoots briefly and overtakes the first car at 60 km/h.

irresponsible   smooth driving ....

(8)   At a party a man drinks only fruit juice because he is driving.

unsociable   intelligent   impolite   ....

(9)   In a museum the signs are in the national language only.

nationalistic   provincial   narrow-minded   ....

(10) Someone asks another person s/he has just met how much s/he earns.

indiscreet   impolite   practical   ....

Adapted from Sercu (1995: 138).

Appendix 7.4   Written Genres

Place washing machine in kitchen

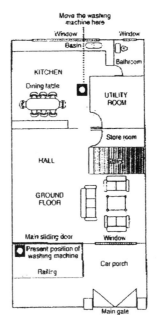

By ALBERT LOW

M Y FINANCES are not stable and I seem to be facing cash-flow problems. Please comment on the *feng shui* of my house.
Karen Loh
Kuala Lumpur

THE front of a house should be cleared of dirty things so that good fortune can flow in. With a washing machine, where dirty linen is washed and dirty water is discharged, placed in front of the house, you can't possibly expect good tidings to come your way.

You can overcome this problem by simply moving your washing machine to the kitchen as shown in the illustration.

Secondly, your house should have a back door otherwise stale *chi* will be trapped inside, resulting in an unhealthy environment.

If you have any query on *feng shui*, write in with your name, address and phone number to:
Albert Low
Feng Shui
Section 2
Star Publications
13 Jalan 13/6
46200 PJ
Fax: 03-7554039/ 7552959

Source: *The Star* (Malaysia), 12 February 1998.

DECO RATING

Q I adore the Art Deco period and would like to decorate my living and dining-room in this style. However, I am having trouble tracking down suitable furniture. Do you know of anyone who sells reproduction Art Deco furniture?

Mrs HN, Kent

A company called Restall Brown & Clennell has pro-duced an Art Deco collection, which I feel is just what you are looking for. They usually supply direct to decorators, but are happy to send you details and

order the furniture for you. The range includes upholstered pieces as well as cabinets, tables and mirrors. The beauty of the furniture of this period was the use of burr veneers, often cross-banded or with intricate marquetry features in rare woods, and these characteristics are reflected in the range. They have also included one or two useful pieces, including a tele-vision cabinet and a range of Art Deco wall lights in silver plate. Prices start at £1,000 for a tub chair. Contact them at 120 Queensbridge Road, London E2 8PD (tel: 020 7739 6626). Lizi

---

Much as we enjoy reading your letters, we are sorry that we are unable to answer them individually, so please don't enclose an sae or photographs. Send your letters to: BBC *Homes & Antiques*/Ask The Right People, 80 Wood Lane, London W12 0TT.

Source: This article first appeared in *Homes and Antiques* (BBC, England), September 2000.

Appendix 7.5   Evaluation Questionnaire

Please tick ONE of the boxes

(1) How many countries other than England have you lived in for more than one month?

None at present	☐	Two	☐
One	☐	Three or more	☐

(2) How many languages other than English can you communicate in?
(a) In a range of situations?

None at present	☐	Two	☐
One	☐	Three or more	☐

(b) At a basic level?

None at present	☐	Two	☐
One	☐	Three or more	☐

(3) Please show the extent of your agreement with the following statements by circling a number:

During/as a result of this session:	Strongly agree	Agree	Neither agree nor disagree	Disagree	Strongly disagree
(a) I have thought more about my own culture	5	4	3	2	1
(b) I have NOT understood more about behaviour, perceptions and values in other cultures	5	4	3	2	1
(c) I have NOT understood implications for my interaction with people from other cultures	5	4	3	2	1
(d) I have become aware of some implications for my classroom management of a multicultural group	5	4	3	2	1

Any comments (please write overleaf...
Thank you for completing this.

Appendix 7.6   Personal Record and Thinking Framework

Activity topic	*What thinking task did you do? (e.g. classifying)*	*How did you feel during the activity?*	*How is it relevant to your classroom teaching?*

Adapted from Wright and Bolitho (1992).

References

Archer, C. (1986) Culture bump and beyond. In J. Valdes (ed.) *Culture Bound.* Cambridge: Cambridge University Press.

BBC (1991) *Crosstalk 2*, series Mosaic (video off-air). London: BBC.

Byram, M. (1995) Acquiring intercultural competence: A review of learning theories. In L. Sercu (ed.) *Intercultural Competence Vol. 1: The Secondary School.* Aalborg, Denmark: Aalborg University Press.

Ehrman, M.E. and Dörnyei, Z. (1998) *Interpersonal Dynamics in Second Language Education.* London: Sage.

Jaeger, K. (1995) Teaching culture: The state of the art. In L. Sercu (ed.) *Intercultural Competence: A New Challenge for Language Teachers and Trainers in Europe.* Aalborg, Denmark: Aalborg University Press.

Johnson, D.W. and Johnson, R.T. (1995) Co-operative learning and non-academic outcomes of schooling. In J.E. Pedersen and A.D. Digby (eds) *Secondary Schools and Co-operative Learning.* New York: Garland.

Schmuck, R.A. and Schmuck, P.A. (1975) *Group Processes in the Classroom.* Madison, WI: Brown and Benchmark.

Sercu, L. (1995) The acquisition of intercultural competence: A teacher training seminar. In L. Sercu (ed.) *Intercultural Competence: A New Challenge for Language Teachers and Trainers in Europe.* Aalborg, Denmark: Aalborg University.

Shirts, R.G. (1966) *Bafa: A Teacher's Guide to a Simulation.* Del Mar, CA: Simile II.

Tomalin, B. and Stempleski, S. (1993) *Cultural Awareness.* Oxford: Oxford University Press.

Woodward, T. (1991) *Models and Metaphors in Language Teacher Training.* Cambridge: Cambridge University Press.

Wright, T. and Bolitho, R. (1992) Language awareness activities workshop, Language awareness conference, Bangor, Wales.

Wright, T. and Bolitho, R. (1993) Language awareness: A missing link in language teacher education? *English Language Teaching Journal* 47(4), 292–304.

Part 2

Beyond the Classroom

Chapter 8

Virtual Intercultural Competence: A Programme for Japanese Elementary School Students

LYNNE PARMENTER AND YUICHI TOMITA

Foreign language learning in Japan is undergoing substantial change including the introduction of an international dimension in the primary school. This provides an opportunity to introduce an intercultural experience in young children's lives, and television offers a means of making this widely available as well as bringing it to life in the classroom. This chapter describes the use of television, the ways in which children respond and the evaluation researchers and children are beginning to make.

Foreign Language Education in Japan: The Current Situation

In Japan, the Ministry of Education (Monbusho) has considerable power in determining and implementing education policy and curriculum. The publication of detailed Courses of Study, a textbook authorisation system, mechanisms of control over the training and employment of teachers and other such measures ensure that central policy is influential in all state schools throughout Japan. Over the past decade, four basic aims have underpinned Japanese education policy and curriculum. One of these four basic aims has been 'to place importance on deepening international understanding and developing an attitude of respect for our country's culture and traditions' (Monbusho, 1989: 2).

Theoretically, foreign language education in Japanese state schools is an optional part of the curriculum. In practice, because a foreign language is one of the main subjects in the entrance examinations for senior high school and university, the vast majority of Japanese students have three to four classes per week of foreign language education for six years. Although foreign language education in the school system does not begin until the age of 12, the well-frequented private language schools offer classes for children as young as 2 or 3 years old, meaning that a significant proportion of children have some familiarity with a foreign language before they enter junior high school.

At present, there is very little choice in foreign language education. Although the Japanese Ministry of Education publishes teaching guidelines for English, French and German and officially allows other languages to be taught, the only language for which textbooks are authorised in junior high school is English. At senior high school, there is a little more diversification, with 5% of senior high schools offering courses in Chinese, 3.5% in French and 1.9% in Korean in 1997. The vast majority of Japanese students, though, learn only one foreign language, and that language is English.

Until the 1980s, foreign language education in Japan was dominated by the grammar-translation method. In education reforms published in 1989 and implemented from 1993/1994, however, there was a new emphasis on developing communicative competence. In junior high schools, teachers are now expected to encourage speaking and listening skills in particular, and a substantial proportion of the textbook is devoted to conversational English. In senior high schools, three new courses in oral communication have been introduced to the curriculum. There exists a problematic contradiction, however, between the official Ministry of Education curriculum emphasis on communicative competence and the omnipotent entrance exam focus on grammar-translation.

In terms of content, the Ministry of Education specifies in fine detail in its teaching guidelines which grammatical structures and functions have to be taught and which vocabulary should be mastered. The textbook authorisation system means that publishers have to follow these guidelines closely in order to have their books authorised for use in schools. Textbooks form the central part of foreign language classes, and this system ensures that Ministry of Education guidelines reach individual students directly. However, there are no teaching guidelines concerning cultural content or the development of intercultural competence. As a result, cultural issues are not included in the curriculum in any integrated or significant way. Although there is no systematic inclusion of cultural content in the curriculum, analysis of textbooks reveals that there is a bias towards the USA, both in terms of language (US idioms, spelling, accent etc.) and in terms of cultural information included.

Another significant aspect of foreign language education in Japan is the JET (Japan Exchange and Teaching) Programme. The JET Programme, the main purpose of which is to employ native speakers of English in Japanese state schools, has expanded rapidly since its implementation in 1987. Currently, over 5,000 native speakers of English (over half from the USA) are employed on the programme. As a result of this Programme, almost every Japanese child over the age of 12 now comes into direct contact with native speakers of English at school.

The 2002 Reforms and their Implications for Foreign Lanuage Education

In December 1998, the Japanese Ministry of Education published national reforms of the education system, effective from April 2002. As before, one of the underlying principles of education policy will be 'internationalisation'. In relation to foreign language education, the biggest changes are that a foreign language, English, will become a compulsory part of the junior high school, with an emphasis on 'practical communication skills'. At the same time, there is a reduction in the number of grammatical and vocabulary items to be studied. Overall, however, there will be few changes in policy or curriculum of foreign language education as a subject at junior and senior high school.

In another way, though, the reforms do have important implications for foreign language education. The major feature of the reforms is the introduction of 'integrated study time' to the curriculum from the third year of elementary school through to the end of senior high school. According to Monbusho guidelines, 'integrated study time' is to be used for education in areas such as international understanding, environmental education, ICT education, welfare and health education. Unlike all other areas of the curriculum, for which the Ministry of Education provides detailed guidelines, the content of 'integrated study time' is to be decided at individual school level. At present, discussion over the use of this new section of the curriculum is raging in Japan, particularly at elementary school level. One of the most fierce areas of debate is between a large group of educators who see 'integrated study time' as an opportunity to introduce English (as a subject) into elementary schools and a smaller group who argue that the focus should be on cross-curricular themes such as international understanding, and that the learning of English (and/or other languages) should be conceptualised within this domain.

Protagonists of the introduction of English as a subject argue that Japanese people's foreign language abilities compare unfavourably with the abilities of people in most other Asian countries, and that the solution is to introduce English from an earlier age. Their general argument is that, to compete economically and politically in international society in the future, Japanese people will have to have a higher standard of proficiency in English. The wider context of this argument is the debate over whether to make English a second official language in Japan, which came out of the recommendations of a Prime Minister's Commission on Japan's goals for the twenty-first century published in January 2000 (Kawai *et al.*, 2000). In general, however, the purposes of foreign language education from this perspective are political and economic, rather than social or individual, and the connection between foreign language education and education for international understanding or intercultural competence is often not considered to be so important.

At the opposite end of the spectrum are those who see foreign language education at elementary school as one element of education for international understanding. In this case, the foreign language does not necessarily have to be English, as other languages are equally valuable for the social and individual purposes of developing children's awareness and appreciation of other cultures and other people. Although this is the official Monbusho position on foreign language education in elementary schools from 2002, this is a minority view among Japanese people, partly because of prior expectations of the reforms (that English as a subject would be introduced to elementary school), partly because of the perceived gap between official and real Monbusho policy, and partly because until now, foreign language has been so closely associated with English, and intercultural understanding has not formed an integral element of foreign language education and policy.

The NHK Project and Programmes

It is within this social and political context that NHK (Nihon Housou Kyoukai [Japan Broadcasting Company], the equivalent of the BBC) has developed an English programme to be used by elementary schools as part of 'integrated study time'. The first series of the programme, whose intended audience is third and fourth grade elementary school children (age 8–10 years old) began broadcast in April 2000. The programme is shown twice a week in a fifteen-minute time slot. Supporting materials include notes for teachers in the 'NHK Schools Broadcast' publication, a textbook published by an associated company and an interactive web site on the internet.[1] Mindful of the above 'English vs. international under-standing' debate, NHK compromise by including a significant proportion of cultural content, i.e. portraying English in its various cultural contexts.

In the information for schools, the aim of the series, which is entitled *Eigorian*, is stated as follows:

Now, a new era of English education is required. Designed for 'integrated study time', *Eigorian* is a new style English programme, made for the purpose of international understanding.

The aim of *Eigorian* is to nurture the communicative competence children need in international society by familiarising them with everyday English expressions.

These 'everyday English expressions' form the basic structure of the series, with each programme focusing on a key phrase and function. For example, the first five programmes follow the structure below:

Key phrase	*Function*	*Other expressions etc.*
(1) Hi, I'm Yuji. Nice to meet you.	First meetings.	Names. Manners.
(2) Hello! How are you?	Everyday greetings.	Feelings.
(3) Who is this? This is my mother.	Introducing people and things.	Family. Occupations.
(4) Do you have a red pencil? Sorry, I don't.	Asking about things.	Stationery. Shopping.
(5) What's this? It's a butterfly.	Asking what things are.	Questions.

Cultural Content in the Programmes

Cultural content is organised to fit in with and complement these key expressions and functions. The programme team's stance on cultural content is influenced by the following policy, outlined in an internal document: 'Include English communication with people whose native language is not English (international understanding perspective)'. In this respect, the programme represents a radical departure from existing English education in Japan, where the overwhelmingly dominant model is American English for communication with Westerners (Americans). It also demonstrates a recognition of English as the lingua franca between non-native English speakers in most situations in Asia and further afield.

To give a concrete example of what kind of cultural content is included and how it is incorporated with the 'everyday English expressions', the key phrase 'I'm (name). Nice to meet you' is the focus of the first *Eigorian* programme. The fifteen-minute programme runs as follows:

(1) Introduction and self-introduction of the main characters. Two actors play the character of Yuji – one as a child (mini-Yuji) and one as an adult. Michael and Janica are American adults.

(2) Main characters play role-play guessing game, e.g. one person mimes a lion, others guess, the person who mimed says 'I'm a lion. I'm from Africa.'

(3) Mini-Yuji visits an international school in Japan. Tapescript as follows:

Mini-Yuji: Hi! I'm Yuji. Nice to meet you.

Teacher: Nice to meet you. I'm Daniel. Welcome to Tsukuba International School. Come on in! . . . So, everyone, we have a special guest today. His name is Yuji.

(Mini-Yuji goes round class

Mini-Yuji: Hi, I'm Yuji. Nice to meet you.

Maithili: Hi, I'm Maithili. Nice to meet you too. (Yuji and Maithili shake hands)

Mini-Yuji: *(goes on to next person)* Hi, I'm Yuji. Nice to meet you.

Alexander: Nice to meet you too. My name is Alexander.

Mini-Yuji: Ale . . .

Teacher: Help him. Say it slowly and clearly.

Alexander: Al-ex-an-der.

Mini-Yuji: Xander. Nice to meet you. (goes on to next student) Hi, I'm Yuji.

Lian: I'm Lian. I come from India. I was born in Birmingham.

(Mini-Yuji looks confused)

Teacher: Lian, he doesn't understand. Say again.

Lian: I'm Lian!

Mini-Yuji: Lian.

Lian: *(spells out)* L.I.A.N.

(Mini-Yuji and other children eat lunch together)

(4) Video clips of chefs from different countries, introducing themselves first in their native language and then in English. Tapescript as follows:

Takashi: *Konnichi wa. Takashi desu. Oita-ken shusshin desu. Hajime-mashite.* Hi, I'm Takashi. I'm from Oita. Nice to meet you!

Oreste: *Ciao, sono Oreste. Vengo dall'Italia. Piacere di conoscervi.* Hi, I'm Oreste. I'm from Italy. Nice to meet you!

Hasim: *Merhaba, ben Hasim. Ben Turkigeden Geldim. Tanistigima memnun oldum.* Hi, I'm Hasim. I'm from Turkey. Nice to meet you.

Solomon: (*in native language*) Hi, I'm Solomon. I'm from Ethiopia. Nice to meet you.

Krisostomos: (*in native language*) Hi, I'm Krisostomos. I'm from Greece. Nice to meet you.

(5) In the studio, adult Yuji, Michael and Janica are talking with visitors. Tapescript as follows:

Ada: Hola!

Yuji: Hola!

Ada: My name is Ada. I'm from Chile, and Chile is right here (points to Chile on a world map). This is our national costume. Nice to meet you.

Yuji: Nice to meet you too.

Xiao: Nihao.

Yuji: Nihao.

Xiao: My name is Xiao-rui. I'm from China. And this is my friend, panda (shows a toy panda). Nice to meet you.

Yuji: Nice to meet you too.

Richard: Hello, Yuji, how do you do?

Yuji: Hello.

Richard: My name is Richard, and I'm from the United Kingdom, near London. This is my good friend, Tom (shows a cut-out beefeater). Nice to meet you, Yuji.

Yuji: Nice to meet you too.

Nena: Zdravo!

Yuji: Zdravo!

| Nena: | Hi, I'm Nena. I'm from Yugoslavia. Yugoslavia is here (points on map). And this is our national costume. Nice to meet you. |
| Yuji: | Nice to meet you too. |

In the teacher's notes available to accompany the programme, the following explanation is given under the heading of 'the programme's perspective':

The actions which accompany greetings differ according to the country and culture. Please draw students' attention to the different expressions and movements which people use when they greet each other in the programme. People bowing to each other, people shaking hands and people hugging each other are all showing their pleasure at meeting.

When we are greeting people in English, we need to be particularly careful not to avoid eye contact, to shake hands firmly and to greet people in a clear voice.

It's difficult to catch foreigners' names when we hear them. In the same way, it's difficult for foreigners to catch Japanese names, so we need to pronounce them slowly and clearly. When we don't catch the name, we should feel that 'I want to know your name' and shouldn't worry about asking again. It's nothing to be ashamed of.

Discussion of the NHK Project from an Intercultural Competence Perspective

In terms of developing intercultural communicative competence (ICC) through foreign language education, several points which emerge from this fifteen-minute programme and accompanying notes are significant and perhaps generalisable to other contexts. In this section, we would like to introduce three points and expand on them with comments from elementary school teachers and pupils who are using the *Eigorian* programme.

The development of intercultural competence from the earliest stages of foreign language learning

The transcript above is taken from the first programme of a series aimed at 8/9-year-old children. The assumption is that the viewers have no previous knowledge of English, and the only phrase they know in English is therefore: 'Hi, I'm . . . I'm from . . . Nice to meet you.' Even within this minimal framework, though, many possibilities for developing ICC are proposed and demonstrated. In response to points which often bother foreigners greeting Japanese people, details such as eye contact and ways of shaking hands are specifically treated. Attention is also drawn to alternative forms of greeting (bowing, shaking hands, hugging) and to the common underlying significance of these gestures (to express pleasure at meeting someone). This approach – maximum intercultural competence through minimum language – proves that the development of intercultural competence can form an integral and effective part of foreign language learning from the earliest stages. It is particularly significant in the Japanese context in the sense that existing foreign language education (in junior and senior high school) pays almost no attention to the development of such competence, overrelying instead on the linguistic and (to a lesser extent) sociolinguistic elements of communicative competence.

The inclusion of such cultural content is welcomed by the majority of elementary school teachers using the *Eigorian* programme. If anything, the complaint of teachers is that not enough emphasis is placed on such content in the programme. One teacher makes this comment:

> I think [the programme] ends up leaning towards English . . . it's teaching today's key phrase, and the key phrase is repeated again and again, and that's what makes an impression on the children . . . and so, like today, the children saw the person from Africa but they didn't remember. In that way, I feel it's not really linked to international understanding.

Other teachers agree, making the point that the 'mini-Yuji' feature (where Yuji as a child visits and talks with people from various countries) is only presented as an opportunity for repeating the key English phrase, when it could be better exploited as a rich source of material for cultural knowledge and international understanding. Such criticisms are apparent particularly in schools which treat English as one element of education for international understanding, and are less often heard in schools which treat international understanding as part of English.

The development of language and cultural awareness

When the foreign language is an international language (and particularly if it is English), the development of language and cultural awareness is of primary importance. As described above, the NHK project has a specific policy of diverging from the current situation in

Japan, which tends to be 'foreign language education = English = USA'. In terms of the 'foreign language = English' part of the equation, the inclusion of other languages in the English programme is an attempt to make elementary school students realise that not all foreigners speak English, and that those who do often speak another language as well. The 'English = USA' part of the equation is also put into question. Although the two main foreign characters in the series are both American, there is a deliberate decision to introduce a wide variety of cultures, races and nationalities by featuring many other guest characters in the series. The first programme, for example, includes fourteen foreign guest characters who between them hail and speak eight foreign languages in addition to English and Japanese. In light of the 'single track American English road' which characterises foreign language education in Japan from junior high school onwards, NHK's aim of developing an awareness of the multicultural and multilingual nature of the world is an important contribution to developing intercultural competence in Japanese children.

This feature of the programme is welcomed by most elementary school teachers, and the following teacher's comment is illustrative:

> Through the programme children pick up naturally the fact that people have their own languages but that they use English to communicate with people from other countries: for example, a Japanese person and an Indian person can communicate in English. In terms of pronunciation, there's not just American English but Indian English and Chinese English and so on, and that's transmitted naturally without actually being stated. And the programme makes the children familiar with the fact that there are people of all different skin colours with different customs, and maybe in that way can help to eliminate prejudice.

At the same time, there is a danger of transmitting the wrong message, as another teacher points out: 'The children have no awareness of the countries . . . They just think everyone speaks English.' As the intended audience of this programme is children whose knowledge of the world is extremely limited (the Japanese National Curriculum excludes world knowledge until fifth or sixth grade (age 10–12)), this danger of distortion is very real, and is something which the programme producers as well as teachers need to be aware of.

Attitudes towards other languages and cultures

One of the key aspects of ICC which is included in the NHK project is the development of attitudes towards and ways of thinking about one's own and other languages and cultures. In the teachers' notes quoted above, the point made about the difficulty for foreigners in catching Japanese names, and the way of dealing with this, will certainly be new to the majority of 8–10-year-olds and maybe their teachers. Realising such a point could serve as a first step in helping children to decentre and relativise their own language and culture – to other people, Japanese is a foreign language and Japan is a foreign culture. At the same time, the recommendation not to be ashamed of failing to understand but asking again because you are interested in the other person, if followed, would be useful both in developing skills of learning, discovering and interacting, and in developing attitudes of valuing the other person by wanting to overcome linguistic barriers of communication to understand him/her. These attitudes are demonstrated repeatedly by the characters in the television programme, who may not understand perfectly everything their interlocutor says (as in the exchange between Yuji and Lian in the school), but who manage to create some shared meaning and communicate.

Turning to what happens in practice, the attitudes demonstrated in the programme seem to be accepted and adopted by the programme's audience of children aged 8–10. The following excerpt is taken from an interview with a group of elementary school children:

Interviewer: Do you ever talk to foreign people?

Child 1: Yes, in our apartment block there are some Korean people and some Brazilian people.

Child 2: And some Americans.

Child 1: And when I see them I say 'Hello' and they understand and say it back.

Interviewer: Really? And what does it feel like when you talk to them?

Child 3: Somehow, it makes you feel refreshed.

Child 1: If you don't do anything, the atmosphere is kind of lonely, so if you say hello it makes it better and it feels good.

Child 4: And once you start talking to people, you can be friends with them.

Interviewer: And before you learned English, was it the same?

Child 4:   No, no, before I started learning English I never used to say anything.

Child 3:   Since we've been learning English, the words just seem to come out kind of naturally.

To what extent this change in attitude is directly attributable to the behaviours and attitudes demonstrated in *Eigorian*, and to what extent it is attributable to learning English in general, is open to question. Certainly, though, demonstration of empathy for the other, willingness to take the initiative in communication and satisfaction at having communicated, even at a very basic level, are shared features of the *Eigorian* programme and of many children's attitudes to intercultural communication.

Problems and Possibilities

All three points discussed in the previous section are important elements in the development of ICC through foreign language education. Their inclusion as key threads in the NHK series provide a clear example of how ICC can be developed with young learners who are in the first steps of foreign language education in the classroom and who often have no opportunities for direct intercultural contact. In this respect, *Eigorian* has received positive feedback from teachers and pupils alike, and can be judged to be successful.

Although *Eigorian* is clearly successful in encouraging the development of ICC through English, one question which lingers is how valid this success is. The whole policy of 'integrated study time', as explained earlier, is officially to introduce foreign languages as part of international understanding which in turn is part of integrated learning, not to teach international understanding as part of English. In schools that are trying to build up a framework of foreign language education within international understanding, some doubts are voiced about the usefulness of *Eigorian*, due to the fact that cultural content is completely subsumed to linguistic objectives. Teachers in such schools suggest that, in order to facilitate the development of international understanding, cultural content in *Eigorian* could be better structured and presented in a more effective manner.

In conclusion, this NHK project highlights the contradictions which exist between ICC or international understanding as part of English education (a common perception of the 2002 reforms in Japan) and foreign language education as part of ICC or education for international understanding (the official position). As far as the former is concerned, the *Eigorian* producers can be justifiably proud of their success. As far as the latter is concerned, there is still considerable room for improvement in the programme. If NHK really wants *Eigorian* to meet Monbusho's stated aims of foreign language education within a framework of international understanding, and its own stated aims of being 'made for the purpose of international understanding', then more careful attention needs to be paid to the structure, presentation and use of cultural content in the planning stages of the series.

In the final analysis, though, a television series can only be effective in facilitating the development of ICC and international understanding if it appeals to and communicates with its audience. For that reason, we would like to leave the final word in this article to a class of 8–9-year-old Japanese children. When asked for their opinion of *Eigorian*, 30 voices in spontaneous unison shouted, 'Suki!!' ('We like it!!').

Note

1. The website URL includes the aims and outline of the series, the full text and images of each programme, teaching plans using the programme, a column where teachers can ask questions which are answered by the programme's advisory board (university professors of English), a section for children's comments on the programme and so on. The URL is http://www.nhk.or.jp/eigorian

References

Kawai Hayao *et al.* (2000) *Nihon no furontia wa Nihon no naka ni aru: Jiritsu to kyouchi de kizuku shinseiki '21seiki Nihon no kousou' kondankai* (The Frontier Within: Individual Empowerment and Better Governance in the New Millennium. Report of the Prime Minister's Commission on Japan's Goals in the 21st Century) Tokyo: Kodansha. (A complete English version of the text is available on http://www.kantei.go.jp/jp/21century/report/htmls/index.html)

Monbusho (1989) *Chuugakkou shidousho: kyouiku katei ippan hen* (Junior High School Guidelines: General Educational Curriculum). Tokyo: Monbusho.

Chapter 9

Students as Virtual Ethnographers: Exploring the Language Culture-Connection

SHEILA CAREL

> *Observing how people of a different culture communicate and com-*
> *paring and contrasting with one's own, and thereby becoming aware*
> *of one's own unconscious and in part non-verbal means of com-*
> *munication, was previously possible only by travelling to another*
> *country. In this chapter it is made possible through the use of video*
> *and the author describes the theoretical basis for this in the*
> *ethnography of communication as well as the experiment carried out*
> *with upper secondary school students in the USA. The effects on*
> *attitude and understanding of another culture are also described.*

Introduction

In 1996, the authors of the *Standards for Foreign Language Learning* (SFLL) published a document intended as a benchmark for foreign language instruction and assessment in the United States (The National Standards in Foreign Language Education Project, 1996). The opening lines of this report convey its basic theme: 'Language and communic-ation are at the heart of the human experience. The United States must educate students who are equipped linguistically and culturally to communicate successfully in a pluralistic American society and abroad.' While this goal is honourable, I have been privy to many discussions with colleagues who judge it unrealistic. The following excerpts are from actual conversations:

> As for the standards, I've done so little with them. I've read them and I give lip service to them but I haven't incorporated them into my thinking and into my methods courses in any kind of a serious way and that's my own neglect. (university professor)

The National Standards just aren't realistic so I ignore them. Everyone at my school does. Eventually we'll have to be accountable for this stuff, but I just don't see how I'm ever going to be able to do that. (high school teacher)

Why do these standards seem unattainable to many of our colleagues? Perhaps the answer lies in two unlike approaches to studying language.

As a graduate student at the University of Texas, I realised that discussions in my department, at conferences, and in journal articles presented human interaction in ways that differed sharply from my real life experiences and from the ways other people in other fields, namely sociolinguistics, communications, and linguistic anthropology, considered communication. I asked myself 'If I had studied French from a more contextualised perspective, would my language learning experiences have differed?' Consequently, for my dissertation research project I decided to observe second language and culture (L2/C2) students as they learned about French interactions through a culturally grounded lens, which included contextual clues in the environment, embodied communication, and native informants' interpretations of the interactions. I borrowed methodology from Dell Hymes, who had successfully studied the language/culture connection.

The Ethnography of Communication

The ethnography of communication is rooted in anthropology and linguistics (Hymes, 1974). Ethnographers of communication analyse patterns which constitute the communicative norms of people at the societal, group and individual levels. At the societal level, communication often patterns in terms of functions, categories of talk, and attitudes and conceptions about language and speakers. Communication also patterns according to particular roles within a society. At the group level, influences include sex, age, social status, occupation, educational level and geographic region. At the individual level, communication patterns at the level of expression and interpretation of personality (Hymes, 1974). These culturally relative practices are a crucial part of what members of a particular culture know and do. (Hymes, 1972).

Ethnographers of communication attempt to analyse speech situations, speech events and speech acts. The situation, the context within which communication occurs, might include a dinner party or a religious service. The event, the primary unit for description, is defined by a united set of components, takes place in the same setting with the same purpose of communication and the same topic, involves the same participants, and maintains the same general tone and rules for interaction. An event concludes with a change in participants, their role-relationships, or the focus of attention. Acts usually coincide with single interactional functions and include requests, commands, gestures and facial expressions (Saville-Troike, 1989). By studying these components, ethnographers of communication attempt to determine the speech community, learn about its social organisation, and hypothesise how these factors manifest themselves in communication. Hymes's SPEAKING heuristic provides a framework for examining human interaction:

S	Setting	Physical circumstances
	Scene	Subjective definition of an occasion
P	Participants	Speaker/sender/addresser
		Hearer/receiver/audience/addressee
E	End	Purposes and goals
A	Act sequence	Message form and content
K	Key	Tone, manner
I	Instrumentalities	Channel
		(verbal, non-verbal, physical)
N	Norms of interaction	Specific proprieties and interpretation
	and interpretation	of behaviours within a cultural belief
		system
G	Genre	Textual categories

Using exercises based on this heuristic, L2/C2 learners may distinguish important elements of communication as they observe and analyse authentic communication between members of the target culture and access native interpretations of those practices. However, since opportunities for contact are often limited, as educators we must search out creative means of reaching members of the target culture. Recent technological advances may afford such opportunities. To investigate the feasibility of virtual ethnography, I designed and implemented *The Virtual Ethnographer* interactive courseware.

The Virtual Ethnographer

The Virtual Ethnographer, a multimedia software package designed to develop L2/C2 learners' interpretative skills and knowledge, consists of a coursework module and a fieldwork module, discussed in this section.

The coursework section is intended to heighten students' awareness of communicative resources they use in face-to-face interactions: spoken language, gaze and gesture. Students explore concepts regarding human interaction in the context of their own communicative practices. For example, the program introduces the notion of emblematic gestures, or gestures that replace entire words of sentences. Then students are asked to describe gestures they would use to say 'come here', 'I'm not listening', and 'quiet'. The module also presents underlying principles of the ethnography of communication, fieldwork techniques, and the SPEAKING heuristic. For example, Figures 9.1 and 9.2 are from the norms segment of the SPEAKING heuristic section. Upon completing the coursework, students begin their virtual fieldwork.

The virtual fieldwork module consists of three parts: tour of Brittany, meet the respondents, and analysis of the clips. The tour includes basic information about Brittany regarding geography, major industries, cultural and linguistic change resulting from contact with other parts of France, language use, and traditions. The second section introduces the primary subject and respondent, Charlotte, a high school teacher, who is seen communicating in several settings: at home with family members, at a dinner party with friends, and in her classroom with her students. It also presents biographical information about five other native respondents (NRs), whose analyses of the interactions are included in the program.[1] These first two sections, intended to familiarise students with Brittany and with the informants they would encounter later in the program, simply asked students to read information, look at graphics, and listen to sound. They were by far less interactive than the third section, which asked students to perform their virtual ethnographies.

Figure 9.1 Page from *The Virtual Ethnographer*

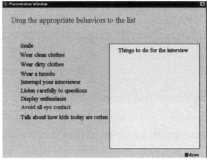

Figure 9.2 Page from *The Virtual Ethnographer*

The third section, analysis of the clips, was designed with three learning concepts in mind: detection (Lewo, 1998), Vygotsky's (1978) zone of proximal development (ZPD), and schema theory (Rumelhart, 1980). The students were directed to analyse each clip by answering questions corresponding to the SPEAKING heuristic. After completing an analysis of a given clip, they could access similar analyses provided by the six NRs. I hoped the structure provided by the heuristic would focus the students' attention to particular aspects of the interaction and thus facilitate detection and learning. I also tried to create a situation similar to Vygotsky's ZPD. Within this zone, numerous developmental processes ensue when people interact with one another. I hoped that the NRs would indicate culturally salient aspects of the communicative events and provide insights regarding culturally mediated meanings associated with those behaviours. By focusing the students' attention, allowing for detection, exposing them to various communicative events, and providing NRs' perspectives, I hoped to help them develop more detailed schemata, or mental pictures, of the French as communicators, and make them cognisant of French interpretations of culturally relative practices. For example, I hoped the student ethnographers would become aware of differences in verbal and non-verbal behaviours, including turn-taking and proxemics, or use of space.

The Study

This pedagogical case study took place in a predominantly white middle-class suburban town in the north-eastern United States. It examined the processes that ensued during ten 45-minute class periods as 23 public high school students of French IV and V college preparatory classes used the *Virtual Ethnographer* courseware. In essence, I hoped to do an ethnography of students as they performed virtual ethnographies.

While fourteen of the students had first-hand exposure to Francophone countries, most of them reported that their contact with the French culture was restricted to French class. By far the most commonly reported contact with France was textbooks, teachers and movies. However, six of the students had actually visited France and nine reported visiting Francophone countries. Four students mentioned they had family members who lived in France, and two students mentioned having French Canadian grandmothers whom they heard speak French. Finally, five of the students had just returned from a ten-day home stay in Chambray, France, which had been sponsored by the school and which took place during the April vacation.

The computer recorded students' behaviours as they performed their coursework and fieldwork (e.g. sections accessed and amount of time spent in each section), responses to questions posed in the coursework section, and analyses of the video clips. Although I originally planned to be a non-participant observer, the students quickly surmised that I understood the concepts they were encountering (e.g. the ethnography of communication and human interaction) and made me an active participant by asking questions, requesting clarification, and sharing their insights with me as they worked on the program. Consequently, acting as a participant observer, I recorded observable behaviours, administered questionnaires, and performed interviews with nine purposefully selected students. The students also wrote guided introspective reports, at the beginning and end of the study, and final summary reports. The qualitative data were coded according to emergent themes. Quantitative data were analysed to establish emerging trends of behaviour. For the purposes of this chapter, I focus on the students' perspectives, including their findings and reactions to the virtual ethnography experience.

Understanding Language in the Larger Context of Communication

The students' remarks gleaned from interview transcripts, the questionnaire and their analyses of the clips suggest they relied upon their existing knowledge of visual communication including use of space, contextual influences, gaze and gesture as they interpreted the interactions they analysed. One commented: 'I realise how you can kind of understand what they are talking about just by watching them . . . I'm more confident now about being able to understand French.' Students who reported focusing on visual aspects generally provided more descriptions for gesture, gaze and proxemics than their classmates. Surprisingly, their analyses included more descriptions of spoken utterances than those of their peers. For example, students who noted Charlotte's pointing gestures (Figure 9.3) and another gesture in which she raised her hand, palm outward and extended towards the students (Figure 9.4), explained that she used them to regulate turns at talk. Many of these students also mentioned that Charlotte increased the volume of spoken utterances when doing so. Conceivably, by focusing on visual cues, they were better able to understand verbal input. Some of the students even mentioned this phenomenon:

Figure 9.3 Page from *The Virtual*   **Figure 9.4** Page from *The Virtual*
Ethnographer   *Ethnographer*

You get past the language barrier. If you can just get past that by seeing what they are communicating to each other or maybe how the circumstance is, that's half the battle. . . . Even though I still have trouble with language, I was able to figure out what they were talking about, which surprised me and then I could concentrate on the language, and so it opened that gate.

Evidently, the students used visual information apparent in the interactions to help them understand the spoken language and formulate rules about French communication.

Positing Rules for Communication

At the conclusion of the virtual fieldwork experience, the students posited rules for French communication. Topics included: variation of communicative behaviour, variation of meaning, and the French as highly engaged communicators. Their findings are discussed in this section.

In all, fourteen students reported that French communicative behaviour varied depending on the situation. They cited lexical choice, speed, articulation, and postural differences. For example, some found that the formality or informality of settings determines lexical choice. 'When with friends it is all right to use slang, but in a more formal setting it's rude. It was certain that they thought talking in slang was impolite because when Charlotte was in a more formal setting, her classroom, she didn't talk with slang.' Some students mentioned the appropriateness of lexical items: 'The word choice becomes important as well, when you are trying to be polite. Words like "dégeulasse, and machin" are not common words you would find in a polite conversation.' Their comments suggest they noticed that patterns of behaviour may vary according to the situation. In some cases, they also found that the conversational participants influence behaviours.

Many students mentioned that participants govern communicative behaviour. Their findings addressed gender and relationships. For instance, two students cited gender specific behaviours: 'The subjects of our study appear to have trends which exist between genders. Our female subjects used hand gestures much more often than our males, and the volume of speech among French females was considerably louder than their male counterparts.'

Native speakers are often aware of transgressions of gender-specified behaviour in their own cultural context, and that such violations can affect interactions negatively. However, foreign language instruction rarely includes such information. Similarly, many students expressed an awareness of variation resulting from the relationship existing between participants. 'Politeness in France is big, really big. In the family and teacher clips you can notice it. There are many levels of it. On a familiar basis with family, and so on but with elders it's the same here. Pay respect and mind your manners!' It is likely that the students formed these hypotheses based upon variation in both verbal and non-verbal communicative behaviours apparent in the clips. While foreign language instruction addresses this issue to some extent, such as forms of address, other telling aspects of interaction, including posture, overlap, lexical choice, and register, are largely ignored. The students' comments suggest they were cognisant of many of these behavioural aspects. However, not only did they notice patterns of behaviour, but they also addressed meaning.

Some of the students concluded that similar behaviours carry different meanings in different situations:

> In the French culture people talk at the same time to encourage the person to continue to talk. I thought this was shocking, however I was relieved when I heard the teacher tell the students to be quiet and let her talk. It made me aware that there is a time and a place for everything and that sometimes it is rude or disrespectful to talk while another person is talking and that is when you are not encouraging that person, but just being plain rude!

The acknowledgement of situational influences on meaning and that 'there is a time and a place for everything' indicates the students noticed important pragmatic information concerning the French communicative system which might prove useful when interacting with members of the target culture. Furthermore, most of them realised that these meanings are culturally mediated. Many students who mentioned communicative behaviours also referred to what they considered the French meaning associated with those behaviours. 'The French definitely have their own definition of politeness. Talking while others are talking, seems to be a big one. They say that it shows the person(s) they're talking with that they are paying attention.' In fact, many of the students acknowledged the L2/C2 perspective of behaviours, provided by the NRs, which might be considered rude if examined through the L1/C1 lens. Others explicitly compared what they considered French and American interpretations. 'I've discovered that the context of everyday conversations are the same in the US as in France, but the way each communicates and the "values" each person has during the conversation is different.' This insight regarding overlapping discourse resembles Kerbrat-Orecchioni's (1994). discussion of cultural interpretations of this phenomenon. Most of the students evidently incorporated the informants' perspectives and acknowledged culturally distinct meanings while forming hypotheses about French communication. However, not every student exhibited this behaviour.

A few students failed to acknowledge the NRs' input and maintained that the French and American cultures were not different. Their comments indicate they did not recognise the French perspectives concerning the overlap in conversation. 'They're just like you and me. I don't have an opinion of them. I don't want to judge a book by its cover. I guess though that they cut each other off when they talk and that's kind of rude.'

These particular students most likely adopted what Lutz and Collins (1993) call a 'National Geographic way of knowing'. In other words, they failed to recognise other realities, and viewed the foreign culture through a lens, which neither compels empathy and identification, nor reveals the differences among cultures. Consequently, they attributed L1/C1 cultural knowledge to the overlap they witnessed and considered the people they observed rude. Conversely, other students viewed their subjects' behaviour more positively.

Some students depicted the French as highly engaged communicators who relish possibilities for interaction. 'French culture involves a liking of communicating. Our subjects seemed to enjoy speaking to one another, much more so than Americans. In fact, enjoying each other's company, at least in my experience, seems to be lacking in much of American culture. The clips also showed the French have respect for one another and are rather friendly.' Many students who voiced this finding believed the

French demonstrated, through visual and verbal behaviours, attentiveness to the needs and wants of their interlocutors. They also found the French more attuned than Americans to communicative cues and surroundings. 'I noticed that our culture seems less friendly than the French. People aren't as concerned. French people seem more cultured, more aware of their surroundings.' This 'concern' was perceived by many of the students as respect for other people and for relationships. 'The French seem to value the relationships that they have with their family. They also talk to family members often and want to know everything that is going on in their lives.' Although these students witnessed verbal and non-verbal behaviours that many Americans might consider rude and disrespectful, they perceived the French as highly engaged communicators who are attuned to the contexts around them and the people with whom they interact. Their findings resemble Hall's (1976) description of the French culture as a high context culture.

Virtual Ethnography for Learning

Before beginning their fieldwork, the students generally expressed curiosity about ethnography, but did not mention finding this approach to studying language and culture valuable. However, after completing the fieldwork, they generally divulged they believed they learned from their ethnographic adventure. In fact, 17 of the 23 students reported they learned from their experience.

> Travelling through France on the virtual simulation, I began to develop an understanding of the French culture. Not only did someone tell me about the French culture, but I was able to observe and actually be a part of the French culture myself. We were just kind of learning for ourselves without being taught. I liked it a lot because we discovered things for ourselves. It's not like they told us the French have their biggest meal in the afternoon or the French don't make eye contact until they want you to talk. Oh and the English do that too. We discover that and then we make our own conclusions from it.

By 'observing' and 'being a part of the culture' many of them discovered aspects of French culture. The perception of learning by 'virtual simulation' might be explained, in part, by the 'realness' of which the students spoke.

Several students mentioned authenticity. By analysing the 'genuine' interactions, many students accessed input that resulted in more detailed notions of the French and French culture.

I think that watching the video I just started to understand the differences. I saw the differences between us and them and a lot of similarities. It didn't exactly surprise me the way they acted but it just kind of closed some gaps of what I thought about French people. It kind of closed up some of those mental holes of what I didn't know about French culture because it was more real. In the movies we see in class, it's not real. They're just acting. It's not really genuine.

Consequently, some students revealed they believed they had a more realistic mental picture of the French and even mentioned specific examples of belief change.

I no longer view the French culture as a highly sophisticated society where people speak in perfect accents with highly articulative [*sic*] speech patterns. I have been exposed to middle-class France, which to my surprise is much like middle-class America. The fractured sentences have proven to me that the French don't always speak in perfect grammar, and they make mistakes.

Most likely, the students' previous schemata for French language resulted from contact with carefully scripted materials and an emphasis on correct grammar and pronunciation. While at times they found the spoken utterances from the 'real' interactions 'a bit tough to understand', many students preferred accessing what they called 'real French', finding it more useful. 'I think it's a lot better 'cause if you go to France then that's how people really talk there.' The students seemingly wanted to speak and understand the French language as it is used by native speakers, a goal clearly in line with the aim of creating competent L2/C2 communicators. They also reportedly acquired more than French language during their experience.

Some students suggested they learned about French values. 'I think that after my fieldwork experience, I am more aware of the things they value in their culture.' By learning about these cultural values, some students acquired an appreciation for recognising others' perspectives. 'Throughout the two weeks, watching and listening to the video clips of conversations, I have gained a further understanding of the French people as a whole. They have several customs that are different from those in America. If these customs are not understood completely they could be misinterpreted and could cause some unnecessary tension.' By directly accessing information which is often implicit in interactions, these students encountered input that challenged their existing constructs of specific behaviours and increased their awareness of multiple perspectives. This cognisance of multiple interpretations is a key element in the development of cross-cultural perspectives.

French people probably get the reputation for being rude because they interrupt. This is where an ethnographer is needed. It is wrong if we look at the French and label them as rude because they interrupt because we can't compare the French to our cultural norms. Instead we have to look only at their culture and decide whether or not interruption is a norm for their culture. When we discover that interruption is normal for the French we have completed our goals as an ethnographer.

By learning to recognise norms of behaviour and interpretation and by critically comparing them with their own, these students learned to appreciate aspects of French communication they encountered in the program from the French perspective. It is likely that their newfound methodology provided the students with a structure with which to explore the French culture and to facilitate the development of cultural sensitivity. Based on their statements, we can conclude that most of the students viewed the ethnography of communication as a valuable method of learning about other cultures and belief systems.

Belief and Attitude Change

The students completed an introspective exercise prior to beginning the coursework and after having written their summary report. Their responses were compared. Attitude and belief change emerged as important themes.

In their second introspective reports, thirteen students mentioned belief change. 'When I used to think about French people, I would always picture high-class fashionable Parisians at discotheques. Now I think of them as being as diverse as Americans are, people form all walks of life.' Moreover, 21 students provided more detailed descriptions in their second introspective report which confirmed this perception. Furthermore, ten students mentioned discovering common attributes between the French and American cultures, and sixteen mentioned noticing differences between the two cultures. 'When asked to describe their personalities, I used to think that they were very élitist and high on themselves. However, they are very similar to Americans, just some things that they do in their culture make them seem snobbish to us.' Finally, four students who originally stated that the French and American cultures were alike revised their statements to account for differences they noticed. By undertaking ethnographic studies, these students became aware of their beliefs and the changes which took place as they negotiated meaning, albeit in a manner limited by space and time, with the NRs. These belief changes may have also resulted in attitude change.

In all, thirteen students mentioned that their attitudes towards the French changed, and seventeen provided value statements in their second introspective reports which substantiated this observation. 'I used to think French people were rude but now I don't think they are. The project changed my view of how polite people in France are. I think they're nicer now.' Some students did not reportedly perceive attitude change. 'In the beginning of this experiment I was under the impression that all French people were loud and obnoxious. This field work pretty much reassured my stereotypes.' Tracking records revealed that three students who neither reported nor demonstrated attitude change during the second introspective exercise did not access the NRs' analyses during their fieldwork. Presumably, they did not gain sufficient access to the perspectives of French people concerning the behaviours they witnessed to change their beliefs and attitudes concerning the French.

Lessons Learned

In my opinion, the value of educational research lies in what lessons we learn and how we apply them. In this section, I list the lessons I learned from my experience with these teenagers in the hope that they will encourage practical change.

1: We should use knowledge from other domains to broaden L2/C2 students' understanding of language and communication. The very nature of our subject, foreign language, has posed several problems for our field. Our classrooms are disconnected by space and time from the people of the target cultures. While our goal of fostering communicative and cultural competence among our students is commendable, the limited communicative resources we rely upon to achieve these aims have thwarted our efforts. We teach our students to use only a small portion of the resources for both producing and interpreting meaningful communication and to ignore contextual clues and visual aspects of communication. The students' findings and insights suggest using knowledge and methods developed by anthropologists, communication scientists, and sociolinguists, who have benefited from extensive contact with their subjects, can lead to rich learning experiences. However, we cannot ask teachers to adopt these approaches without providing appropriate materials and without incorporating them into the curricula. In addition, I was fortunate to find a school system that would allow me to take ten class periods of precious teaching time. Realistically, most classroom teachers are constrained by tight schedules and cannot afford to stray from the existing curricula. Consequently, as a profession, we must reassess what we teach our students and what methods we utilise to do so. We must also modify existing curricula and materials to meet the new demands.

2: We should explore creative uses of technology to meet our goals. This research project illustrates one way in which we can use technology as a means of overcoming some of the barriers that have traditionally hindered the development of communicative competence in foreign language classrooms. In this case, I tried to create a virtual culture contact situation. The students experienced French communicative practices in various contexts and accessed native informants' interpretations regarding these practices. As foreign language researchers, teachers, and materials designers, we should explore the various means afforded by technology in order to create learning environments that help our students achieve the goals we have set for them.

3: We must equip our schools with the necessary technology. To date, many school systems lack technological resources for innovative projects which rely upon digitised film and other materials requiring large amounts of computer memory and fast processing power. If we are going to introduce technology-enhanced learning into the curriculum, then we must equip our schools with adequate facilities and tools to support pedagogically sound learning experiences.

4: L2/C2 teachers should receive training in language and culture issues. This study documented the benefits of introducing students to basic information about ethnographic techniques and about human interaction. To date, since few teacher training programmes require their prospective teachers to take courses in sociolinguistics or communication sciences, few high school and middle school teachers are familiar with these concepts and methods for exploring language and culture. Accordingly, if we expect teachers to develop intercultural skills among their students, teacher training and development must address these topics.

5: We should trust our students and listen to them. Rather than going into this project with established categories that I was going to study, I listened to the students' comments and allowed them to shape the study. I also allowed them to change my role as a researcher. Based on their comments and insights, I was able to mine my data and substantiate their claims, which were remarkably perceptive and revealed how they learned. Furthermore, before working with the students, I received many warnings from well-wishers who felt high school students would be incapable of understanding the concepts presented in the courseware and of undertaking virtual ethnographies. These students proved them wrong. We must trust that our students are intelligent and capable. Furthermore, in order to create effective learning environments and understand their learning experiences, we must enter into dialogues which allow them to become active participants in the construction of their education.

6: We must examine the foreign language culture to understand why we do what we do. Like any culture, the foreign language culture has been shaped by its environment and the resources available to its members. As a result, notions of language and language teaching have been moulded and constrained by these factors. As members of this culture, we must adapt and profit from the new resources available to us. We must learn to use these tools intelligently and purposefully so that our understanding of communication, culture, and language teaching evolves.

Note

1. In choosing the informants, I tried to allow for diversity. In all, there were three men and three women ranging in age from 20 to 60 years of age. They hailed from different regions of France and from different socioeconomic backgrounds. However, they were all college educated.

References

Hall, E.T. (1976) *Beyond Culture*. New York: Doubleday.
Hymes, D. (1972) On communicative competence. In J.B. Pride and J. Holmes (eds) *Sociolinguistics*. Harmondsworth: Penguin Books.
Hymes, D. (1974) *Foundations in Sociolinguistics: An Ethnographic Approach*. Philadelphia: University of Pennsylvania Press.
Kerbrat-Orecchioni, C. (1994) *Les Interactions Verbales*. Paris: Armand Colin.
Lewo, R.R. (1998) Toward operationalizing the process of attention in SLA: Evidence for Tomlin and Villa's (1994) fine grained analysis of attention. *Applied Psycholinguistics* 19, 133–159.
Lutz, C. and Collins, J. (1993) *Reading National Geographic*. Chicago: University of Chicago Press.

Rumelhart, D.E. (1980) Schemata: The building blocks of cognition. In R.L. Spiro, B.C.Bruce and W.E. Brewer (eds) *Theoretical Issues in Reading Comprehension*. Hillsdale, NJ: Erlbaum.

Saville-Troike, M. (1989) *The Ethnography of Communication: An Introduction*. Oxford: B. Blackwell.

The National Standards in Foreign Language Education Project (1996) *Standards for Foreign Language Learning: Preparing for the 21st Century*. Lawrence, KS: Allen Press.

Vygotsky, L. S. (1976) *The Development of Higher Psychological Processes*. Cambridge, MA: Harvard University Press.

Chapter 10
Working in Tandem:
An Anglo-French Project

CLARE DODD

*The integration of cultural and linguistic learning, of the develop-
ment of intercultural competence with linguistic competence, is
demonstrated in this chapter, which also deals with issues of
motivation. In an English school boys with little motivation were
linked in a tandem project through e-mail with their peers in
France. The chapter shows how they developed language skills and
acquired more cultural awareness whilst the teacher ensured that
limited curriculum time was used to best effect.*

Introduction

The English school in which this tandem e-mail project was undertaken is a rural comprehensive school for students aged between 11 and
16 years old. It has Technology College status which means that extra
funding was granted from the government in order to put greater
emphasis on the teaching of science, maths and technology. Targets in
these subject areas, such as the raising of the number of passes in GCSE
examinations, have to be met in order for the extra funding to be made
available. Other implications are that technological advances both
theoretical and practical should enhance and develop the students'
education in all subject areas and also benefit the pupils in neighbouring
schools and in the wider community.

The school has three networked computer rooms each allowing for the
teaching of 30 students. During the project there were two networks and
only ten of the computers had internet access. There are three foreign
language teaching rooms and 670 students in the school, with over a third
of the students having special educational needs – twice the national
average.

The Nature of the Foreign Language Curriculum

In terms of curriculum time given to subjects in the college, a comparison between the core subjects and French during the tandem project is as follows:

Key Stage 3 (KS3) (students aged 11–14):

English: 16.7% (Yrs 7 & 8); 13.3% (Yr 9)
Mathematics: 13.3% (Yrs 7, 8 & 9)
Science: 10% (Yrs 7 & 8); 13.3% (Yr 9)
Technology: 6.7% (Yrs 7 & 8); 10% (Yr 9)
French: 6.7% (Yrs 7, 8 & 9)

Key Stage 4 (KS4) (students aged 14–16):

English: 13.3%
Mathematics: 13.3%
Science: 20%
Technology: 10%
French: 10%

For French, students are taught in mixed-ability groups in Year 7 and banded into five ability sets for all subsequent years (12–16). In the academic year in which the project took place the contact time in KS3 (Years 7, 8 and 9) was one 50-minute lesson and one 45-minute lesson per week. As this amounts to approximately 6.7% of curriculum time, it is well below the nationally recommended amount of 10% and this of course does have implications for the effective teaching and learning of a foreign language. During the course of the project students were studying only one foreign language. Their course was topic-based and for the duration of the project the students followed a programme of study involving the topics of: personal details and descriptions, family and pets, school, home town, shopping, Christmas, and television programmes and films.

The National Curriculum for Modern Foreign Languages (DfEE and QCA, 2000: 162) stresses the importance of learning modern foreign languages by stating that:

Through the study of a foreign language, pupils understand and appreciate different countries, cultures, people and communities – and as they do so, begin to think of themselves as citizens of the world as well as of the United Kingdom. Pupils also learn about the basic structures of language. They explore the similarities and differences between the foreign language they are learning and English or another language, and learn how language can be manipulated and applied in different ways. Their listening, reading and memory skills improve, and their speaking and writing become more accurate. The development of these skills, together with pupils' knowledge and understanding of the structure of language lay the foundations for future study of other languages.

In terms of the statutory Programme of Study, pupils should be taught the following, amongst other things:

Knowledge, skills and understanding

Acquiring knowledge and understanding of the target language
(1c) how to express themselves using a range of vocabulary and structures

Developing language skills
(2c) how to ask and answer questions
(2g) strategies for dealing with the unpredictable
(2h) techniques for skimming and for scanning written texts for information
(2i) how to summarise and report the main points of spoken or written texts
(2j) how to redraft their writing to improve its accuracy and present-ation, including the use of information and computer technology (ICT)

Developing language – learning skills
(3b) how to use context and other clues to interpret meaning
(3c) to use their knowledge of English . . . when learning the target language
(3d) how to use dictionaries . . . appropriately and effectively
(3e) how to develop their independence in learning and using the target language

Developing cultural awareness
(4a) working with authentic materials in the target language
(4b) communicating with native speakers
(4c) considering their own culture and comparing it with the cultures of the countries and communities where the target language is spoken
(4d) considering the experiences and perspectives of people in these countries and communities

Breadth of study
(5c) expressing and discussing personal feelings and opinions

(5e) using a range of resources, including ICT, for accessing and communicating information

(5h) using the target language for real purposes

(5i) working in a variety of contexts, including everyday activities, personal and social life.

The National Curriculum obviously underpins our Scheme of Work (SOW). but there is evidently much work to be covered to achieve these aims. Thus we would not have been able to complete our SOW for Year 8 in the curriculum time available if we had not integrated the tandem project into it. However, the project also presented us with an ideal opportunity to achieve the requirements of the National Curriculum. The tasks our students were set therefore linked directly to our SOW and to the *Camarades* 2 coursebook. This was not the case for my colleague in France, who seemed to judge the project more as added language practice rather than as work which was integral to their programme of study. I and my French counterpart explained to each other what was required for each of our classes, and we managed to arrange things so that we were both happy with what we were doing.

Description of the Learners and their Linguistic Competence

One of the target groups with whom I decided to undertake the tandem e-mail project was a Year 8 class of 24 boys (aged 12–13 years old). They had already been studying French for one year, although some of the students had also learned some basic French in their primary school. The English Faculty had decided prior to the beginning of the academic year that they would like to teach Year 8 in single gender classes in order to see if this would help to raise boys' achievement. The Modern Foreign Languages Faculty was timetabled against English, and we agreed that teaching boys and girls separately would be an interesting 'experiment' as the problem of boys' under-achievement has long been a concern for foreign language teachers.

The Year 8 cohort was therefore divided into five sets – sets 1 and 2 (boys) and sets 1 and 2 (girls), with a single set 5 (mixed gender). Many of the boys in the set 1 class which undertook the project would not have been in set 1 had it been a mixed gender class because the girls as a whole had achieved much better results than the boys in Year 7. Also, in terms of behaviour many of the boys were much louder and seemingly lacking in their ability to concentrate properly on the task in hand, which is not so apparent in a mixed gender class. Many boys also displayed a distinct dislike of writing and much of their written work was not neatly presented. Several were not keen to learn a foreign language, particularly French. A few boys had repeatedly asked the question 'Why learn a foreign language as everybody speaks English?' Several of the boys displayed a dislike of the subject French, the French people and France in general – mainly, I believe, because they come from farming backgrounds and there were ongoing problems concerning agriculture between the two countries which were particularly acute during the BSE crisis affecting British beef farmers.

The Tandem E-mail Learning Project

The tandem e-mail project was originally conceived as a two-year European Comenius-funded project. Each country taking part has a national co-ordinator. Tandem learning has been in operation for many years. It was first conceived as face-to-face tandem: a way of helping university students to learn a foreign language. The idea is that two native speakers of different languages help each other to learn each other's language. They therefore get together and spend 50% of the time talking each other's language, with the native speaker helping to correct mistakes and also to provide a model of their own language for the learner to use as a template. The present project was designed to see if the idea of tandem learning could be extended into schools, including primary schools, through the use of e-mail to facilitate more effective, motivating language and cultural learning. The basic premises of reciprocity and autonomous learning were to be maintained, as this is what separates tandem from other sorts of e-mail type correspondence between individuals, groups or classes. The countries involved in the project were France, Germany, Italy, Spain and the UK.

Aims and objectives

My objectives in selecting the class of Year 8 boys to take part in the project were as follows:

- To motivate the boys.
- To raise achievement and aspirations.
- To encourage independence in their language learning.
- To bring about the learning and application of new vocabulary using a 'real' communicative situation.
- To make the students more culturally aware.

- To increase language awareness (in own and foreign language).
- To promote reading and writing skills.
- To promote language-learning skills, e.g. to use dictionaries, to infer meaning, etc.

Before we began the project the boys were made aware that they were privileged to be able to take part. They were reminded that they should not write anything offensive or silly which could be misinterpreted. They were also to take into account that they were in a way representing England as what they wrote would give an impression of what English people were like. They were told that they were helping another person to learn English and that they had to respect their French partners. A letter was sent home to parents explaining the project and setting out what was expected of the boys. They were also informed that the boys would no longer be able to take part in the project if they deliberately did not respect the rules.

In order to manage the project and for it to have a chance of success, I decided, as aforementioned, that I would have to integrate the tandem project into my scheme of work because of lack of curriculum time and also to ensure access to the computers. Fortunately I was able to choose when I could have access to the computer network and I therefore chose last lesson on a Friday as my slot! When I began the project the students did not have their own e-mail addresses and we had to send their e-mails in a group folder. However, this was remedied later in the project when they were given their own individual e-mail address.

Process

I was put in contact with a teacher in Rouen who was also interested in the idea of tandem learning. I told her what age the boys were and she found a class of comparable age (mixed gender). The first e-mail came from my tandem partner's school. It was all in French and described her school and the area. It was sent as a class e-mail so I printed copies for the class and we read it. I then set it as a homework task, asking the boys to translate the main points, using a dictionary. The following lesson we began the project in earnest. Many of the boys had said that the French e-mail had been too difficult for homework but some boys had translated it perfectly (I suspect that there had been some parental involvement!). The students wanted to know whether they had their own e-mail partners yet and they were mostly keen to take part. That lesson in the classroom we continued with work about our town in French, as in the scheme of work.

The following lesson in the network I explained the rules of tandem learning again and then gave them their e-mail partners from the partner school in France. They were really excited, and as can be imagined they mostly clamoured to have girls as their partners! This was not possible for all of them as we were communicating with a class of mixed gender. I was therefore selective in that I gave girl partners to those boys who really needed motivating, and boys to those boys who did not really seem to mind and who seemed motivated anyway. I also assured them that it would be possible to change partners after half-term. I thought that they should continue with the same partner for six to seven weeks in order to have continuity and to develop a relationship of trust in which to correct each other's mistakes.

The boys wrote an e-mail to their partner telling them about their town and school in English, so that the French students would have a topic to work on. Some of them also downloaded pictures of the school and the school badge, and wrote the other half of the e-mail in French, talking about themselves. It must be remembered that most were only beginning their second year of French so we had to be realistic in terms of what they could produce autonomously.

Content of the task

The content of the task was to respond to the e-mail stimulus. Thus the French students wrote about their school in French. The English students read the e-mail in French using dictionaries and then made notes in English. The next lesson we worked through the e-mail and then I asked the students to write about our school in English so that the French students would have the same sort of reading exercise. The English students also wrote some things about their town and themselves in French so that their French partners could correct their mistakes or help them in some way – in providing cultural information about schooling in France, for instance. The English students did the same for their partners when they received their next e-mail and so on. The information they gathered from the e-mails served to help the students with their current topics, to increase cultural and language awareness and to improve their reading, writing and language-learning skills. They were also given the opportunity to write about a topic of their choice, so there was a degree of learner autonomy as well. Differentiation of the tasks for the students was by outcome. The more able students wrote more accurately, although not always more fully in terms of content. There were some mismatches between the partners in terms of ability but this was not very striking or evident as much of the work was 'controlled' in a classroom context.

Obstacles to effective learning

From a technical point of view there were initial difficulties with the project. Although there is an ICT technician in the college we had faced the following problems:

- There was no individual internet access for students. They had to write their e-mails and save them in Word; we then collated the e-mails and sent them as one file to the teacher in Rouen.
- Some students did not save their work correctly.
- Some students did not write much in the allocated time or finish their e-mail.
- Students kept forgetting their partner's e-mail from the previous network lesson and therefore could not remember their partner's name and/or address.
- Students forgot their password, especially if they had recently changed it and therefore could not access the computer. I still have not found an answer to this one!
- Some students did not have adequate computing skills.
- It was time-consuming.
- There were mistakes in both languages.
- There were linguistic difficulties. The boys did not have enough French in order to communicate according to the tandem learning principles. They made mistakes in their English and there were mistakes in the French e-mails they received.

The boys' opinions

I decided that I would like to find out what the boys thought about the project and therefore, after six lessons, I asked them for their opinions. They came up with positive opinions for the most part, responses such as: 'Totally excellent. A good experience', 'Excellent. Better than doing work' (!), 'It's much better than doing writing', 'It's excellent. Much better than being stuck in the classroom', 'It's brilliant! I love computers and e-mail', 'It's ace!', 'Fabulous', 'It's OK 'cause we get to muck about!' (!) Others were less enthusiastic in what they said: 'It's OK', 'It's quite all right', 'It's good'.

There was, however, no distinctly negative feedback. Of course, as I was asking them as a class, it is highly probable that the students were influenced by their peers and I also did not obtain every student's opinion. Before half-term, therefore, I gave them a simple questionnaire and asked them to complete the three sections honestly and on their own.

The three headings were:

- Things I like about the project (if any).
- Things I don't like about the project (if any).
- How the project could be improved.

I analysed the information gathered and put the results into three categories (the third category being used for the 'Development' section of this chapter):

Positive points
- It helps with students' ICT skills through giving a practical focus.
- They like the break from 'traditional' writing.
- It provides the opportunity to know what people really do in France.
- It helps with the learning and broadening of French vocabulary and grammar.
- They find a real need for using dictionaries and other reference material.
- It allows the students to use the internet constructively and purposefully.
- They think that they do not have to write so much.
- They find it fun.
- They like to get out of the classroom and do something else for a change.
- It has helped some students to realise that we are not the only people in the world.
- Students have expressed surprise that 'we are nearly all the same', 'like we enjoy television' and 'they even have programmes like ours'.
- They had been sent words that they felt they would never have learned in a 'real' lesson. (I am not sure which ones!)
- Some students also felt that it helped to space out the week, adding, however, that they thought that two lessons of French a week was 'a bit too much!'
- Some students stated that they had been to France before but that they had never got an impression of what a person their age was like, adding, 'now I know!'

Negative points
- Some students thought that it did not help them much because they wrote their e-mails mostly in English and got someone else to translate the French part of the e-mails they received.

- They felt they needed more time to write the e-mails.
- Some felt that they did not know how to use the internet properly.
- Some students said that they did not receive enough e-mails and that this was boring.
- The students did not like having to wait to use one of the ten computers which have access to the internet.
- Some felt that other students in the class showed a lack of interest and did not give the project the concentration it deserved.

My own evaluation of the project

We undertook tandem work with this class in France during a six month period, until we suddenly and without warning heard nothing more from the French teacher and her class. So the tandem partnership worked relatively well for a time. The French teacher had said on one occasion that they were experiencing many difficulties: logistically, they could only gain computer access once a fortnight and their ICT technician was not readily available. She also felt it necessary to check the e-mails before she could allow them to be sent, which is not really in the spirit of tandem learning. The students in my class had begun to feel frustrated because I was making them send e-mails although they were not receiving any new messages from France.

In spite of this, as can be seen, the boys were much more positive about the project than they were negative. In fact, in terms of future development, they wanted to extend what they were doing rather than change things, and they definitely wanted me to find new tandem partners.

Outcomes

Linguistic outcomes

The project did achieve to a great extent the objectives I had had in mind when we started it. The students were able to use material from the e-mails they received in their own work and they practised their reading and writing skills in an authentic communicative situation. They learned new vocabulary and were able to use it in their own work. Language learning skills were promoted with, for example, a genuine need for dictionaries and a desire on the students' part to understand. The students also scanned their e-mails for information and to a lesser extent were prepared to redraft their work to improve its accuracy and presentation.

Intercultural outcomes

Participants gained a greater awareness of both French and English cultures; particularly, they gained an insight into the life of French students of their own age. They also gained greater language awareness not only of French but also of English – they were surprised by some of the mistakes the French students made in English and there was a dawning realisation about meaning and communication in different languages. This was particularly interesting to me as it highlighted the fact that teaching a foreign language cannot be taught in isolation: it is not just a 'linguistic thing'. There are always cultural dimensions which need to be addressed. For example both French and English students were affected by media reports of the beef crisis and by popular conceptions ('they all wear berets'; 'they're called Frenchies') and prejudices about each others' cultures ('they don't eat the same things as us'; 'they eat frogs' legs, snails, onions and garlic'). These sort of cultural preconceptions can be countered by an initiative such as the tandem learning project. By experiencing the cultural differences at first hand in this way, working with their partner, the students can explore differences and similarities; hopefully this will help to break down barriers and false perceptions.

However, one of the more delicate issues is that of parental involvement and their possible prejudices, and some of the boys were obviously influenced by their parents' somewhat negative opinions of the French. As a teacher it is often difficult to get the students to have a balanced, independent opinion of others when there is so much prejudice in their personal backgrounds. Hopefully with a project such as this they can begin to see that they cannot generalise about people and their way of life and that both similarities and differences may be seen in a positive light.

The following examples from the e-mails illustrate some of the intercultural aspects of the project, taking the topic 'School' as an example:

- Vanessa: *Je suis en 4ème et je n'ai jamais redoublée* (I am in Year 9 and I have never had to re-do a year). The boys were surprised that this system operates in France.
- Antoine: *Il met tous le temps des baskets* (He always wears trainers – talking about his friend). The boys liked the fact that the French liked wearing trainers too and that they do not have to wear school uniform.
- Jack: *We have uniform and it's really boring*.
- Monia: *Avez-vous une permanence et que faites vous avez des heures libres dans votre emploi du temps?* (Have you got a private study

period and what do you do during your free periods?). This was interesting for both schools because we do not operate a system of free periods for our students in state schools and of course they do in France.

- Lise: *Pourquoi êtes-vous séparés des garçons et filles?* (Why are boys taught separately from girls?). The French students had thought that this was common practice in English schools.
- Rachid: *J'espère que les professeurs là-bas ne sont pas sévères* (I hope the teachers aren't strict over there).

Motivation of boys

The boys aspired to writing more French than usual during the project, and were also able to work more independently. The project was undoubtedly motivating for the boys and in that sense I think that it raised achievement. They definitely enjoyed using computers and it did mean that they were actively involved in their work. All the students were able to produce good work, no matter what their ability, once they were prepared to re-draft their work. They liked to find out things about their partner and they talked about their partner to other students: they were, in fact, genuinely interested in what they were doing.

The following examples from the e-mails illustrate some of the motivational aspects of the project:

- Guillaume: *Ce que j'aime aussi c'est aller à la patinoire, au cinéma, au McDonald's et surtout sortir avec mes amis* (What I also like doing is going skating, to the cinema, to McDonald's and most of all going out with my friends). The boys responded, 'that's just like us!'
- Guillaume: *I love video games. Do you have video games and if yes how do your parents react?* The boys realised that French children have 'problems' with their parents too!

Development: Future Possibilities and Directions

We are continuing with tandem e-mailing to a new class in a new school because we have found it to be a good way of teaching and of motivating students. Closer co-operation between the partners and greater preparation of the topics and tasks will, it is hoped, improve students' language acquisition and motivation. It will also necessitate greater commitment to the e-mail partnership. We would like to extend the e-mail project to other classes and to make sure that it forms an integral part of our schemes of work for all students, building in proper assessment procedures as well. Increased learner autonomy, which we must not forget is one of the basic principles of tandem learning, should increase as the students get older and have learned more of the foreign language. I have found that the Year 11 students with whom I have also undertaken this project were much more able to be autonomous in their tandem learning.

Teachers need to accept that their role will be different when doing an e-mail project like this and to take the following points into consideration:

- Teachers will become facilitators of learning and they need to realise that they have to 'let go' of the usual control that they have over lessons.
- Teaching will be more student-centred.
- Teachers are no longer 'the font of all knowledge' in the classroom.
- Students will learn from other students who are native speakers.
- Teachers no longer correct every mistake.
- Teachers no longer see or assess every piece of work.
- Genuine communication and social/cultural awareness are more important than linguistic accuracy.
- Teachers will need computing skills so as not to be 'scared' of ICT.
- Students must be allowed to communicate what they want to communicate (within reason) so that interest can be maintained.
- Reserve worksheets or other resources should be available should the computer system crash.
- Regular communication is essential to maintain motivation.
- Teachers should contact one another on a regular basis to alert each other of such potential impediments as mis-matched holiday dates or students' absences.

At the moment we are planning to have a chat line with our newly established contact school at a mutually convenient time. We are also hoping to start video-conferencing as our partnership continues to develop, again requiring close co-operation between the teachers. I am sure that the students would love to communicate with their partner face to face, especially as some of the relationships develop into closer friendships as has happened with my Year 11 tandem class.

Conclusion

Having taken part in the project I think that class-to-class tandem learning is an excellent way to motivate the students to communicate and to learn about each other's cultures. I am sure that this sort of learning will become more and more widespread with the extended use of technologies in schools. It is yet another effective method of teaching foreign languages and it is obviously encouraging a very authentic means of communication. It does, however, require thorough preparation and close co-operation between the teachers involved. Tandem learning can fit in with any scheme of work and can help to make its application effective. Teachers can also help one another by tandem learning, and may themselves benefit greatly from the up-to-date cultural information and new vocabulary.

Chapter 11

New Tools for Old Tricks: Information and Communication Technology in Teaching British Cultural Studies

PAUL WHITTAKER

The use of information technology is very promising but needs to be contextualised with technology specialists and teachers working together. This chapter describes some of the pleasures and problems of working with advanced technology to produce ways of introducing university students to a new culture and to develop their insight and understanding. The author has sometimes been frustrated by the difficulties but recommends ways forward and the advantages which new technologies can offer.

Introduction

For the last five years the Centre for Comparative Cultural Studies at Palacky University has been exploring ways to use new technologies in teaching and learning about other cultures. The Centre was established with a grant from the Czech Ministry of Education in 1995 and since then has received support from a variety of other sources. One of the main aims of the Centre is to research into the new relationships that are emerging between the cultures of the English speaking world and the culture(s) of the Czech Republic following the fall of the communist regime in 1989. A further role of the Centre is to develop new ways of teaching and learning about those relationships. The people who wrote the application for support had to establish as a fundamental objective what, if anything, the emerging information and communication technologies (ICTs) had to offer to the specific tasks of the Centre and to cultural studies in general.

Technical Terms

It is necessary to explain terms before being to be able to discuss the new technologies. Computers are famous for generating jargon and acronyms and it is probably best to ignore both jargon and acronyms until they cannot be avoided. To avoid them in this article I want to use words that are non-technical but at the same time accurate. The options that exist at present are:

- *Information and communication technology* (ICT): this has a lot to recommend it, since most of the time we are trying to pass information or communicate. However, sometimes we are trying to get people to think or react intuitively and I am not sure how well that fits in. The other problem is that it creates a new domain; there is no clear link to what went before.
- *Information and scientific technologies* (IST): this does not seem appropriate for teachers working in cultural studies or language learning, although it is sometimes used by people working in the Humanities, presumably in the hope of increasing grant income. However, it leaves little room for the empathetic learning that cultural studies often requires, or for what has gone before.
- *Virtual classrooms*: I have spent a lot of time over the last four years struggling with the idea of what 'virtual' means and recently I have come to the conclusion that it may mean a lot for people working with physical objects but for people working on the relationships between human beings it probably does not mean a lot.

William Gibson, the author of *Neuromancer* and the most popular and influential of the new cyber-punk novelists who have done so much to popularise the idea of 'virtual reality', has a lot to answer for. Or, to be fair, the people who took William Gibson's work as predictive rather than imaginative have. William Gibson had never seen a personal computer when he wrote *Neuromancer* and it gave him a great deal of freedom in creating a fictional world in which virtual realities played a powerful role – but it has rather inflated people's perceptions of what is possible. An image on a computer screen is no more 'virtual' than an image in an art gallery or in a magazine or on a cave wall. The addition of interactivity is used to justify the creation of this extra layer of reality. However, interacting with other people in responding to culture is nothing new. Who goes, consistently, to the cinema or art gallery alone? How many people think the best part of a film or a play is the discussion over a drink afterwards, especially with the risk that it might be a bad film or play?

How many conversations at work are about what was on television last night? How many people dance alone? What happened when the person finished painting the pictures on the cave wall?

Virtual reality is an oxymoron – but it has sold a lot computers. Combined with those we had before, we have a set of new tools that is allowing us to do some things better and opening up some new possibilities. Where those possibilities will take us we have as little knowledge of as Thomas More did of America when he wrote *Utopia*. *Neuromancer* will be a successful book if it is viewed in the twenty-sixth century as *Utopia* is now – as an invaluable insight into the mindset of its era.

New tools seems the best way of describing what we are being offered by the flood of computer-based products available. It links us to the past but reminds us that something new is happening and demystifies what some people see as a threat to humanity. These new tools are no more likely to turn us into mind-deadened zombies than television, cinema or painting on cave walls did. It is a set of new tools that, like the old tools, need time and effort to use well. I may slip occasionally but I will try as far as possible to stick to using the term 'new tools' throughout this chapter.

Developing a Course for Students

The fact that the Centre received its initial grant in 1995 was a peculiar piece of luck as one of the most powerful of the new tools, the World Wide Web, was in its infancy and only just becoming widely available, offering however, even as baby, a wide range of possibilities for improving education. The Centre had a role and, thanks to the grant from the Ministry of Education and further support from Palacky University and the British Council, the financial resources to explore the possibilities of the web for cultural studies. The initial design for the Centre's ITC systems did not actually involve an internet connection. However, this omission was rectified very quickly. The situation was made more unusual in that resources were available in the Czech Republic, a country where resources are considerably harder to come by than they are in many countries to the west of the Czech lands.

Following its brief to find out what benefits ICT offered to teaching cultural studies, we decided to try a variety of methods using ICT on a course in British cultural studies for undergraduates studying on a five-year programme leading to a Magister's (Masters) degree. The degree can have English as a main or second subject. Students are part of the Department of English and American Studies at Palacky University. The course has the inspiring title of 'British Studies II'.

The course is taken by second-year and third-year students, usually between 20 and 23 years old, around 70% of whom are women. The course is compulsory for all students on the magister programme and roughly 70 students every year take the course. The course is offered in both semesters of the school year and is taught in classes with a maximum of 15 people attending.

The language level of the students is high. The most linguistically competent students have almost complete fluency. Some students have studied on postgraduate courses at universities in the US or UK at the end of their third year of study. Others have a high level of competency but lack confidence in their ability to use the language as they have only ever used it in a school setting or on very brief trips to English-speaking countries.

One of the major problems students on the degree face is access to resources. Although the situation has improved enormously since 1989 there are still bottlenecks and gaps in providing students with enough copies of texts and with the wealth of reference resources that would be expected by students at Western institutions.

Our attempts to use ICT in teaching 'British Studies II' took two forms. The first was to improve the range and accessibility of conventional resources for students, and so overcome the immediate problem facing students of a lack of access to resources caused by the level of economic development in the Czech Republic. The second was to try and use ICT in the most innovative way possible to teach Czech students about Britain and to give them the widest possible range of competencies we could in understanding other cultures.

To achieve this we had to try to understand what the new tools were capable of and how we could use that technology to further our ends – increasing the resources available to our students and increasing their understanding of other cultures.

Technical Skills

Not many people working on cultural studies understand technology, and a fair proportion positively dislike it and the same is true of technical people and their understanding of cultural studies. One of the main bones of contention is often about who is dealing with reality and who is being fantastic. However, unfortunately or fortunately, we live at a time when the gap between fantasy and reality is the smallest it has ever been since the arrival of Europeans in America. The sense of wonder that Columbus felt when he arrived in America is being re-experienced 500 years later.

The only way we could see of realising the potential, or at least come to understand the potential of our 'marvellous possession' (to borrow Columbus's description of America), was to create a team of people that contained both those with a background in cultural studies and those with a background in working with technology – and to create a language in which they could talk to each other. A survey of existing web sites had shown us that more ICT expertise than could be gained by reading the 'The Dummies Guide to Computers' (IDG Books) series was going to be necessary, very useful though these books are, to use the new tools that are now available.

To use the new tools well requires teamwork. Our experience has convinced us that the future of education lies with people of different competencies being able to work together successfully. Scholars, teachers and technicians will have to work together as equals. This may well be the most revolutionary thing that the new technologies achieve. Or possibly reactionary, as it often seems to me that it will be a return to the monastic workshops that produced the original texts of the Humanities.

This is a rather round-about way of getting to the point that what is important about the new tools is not the tools but the people using the tools. From this comes the best recommendations I can give about using the new tools: do not try to do it alone, and spend as much time and money on people as you do on the new tools.

People

For the cultural studies person entering Terra Technologia the best advice I can give is to approach it as an ethnographer. Assume that there are language and rituals you must acquire and that finally, however bizarre it may appear, the behaviour you see is rational in terms of the cultural values of the people who inhabit this exotic region. Equally, when welcoming the visiting ethnographers from Terra Technologia assume no prior knowledge and treat them with the same kindness with which early ethnographers were treated by the tribes they studied and on the same basis, i.e. that these are well-meaning, but slightly demented six-year-olds. Be willing to explain all the things that you take as basic assumptions, such as cultures only being explicable in their own terms, and if you have a belief in 'universal deep structures' avoid explaining them during the first meeting – save it as a nice surprise.

The time and money spent will be well worth it as you will avoid two things I have come to dread: the 'programmers' inhale' and the 'cultural studies bottom-shuffle'. The programmers' inhale is one of the most fundamental warning signs I have learnt to watch for of a breakdown of understanding between 'Techies and Culties'. It is the deep breath that a person from a technical background takes when they are trying to explain to a non-ICT professional that their idea, while wonderful and possible, would require the computer power of NASA and the research budget of Microsoft to be turned into reality.

The cultural studies bottom-shuffle is a warning sign to those from a technical background. It is the rotational movement of the buttocks a cultural studies professional performs in their chair when asked what the word 'culture', or virtually any other word attached to cultural studies, means in terms that can be turned into a multi-media interactive presentation.

Put simply, be ready to spend hours talking but ensure that the talk is constructive and moves you forward to your goals. A training programme for the people involved is essential, and not just for the cultural studies people trying to come to terms with the new tools. Members of the team must appreciate and understand each other's talents and know the disciplinary limitations within which other members of the team work. Understanding the limitations we found was much more important than understanding the possibilities. ICT can do amazing things, but it can take up an awful lot of time and money before being amazing. Equally, cultural studies is unsure about most things but it has set up disciplinary practices that seem more valid than other possible practices.

I would understand if the reader at this time gives up and decides to stick to chalk and talk. So let me say at this point that our efforts to use new tools have produced very great benefits for our students that have made the effort more than worthwhile. Also the new tools are here and those who hold the purse strings are expecting them to be used. If we hope to maintain the values that most people I know who work in cultural studies share, then we must engage with the new tools. The Luddites are an admirable historical failure, not a model for the twenty-first century.

Practicalities

Given the concentration on difficulties in the last sections, I will spend the next section trying to be as practical as possible. I am afraid this means often saying 'I don't know', but that is just one of things about these new tools – they are new and there is a lot to learn.

Improving Resources

The Centre's plan already included creating a computer classroom for students. The question that had not been answered was how to use this equipment to provide resources to students. The availability of the World Wide Web answered this. We decided to create a website (www.compare.upol.cz) that would promote the Centre's work and provide a means of delivering resources to students, but for copyright reasons most of the teaching resources on the site are only available to students studying on courses supported by the Centre.

Copyright and the absence of any quality control of the wealth of materials the internet makes available to students are the two biggest problems we have faced in making resources available to our students. The good news is that one problem we expected did not occur: students without the technical ability to access the web. As with so much technical learning at present this was dealt with by students providing each other with the skills. Even so we did attempt to make the environment as simple to use as possible.

Copyright

This really is our single largest problem. The law on copyright was designed for print and television. It does not provide clear guidance as to what is and is not allowed on the web. When we asked people who work in this field for advice we got a general feeling of confusion and I have seen no sign of this clearing. A recent interesting development is for some people to give away electronic versions of their products.

There seems to be a growing realisation amongst copyright holders that once something goes digital there really is no way of defending copyright. The *Guardian*, for example, recently gave permission for a large amount of content to be used from its website if a number of simple conditions were met and as long as the material remained in an electronic form.

After a great deal of consultation we came up with a strategy that has worked so far. Firstly, we make sure that we know who has the copyright of any material we use. Secondly, we try to create as much of our own material as possible. Thirdly, we have created a secure section of our website which can only be accessed by people with the correct pass-words. On this section of the site we assume that we can operate under the same conditions that we would use for creating conventional course materials. We are not at all sure if this is legal or not, but we hope that it is. I think the best advice that can be given at the moment is to be very careful about moving anything between forms, i.e. from print into electronic versions or vice versa and to obey the rules and common practices for both areas.

One benefit of copyright might be in forcing universities and schools to co-operate. If we share what we create we all may be able to move forward much more quickly. Happily, more and more materials are available electronically and this is making life simpler for all concerned.

Overload

However, the increase in material available electronically leads to a new problem. As everybody is going digital how do you differentiate amongst sources? How long did it take to develop the elaborate systems we now use for quality controlling printed material, and can those mechanisms be transferred into the global digital world?

This is especially a problem for students who are still acquiring the skills that enable them to make judgements about the value of a particular source of information or ideas. As William Dutton (1999: 215) has warned: 'In a world exploding with electronic and published information, a positive gatekeeping role will become more critical than ever in determining what educational material is best for students'. The role of teachers in supporting students in dealing with the amount of information available to them, in helping them to understand the value of the information they find and in providing them with techniques for dealing with the different types of information they come across seems certain to expand. As a student my access to information was bounded by the resources in the library and my teachers, whereas students today have an immensely larger information burden available.

Eventually, hopefully, we will have the same kind of guides to electronic sources as we have in printed sources. This is already happening with universities becoming more selective about what goes on their websites and refereed journals becoming commonly web-based. One thing we have tried to avoid is giving lists of websites without giving guidance as to what students can expect to learn from those websites. Already tools are emerging to provide students with guidelines to evaluating the information on the internet. One of the best I have seen is Internet-Detective (http://www.sosig.ac.uk/desire/internet-detective.html), which provides basic guides to using the internet and a simple test to advise students on how well they have grasped the value of the information with which they have been working.

Using the New Tools

One of the best pieces of luck we had when setting up the Centre was that the financing kept being postponed. This gave us much longer for planning and discussion than would have been possible if funding had arrived when it was promised. It also gave those of us with little experience of using the new tools a chance to learn from our more experienced colleagues What we learnt can be reduced to the following points. First, it is possible to do anything within the space of the monitor of a computer screen; however, the more you do the longer it will take to tell the computer what to do and the longer it will take the computer to do it. And secondly, once a resource is in a digital form it can be used in a wide range of ways; it is important to understand the way computers move information around.

The delays also gave us a chance to read about other people's experience in using the new tools and to talk to people with more experience than ourselves. A chance meeting with Dr John Rae of Salford University, who has extensive experience of using the new technologies in teaching and education, led to discussions that helped a great deal to clarify our thinking about what we would do. One thing that became clear was that using the new tools successfully in education required a clear objective that was defined not by the technology but by the learning needs of students and by the skills available to teachers. The new tools are just tools – you must know what you want to do to be able to pick the correct tools to achieve your objective.

As we had been teaching about other cultures for some time we were clear about what we wanted to do – create the richest learning environments possible for our students to be able to explore the difference between their own culture and the culture they were studying. This just left the question of how to do this. By looking at other people's experience in using the new tools, we learnt that the 'how' had to be in two parts that had to be considered jointly. These were the pedagogical 'how' and the technological 'how'.

The pedagogical 'how' meant thinking about how we could create learning-rich environments that our students could use and that would provide us with learning outcomes that could be defined and tested. What we really needed was a set of ideas about learning and teaching that would act as a guide as to how we used the new tools. It surprised me at first that people interested in using the new tools in education spend much more time discussing the philosophy of education and the psychology of learning than they do discussing what the latest gadget will do. However, the longer I work with the new tools the less surprised I am. If you are not clear about what you want to do and how you are going to do it, then choosing the right tools and using them well is very difficult.

John Rea had spent a lot of time working with the Kolb learning cycle, a set of ideas about learning developed by an American management specialist, and this was the set of ideas that we drew on to develop learning rich environments for our students. The Kolb (1984) learning cycle divides learning in to four stages:

(1) *Experiential learning*: this is when we attempt to work with something new, like pressing the buttons on a new piece of equipment to see what happens.
(2) *Observation and reflection*: this is when we learn by watching and thinking about something, e.g. watching somebody else with more experience work with a new piece of equipment.
(3) *Concept formation*: This is when we try to establish a theory to explain a new phenomenon, for example by trying to guess how a new piece of equipment works by guessing what the different knobs, buttons and slots are for.
(4) *Testing implications in new situations*: when we realise that we do not understand something completely we will try to develop new ways to understand it more completely, for example, once we have learnt the basic features of a new piece of equipment we will see if we can get it to do more things.

As an example of the Kolb learning circle, consider how my wife and I took different approaches to learning how to drive our new car. My approach is to get in the car and push every button in sight to see what happens – experiential learning. If there are buttons that seem to have no effect then I will look at the icons on the buttons and the buttons' general position in the car and guess what they are for – concept formation. If this does not work then I will read the manual or ask the dealer – observation and reflection. As far as cars go I tend to see them as a means of getting from A to B and so tend not to involve myself in guessing what other potentials they may have, but if something goes wrong or if I want to move an unusual load I might have to involve myself in some testing.

My wife takes a different, and probably more sensible approach. She reads the manual and talks to the dealer and any friends who have a similar car – observation and reflection. Based on this she looks carefully at the car and matches things up to the manual and her past experience – concept formation. Next she will try things and see if they work –

experiential learning. We tend to share the same approach to the testing stage. Both of us end up being able to drive the car. I manage to make it move in less time; she manages to make it move without ending up with bits of the car dangling in her hands. Of course the best thing that happens is when we share learning to drive the new car and benefit from both learning styles.

What my example is intended to show is that the Kolb learning cycle describes a set of experiences that we must all go through to learn something new, but does not dictate the order in which we must go through them. This is a very brief introduction to Kolb's ideas and for those who are interested in more detail an internet search using the keywords 'Kolb learning cycle' will provide a wealth of other resources.

So, at the Centre we had now settled in our minds the educational objective (to create learning-rich environments that would allow Czech students to explore British culture and society), and the major pedagogic method we would use (the Kolb learning cycle). What we needed was a way of bringing these together using the new tools.

To do this we used 'story boarding', a technique borrowed from the film industry and widely used in producing multi-media products. A story board is a piece of paper that represents graphically and with brief descriptions in words what is going to happen on screen. The most important thing about using this technique from our point of view was that it meant that technical and subject specialist people had to agree what students were going to see, hear and do and describe this in the briefest way possible. The amount of paper this used was horrifying but the clarity of understanding it produced between people coming from radically different professional backgrounds was very satisfying. A fuller description of story boarding and how it is used to produce multi-media products is in Fisher's *Creating Dynamic Web Sites* (1997).

What story boarding resolved for us was that it was going to be impossible to do everything that we wanted to do on screen and that we would need to produce a workbook/reader to go with what the students viewed, heard and did on screen. It also clarified how we would deal with each of the three parts of the Kolb learning cycle that we would be trying to represent in our project: experiential learning, observation and reflection and concept formation.

Experiential learning

This was the most difficult part of the project. The normal way to think of experiencing a culture is to visit the culture *in situ*. A visit to another culture is an enormously rich experience involving all our senses as well as our emotional and intellectual capacities. Trying to replicate this experience on a computer screen is probably impossible. Indeed it was our efforts to work out ways to provide students with experiential learning that led to our sceptical view of the claims for virtual realities – at least as far as these relate to cultural learning.

Initially we went back to tried and trusted methods, role plays. We videoed two people, taking on the roles of British parents, discussing the kind of issues that British parents have to take into account when deciding to which secondary school to send their children. This raised issues such as class, the British attitude to education, perceptions of the difference between private and state education, the importance of catchment area, etc. It also gave a natural opportunity to ask students to take on the role of parents in Britain and the Czech Republic and to consider the different sets of values that come into play when people have to make such decisions.

Students would watch part of the video on screen and then be referred by on-screen instruction to the page in their workbooks with questions relevant to what they had just seen. Of course this is no different from giving the students a workbook and video. However, there are significant differences in how it was prepared, with all the editing of video and audio material taking place within one office. This is probably the greatest advantage the new tools give to teachers: the ability to create types of material that would only have been possible in the past with large amounts of funding and a wide range of resources available. This also means that as we learn how students respond to the material we can add or edit features without substantial further expenditure. A further difference is in the way it was delivered, on one CD-ROM containing not only the video but a wide range of other learning activities.

Since this first attempt at experiential learning we have begun to look to computer games as a way of increasing experiential learning on our course and have built a prototype version of a game comparing the life chances of young people in Britain and the Czech Republic as they leave school. This seems to be a very promising way of achieving experiential learning for students but a lot of work still needs to be done.

Observation and reflection

What we wanted to do in this section of the course was replace all those parts of a class in which a teacher says 'A British teacher/student etc. would say . . .' with a British teacher/student saying it. Additionally we added video and still photographs of the places these people came from and, when we could, the sounds of the place. The other way in which we sought for students to be able to observe other cultures was by visiting the websites of schools and seeing what those schools felt it was important to tell the world about themselves.

Concept formation

In this we were very traditional. Our course is an academic course and we wanted students to gain an insight into the academic discourses that have been used to explain what they have experienced and observed. So on the CD-ROM we recorded two academics talking about British and Czech education and in the workbook we included a text that covered some of the major academic debates there have been about education in the two countries. This was not tremendously exciting or innovative but I have my doubts if it is possible to come to an understanding of difficult ideas except by reading, thinking listening and talking in a balanced way.

Conclusion

Recently the Centre has been asked to take part in two projects working on using the new tools in cultural learning. One project is from a group of cultural studies specialists who have outlined very clear learning objectives and have the abilities to make the content very rich. Unfortunately, the technical methods they have suggested to achieve their aims are less than perfect, and the budget they have asked for to achieve their goals is about one tenth of what they need.

The other project is from a group of specialists in information technology. The technical delivery they are suggesting is wonderful but I really do not understand what it is they are trying to teach. However, the budget they have asked for means I am sure that they will be able to teach something, even if it is only themselves learning how to manage money.

If the new tools are going to be used successfully in cultural learning, the age-old divide between 'techie' and 'cultie' has to come down and we all have to accept the value of each other's work. Even when we do not understand them.

References

Dutton, W. (1999) *Society on the Line*. Oxford: Oxford University Press.

Fisher, S. (1997) *Creating Dynamic Web Sites*. Berkeley: A-W Developers Press.

Kolb, D. A. (1984) *Experiential Learning*. Englewood Cliffs: Prentice Hall.

Chapter 12
Tandem Learning as an Intercultural Activity

JANE WOODIN

The purpose of this chapter is to show how learners can benefit from reciprocal arrangements to develop their intercultural competence in the context of tandem learning in a university They work face-to-face or through e-mail. In this chapter the diaries kept by those meeting in person are analysed to describe the development of their intercultural competence. The chapter thus suggests ways in which tandem learning can be developed to put emphasis on intercultural competence.

Introduction

The Modern Languages Teaching Centre at the University of Sheffield was set up in 1993 to provide service language teaching to non-specialist undergraduates (i.e. those taking degrees in science, engineering or social sciences).[1] We take a broadly communicative approach to language learning, with an emphasis on practical language skills. In the year 1999–2000, approximately 700 undergraduates took language courses with our Centre.

The University of Sheffield operates a modular system, which means, for example, that a first-year engineering undergraduate who takes modules to the value of 120 credits may be required to take modules to the value of 100 credits from courses offered within his or her department. The remaining 20 credits can be taken from any course which is offered from other departments across the university; many students choose to take a language with the Modern Languages Teaching Centre (MLTC).

Tandem learning – collaborative learning between speakers of different languages – is particularly relevant to higher education contexts, as it is practically very easy to organise. Large numbers of students come from many countries in Europe under the 'Erasmus' scheme. In particular, Erasmus students from French, German, Italian and Spanish-speaking countries are highly sought after, these being the most commonly studied languages in UK universities.

The concept of tandem learning[2] is complex but its overarching principles are as follows:

Autonomy: You are responsible for your own learning;
Reciprocity: You are responsible for ensuring mutual benefit.

(http://www.slf.ruhr-uni-bochum.de/learning/idxeng11.html)

Students are therefore active participants in their own learning and clearly have the opportunity of setting their own agenda.

Students studying with the Modern Languages Teaching Centre can take part in tandem learning either face-to-face or through e-mail, and either as an informal activity or as an assessed part of their degree course. The project described here is concerned with the experience of students undertaking tandem learning face-to-face, as a formal ten-credit module. This is available to students with language proficiency equivalent to Advanced level or higher, i.e. a level usually reached after six to eight years of language learning in secondary school.

The tandem module[3] has proved hugely successful in particular because students have a high degree of control over what they choose to learn and how they go about it, and they have far more opportunity to practise their speaking than in a language class. By way of illustration, here are some students' responses to the question 'What do you like best about the tandem module?':

The ability to manage your own learning and learn from a native.
Manage own learning and at my own pace and in my own way and choose what I wanted to talk about.
You can talk about things which aren't in books.
You choose what you learn – no restrictions.
Autonomy and access to native speakers.
Improve my language learning skills in a relaxed atmosphere.

The students from other European Union countries, studying under the Erasmus scheme, consistently report that they find it hard to make English friends when they come to study in the UK; this is particularly difficult for those who only come to study for one twelve-week semester. Tandem learning, therefore, is a real opportunity to get to know English students, practise English and (as is often the case) socialise more closely with them.

Outline of the Tandem Module

The face-to-face tandem module runs over one twelve-week semester. Its format is broadly as follows:

Week 1: Get to know your partner. Prioritise your main learning aims for the semester. Plan your personal learning goals, methods and materials to help you achieve your aims, together with advice from your tutor. Agree time and place for tandem session, discuss effective ways of working with your partner.

Weeks 2–5: Attend (optional) session with tutor for advice on filling in diary. Continue with tandem sessions with partner. Complete tandem diary page after each tandem session (ten pages to be completed over the semester). Use ready-made tandem learning sheets if desired.

Week 6: Together with your tandem partner, attend a counselling session with your tutor, to review your learning and your goals, making changes where necessary.

Weeks 7–10: Continue with tandem sessions and diary completion.

Weeks 11–12: Undertake speaking test (mini tandem session). Hand in diary together with a report of the semester, self- and peer-assessment grades. Speaking test and diary are graded by tutors (each worth 35% of the final grade). Self-assessment is on your development of autonomy (worth 10%) and your progress in language learning (10%). Peer-assessment is on your partner's development in the language (also worth 10%).

The tandem diary[4] offers students a basic structure for them to follow. Initially they are required to prioritise the main areas of learning for themselves (they are asked to rank the following in order of priority for them: range of vocabulary, sentence structures, accuracy, pronunciation/ intonation, listening, cultural knowledge, techniques for language learning and independent study skills). They can also choose their own areas to focus on; one of the most popular areas chosen by students themselves is 'Fluency'. Once the general learning areas have been prioritised, students are then required to translate their 'wish list' into realistic, manageable goals. This is done with the aid of the tutor. For example, a student who has chosen 'range of vocabulary' as one of their priorities will identify specific areas where they would like to develop their vocabulary (such as informal language spoken by students, or vocabulary related to engineering). They will then devise activities together with the tutor which will enable them to achieve their goals by the end of the semester. Such activities, in the case of engineering vocabulary, might include finding a written text on an aspect of engineering from the World Wide Web, reading it before the tandem session and then summarising it to their tandem partner. The tutor also helps students to devise activities which are commensurate with their level of language proficiency, enabling them to progress without setting goals which are too easy or difficult for them to achieve.

The process of turning priorities into manageable learning goals is one which is difficult for many students, particularly those who are not used to evaluating and monitoring their own learning. Once the process of setting goals and the means by which they will be achieved is completed, students arrange with their tandem partners the tandem sessions themselves; these take place at times and places mutually agreed between partners. Each week, students fill in a page in their learner diary, recording their progress. The diary pages contain the following headings to help guide them:

> Vocabulary and new expressions
> Cultural information
> Sentence structures/Accuracy
> Did I fully achieve today's goal or not?
> Next step;
> Observation of self and partner (How can I learn from the way I learn and from the way my partner learns?)

Students are informed that these headings serve as a guide; they can write their diary on separate pages if they prefer, or they can leave out certain sections some weeks if they are not relevant. It is the students' diary entries which have revealed evidence of the intercultural nature of tandem learning.

Evidence from the Tandem Diaries of the Development of Intercultural Communicative Competence (ICC)

One of the aims of the tandem module is 'To enable students to develop proficiency in . . . intercultural awareness' (MLTC Student Guide, 1999–2000).

In fact, the tandem learning module does not directly assess students' intercultural communicative competence, although it is implicit in some areas of assessed work.

For example, if students have chosen the development of cultural knowledge as one of their goals, then they will be assessed on whether they have achieved this or not.

However, regardless of whether students have chosen the development of cultural knowledge as their goal, there is evidence that they are in fact developing their intercultural communicative competence through tandem learning. The fact that most of them do not tend to choose cultural knowledge as one of their main priorities means that one can assume that the evidence which they provide of developing their ICC is not driven by a desire to succeed in the module, but is a genuine product of the tandem relationship.

The evidence of aspects of ICC comes from a number of tandem diaries, seventeen of which were examined in detail; these were all from students undertaking the tandem module during the autumn semester of 1999. Nine were from native English students and eight from native Spanish students.

By its very nature, tandem learning is an intercultural activity; in order to achieve their learning goals, learners must exchange ideas, opinions and negotiate ways of working with their partners. In undertaking all of this, they are communicating directly with speakers of another language/ culture. One area which provides evidence for the development of ICC is that of the choice of topics discussed by students.

The choice of topics discussed was extremely varied, ranging from an exchange of personal information, to debates on homosexual parenting. A rough categorisation has been attempted below, using the work of Robinson (1985: 7). She found that when teachers were asked the question 'What does culture mean to you?' the following categories were most commonly reported:

- products (literature, folklore, art, music, artefacts);
- ideas (beliefs, values, institutions);
- behaviours (customs, habits, dress, foods).

A rough analysis of the topics mentioned by tandem learners in the 'Cultural information' section of their diaries revealed that certain topics were more popular than others. The number of times each topic was mentioned is noted below:

Products:	Ideas:	Behaviours:
Literature – 3	Beliefs – 10	Customs – 14
Folklore – 7	Values – 18	Habits – 15
Art – 4	Institutions – 29	Dress – 5
Music – 0		Foods – 9
Artefacts –0		Leisure – 10

The lack of emphasis upon products is interesting. Some of this may be due to the fact that all of the students had visited Spain, some for holidays, others for a period of study. Other possible reasons for this could be that many of the students were also following courses in Spanish/English literature and cinema, or had access to this kind of information in other places. The relationship with their tandem partner, however, allowed them to exchange views on the way Spanish/English people think, and similarities and differences between institutions (by far the most popular being the education system, but covering also the job market, government and politics).

Topics which were brought up by students which do not appear to fit into the above categories include:

- getting to know your partner (9) (for obvious reasons, this was the most common topic for the first tandem session);
- geography of each other's country (7) (for example, regions, climate, principal cities);
- history (3);
- transport (2);
- language/gestures: (15);
- feelings (2);
- practicalities and conventions (3) (for example, travelling in another country, structuring essays).

It is interesting to note that quite a number of students wrote aspects of language under the section 'Cultural information'. Typical instances include the use of idioms, and phrases related to card playing or drinking, as well as the use of gestures. Possibly at the time of Robinson's study, teachers saw language as an area separate from culture, whereas nowadays the cultural weight of language is far more accepted (see for example, Kramsch, 1993).

The students' contributions under the heading 'Cultural information' were also analysed in the light of Byram's factors of intercultural communication (see Figure 12.1).

The criteria for each of these five *savoirs* were used to evaluate the kind of experience that tandem learning was giving the students. Below are some examples from the students' entries which illustrate how they are developing some of the aspects of ICC.

Attitudes (*savoir être*)

Simply by taking part in tandem learning, the student is fulfilling an aspect of Byram's criteria, covered in *Attitudes*: (*Willingness to seek out or*

	Skills Interpret and relate (*savoir comprendre*)	
Knowledge Of self and other; of interaction; individual and societal (*savoirs*)	**Education** Political education Critical cultural awareness (*savoir s'engager*)	**Attitudes** Relativising self Valuing others (*savoir être*)
	Skills Discover and/or interact (*savoir apprendre/faire*)	

Figure 12.1 Byram's factors of intercultural communication (1997: 34)

take up opportunities to engage with otherness in a relationship of equality, distinct from seeking out the exotic or to profit from others, Byram, 1997: 57). The relationship of equality is defined by the nature of the tandem course and the tandem principles themselves. Byram also states that the Attitudes category involves the speaker being interested in a range of social groups within a society and not only that represented in the dominant culture (ibid.: 58). With such topics discussed as those mentioned above, students are clearly demonstrating interest in a wide range of social groups.

Similarly, the native Spanish tandem students are displaying a readiness for experiencing different stages of interaction and adaptation with another culture (criteria (d) of Byram's *Attitudes*). For example, Jaime[5] commented that he and his partner discussed personal feelings about being in the UK: 'We talked about the changes for me in Sheffield . . . all those little things which you don't realise you miss until they are not there' (Jaime, Week 9).

Knowledge (*savoirs*)

This is the category for which there was the largest amount of evidence in the tandem diaries. This is possibly not surprising; students with largely linguistic goals often choose different aspects of society to discuss with their partner in order to improve their language. They are, of course, improving their cultural knowledge at the same time.

Some examples of evidence which satisfy the Knowledge category are presented here. One pair of students discussed legends: 'We also discovered that the English think that St. George saved England from the dragon, and the Spanish think he saved Spain' (Gail, Week 8). The same student also commented that she and her partner discussed Spain and Britain entering the European Union, but did not give details as to exactly what was discussed (Gail, Week 2). This is evidence of the development of an understanding of historical and contemporary relationships between one's own and one's interlocutor's country (criterion (a) in the *Knowledge* category, ibid.: 59).

One tandem pair decided to study gestures; they used a ready-prepared tandem sheet as a basis for their discussion (Nadia, Week 2). They came to the conclusion that the majority of gestures are similar between Spanish and English cultures, but that kissing is used very differently. This activity clearly contributes to students' knowledge of the types of misunderstanding between interlocutors of different cultural origins (criterion (c) in the *Knowledge* category, ibid.: 59).

Through the comparison of heroes (stimulated by a tandem sheet on legends), one tandem pair discussed how some of Spain's heroic legends are quite recent, for example from the civil war or the war with France: 'David and I discussed how this wasn't true for England and came to the conclusion that most war heroes come from either civil wars or from wars which are fought on their own land. English war heroes are from a time when we had civil wars, so our heroes/legends are principally from hundreds of years ago' (Gail, Week 8). This is evidence of their having considered the national memory of each others' country (see critera (d) and (e) of the *Knowledge* category, ibid.: 59).

Another student discussed with her partner the regional stereotypes in Spain (Alice, Week 7). Another commented on how it is interesting to know the different regional accents 'although trying to identify them would be difficult' (David, Week 6). Still another pair discussed the different countries which make up the United Kingdom (Rocío, Week 2).

Education systems are compared by a number of tandem pairs, some in direct relation to the courses which they are currently studying (Annie, Weeks 7 and 8; Charlotte, Week 9). The topic of religion is also considered by a number of tandem pairs, particularly in terms of its importance at Christmas (Marisa, Week 2) or comparatively with the UK (Caroline, Week 6). (This is evidence for criterion (h) of *Knowledge: The processes and institutions of socialisation in one's own and one's interlocutor's country*, ibid.: 60).

Byram's criterion (f) in the *Knowledge* category covers social distinctions and their principal markers, in one's own country and in one's interlocutors (ibid.: 60). Evidence of this is apparent in the tandem pairs who discussed the roles of women (Caroline, Week 3), homosexuality (Cathy, Week 6), under-age sex (Alice, Week 11), or the British attitudes towards certain professions, such as waiters and teachers (David, Week 3). These kinds of topics appear to be relatively popular with the tandem partnerships.

As revealed in the rough analysis of topics earlier, a large number of institutions and perceptions of them are discussed (fulfilling criterion (j) of *Knowledge: Institutions and perceptions of them, which impinge on daily life within one's own and one's interlocutor's country and which conduct and influence relationships between them*, ibid.: 60). Some examples include the following. One student reported how the police in Spain are cracking down more on drink driving than before, information which she gleaned from her partner. (Polly, Week 4). Another student specifically chose to discuss banking customs, as he felt he needed to understand them better in England (David: Week 4). The same student chose to understand more about the relationship between the House of Commons and the House of Lords in England, at a time when this topic was in the news. (David, Week 9). Another pair chose to compare the Spanish and the British royal families (Annie, Week 10). Public behaviour in terms of meals is discussed (María, Weeks 1 and 5), as are forms of public meeting (Charlotte, Week 7; Gail, Week 7; Alice, Week 1).

Less is reported with regard to taboos, which Byram includes under criterion (k) (*The processes of social interaction in one's interlocutor's country*, ibid.: 60).

Taboos are possibly a risky topic to discuss with one's tandem partner.

Skills of interpreting and relating (*savoir comprendre*)

The aspect of this category most evident in the tandem diaries is the ability to identify ethnocentric perspectives in a document or event and explain their origins (ibid.: 61).

One student reported that the television in England is of higher quality than in Spain, but notes that the news in England is 'self-centred', that there is little information about Europe (María, Week 3). She did not, however, report having attempted to explain the origins of this difference.

Skills of discovery and interaction (_savoir apprendre/faire_)

Many students discussed documents, whether written or recorded, with their tandem partner; some also identified the significant references within and across cultures. (See criterion (a) _Elicit from an interlocutor the concepts and values of documents or events and develop an explanatory system susceptible of application to other phenomena_, and (b) _Identify significant references within and across cultures and elicit their significance and connotations_, ibid.: 61–2.)

One student compared student life in Spain and England with her partner and then came to the conclusion that the reasons for the differences largely come from the fact that Spanish students tend to study near where they live (Cathy, Week 5).

In a discussion about homosexual families, the same student reported in her diary:

'One of my arguments for adoption by homosexual couples was that two mothers or two fathers are better than the 'one parent family' which is so common in Britain nowadays. Carolina disagreed with me on this point – she thinks that the concept of the single parent family is not as widely accepted in Spain as it is here – and that there are few.' (Cathy, Week 6)

Another commented, on discussion with her partner on the topic of tobacco and drink:

'Interesting to debate these – it gave me an insight into Spanish young person's opinions on these topics. Despite our cultural difference we saw eye-to-eye on almost all of the topics. . . . We decided that European young people are much more alike than a few generations ago. For example, the fact that Spain is a Catholic country no longer seems to affect the opinions of the young people.' (Gail, Week 6)

Critical cultural awareness/political education (_savoir s'engager_)

This involves: _An ability to evaluate, critically, and on the basis of explicit criteria, perspectives, practices and products in one's own and other cultures and countries_ (ibid.: 63).

As mentioned previously, although all the _savoirs_ overlap, this is the one category which underlies all the other ones, focusing on comparison and evaluation.

Evidence exists of students' evaluating information which they have gleaned. One example is that given previously of Cathy, who concluded that the differences in studying habits between Spain and England stemmed largely from the fact that Spanish students tend to study near where they live. Another student reported that she and her partner discussed the availability of alcohol, bleach etc. and related this to the attitudes towards safety in each country (Annie, Week 3).

While there does exist significant evidence from the tandem diaries of some aspects of critical cultural awareness, there is little evidence of students' having evaluated on the basis of *explicit* criteria.

Developments

To summarise, it certainly appears that the face-to-face tandem relationship does offer opportunities for developing intercultural communicative competence. The evidence from the tandem diaries does not fit neatly into all the categories, however. Neither does it necessarily fulfil each of the criteria in their entirety. For example, concepts and values were elicited from documents, but students did not apply explanations to other phenomena (see *Skills of discovery and interaction* (a)).

It appears that students are interested in their partners' culture coupled with a desire to know more, but students do not seem to take the further step of a deeper analysis, such as questioning attitudes or drawing conclusions from information. It may be that in order to achieve these, students will require further support from their tutor.

This begs the following questions:

(1) To what degree can a student who partially fulfils criteria be considered interculturally competent? Byram argues that the ideal to be reached will depend upon the context, and that different contexts will require different descriptions of intercultural competence (ibid.: 79–81). The evidence, as described above from student diaries, could therefore inform the future development of a tandem learning syllabus designed for developing intercultural communicative competence.

(2) How much does the layout of the diary dictate what students actually report is happening? As mentioned previously, the sub-heading 'Cultural information' may well give them the impression that they should largely report facts and knowledge. What is interesting from their entries is the emphasis on the *Ideas* and *Behaviours* topics as opposed to the *Products* (see earlier). Scrutiny of diaries along with video evidence of tandem sessions could well provide some answers to this question.

(3) Clearly with tutor input it would be possible to enable students to fulfil criteria more fully. For example, with prompting from the tutor, students could take steps to reflect on how their own country is perceived by others (See *Knowledge* (g)). But to what degree will this tutor interference inhibit students' development of autonomy? Since, together with language learning, this is the main aim of the tandem module, it would appear that an insistence of undertaking certain intercultural tasks would remove some of the emphasis on autonomous learning. It might be fitting, therefore, to consider tandem modules with different aims, or a broader intercultural syllabus which incorporates tandem learning as one of its components.

In order to enable learners to take the necessary steps with regard to analysis and evaluation, one may well wish to consider some of the following possible modifications:

(1) At the start of their tandem learning venture, students can be sensitised to the possibilities of development of their intercultural communicative competence. This could be done by the inclusion on the list of priorities of aspects such as:
   • identification of differences and similarities between my country and that of my partner;
   • identification of the main stereotypes which exist of each of our countries as seen from the other;
   • understanding of possible reasons for the existence of these.

(2) Similar questions to cover other aspects of ICC could well be devised, to make it easier for students to analyse and evaluate.

(3) Tandem learners could be encouraged to analyse more through the simple inclusion of further questions in the diary sheets; for example the inclusion of a heading of 'Cultural aspects: your analysis and/or conclusions' might draw out a slightly deeper reflection on the topics discussed.

(4) Some tandem sessions could be extended to involve two or more tandem pairs in group discussion. This could provide students with situations which take them further than their tandem relationship normally allows. For example, a group of English students and a group of Spanish students could be given different points of view to argue on a topic, and be encouraged to identify at the end of the debate any differences in interaction patterns between the English and the Spanish students.

If cultural aspects of tandem learning are more directly assessed, students may well be more inclined to focus more closely on intercultural aspects. This would of course have the effect of lessening the degree of student autonomy over the tandem process.

Ironically, however, what has been particularly interesting about this study has been the fact that students have not seen the cultural aspects as being assessed (except in the case of one or two who chose cultural aspects as a personal learning goal) and so what they have reported is clearly what they have gleaned regardless of outside requirements. This has offered the unique opportunity to understand further the points at which intervention from the tutor may be necessary in order to enable them to develop their ICC further.

What is certainly clear from the evidence presented above is that the acquisition of intercultural competence is a process. Learning is not necessarily a linear process, but students may well wish to revisit these issues at a later date, possibly outside the tandem relationship (see Byram, 1997: 75) The definition of culture itself as a process is supported by many (see for example, Robinson, 1985, or Street, 1991). Tandem learners, whether consciously or unconsciously, are engaging in this process actively. To cite a Spanish student:

> From my point of view . . . the most important goal for me and which I am really proud of having achieved, is having integrated fully into my group of friends . . . because this means that I am like one of them, and so I can talk about anything, any topic or problem which I like, freely, and it's this way that I have learnt the street language, the language which is used by young people; that is, the language which you can't learn in any book, no matter how good it is.' (Marisa, Tandem Report, end of semester 1999).

Notes

1. Some of the information and data presented in this chapter was also used as the basis of a paper presented at the conference, The New Communicators: Graduates with Languages (University of Nottingham, July 2000).
2. A comprehensive bibliography can be found on the website of the International Email Tandem Network, address: http://www.slf.ruhr-uni-bochum.de/email/infen.html
3. The framework for the face-to-face tandem module was developed by Lesley Walker with input from the Centre's core teaching team.
4. The tandem diary was also developed by Lesley Walker at the University of Sheffield; copies of the diary can be obtained from the Modern Languages Teaching Centre at the university.

5. All names of participants have been changed to ones in keeping with their sex and nationality.

References

Byram, M. (1997) *Teaching and Assessing Intercultural Communicative Competence.* Clevedon: Multilingual Matters.

Kramsch, C. (1993) *Context and Culture in Language Teaching.* Oxford: Oxford University Press.

Robinson, G.N. (1985) *Crosscultural Understanding.* Oxford: Pergamon.

Street, B. (1991) Culture is a verb. In D.L. Graddol, L. Thompson and M. Byram (eds) *Language and Culture.* Clevedon: Multilingual Matters.

Chapter 13

'Why do Danes put Their Elderly in Nursing Homes?' - Working Outside the Classroom with Adult Second Language Learners

JUDITH PARSONS AND PETER JUNGE

This chapter describes work with adult immigrant students of Danish as a second language and the use of an ethnographic method in fieldwork to develop their intercultural competence. The learners are first intrigued by difference in their new environment and their teachers devise ways in which they can explore not only the society around them but also the underlying beliefs and values which explain what their learners had found strange. The learners thus acquire knowledge about their host society and also ways in which to 'discover' the world around them.

Introduction

We teach Danish as a second language for adults at a language centre which is situated in a thinly populated area in the north-west of Denmark. Here we service the needs of nine municipalities spread over a large geographical area. At any one time there are about 250 students from 40 to 45 different countries enrolled at the centre which caters for the needs of learners with very different learning capabilities – from people who can neither read nor write in their mother tongue or are unfamiliar with the Latin alphabet to university graduates who are fluent in several languages.

There are 275 municipalities and 53 language centres (*Sprogcenter*) in Denmark, each language centre serving one or more municipalities. All learners are referred to the centres by their local municipality, which also pays tuition fees, making it cost-free for learners. At our language centre learners are offered eighteen lessons of 45 minutes duration per week. It is also possible for learners to take part in extra activities such as ICT, sport, handicrafts, study workshops, basic maths, etc. for up to twelve lessons (three lessons per subject).

The law governing second language tuition in Denmark (Law no. 487 of 1 July 1998) states in section 1 that the aim for tuition of Danish as a second language is that learners 'on the basis of their linguistic and cultural premises' acquire knowledge of the Danish language while developing their ability to understand and use it. Tuition should 'encourage active use of Danish and develop awareness of Danish culture' so that the learners can go on to study and/or work and in doing so 'play an active role in Danish society'.

In Denmark there is a long tradition of allowing teachers free choice of methodology and pedagogy within the framework of the law governing all forms of tuition. Furthermore there is no fixed curriculum for Danish as a second language for adults, so teachers are not bound in any way in relation to the choice of subject matter and materials.

In the guidelines for teachers (Handbook no. 27, 1999, The Ministry of Education) it is further stated that 'the cultural complexity in Danish society should be visible in tuition' and learners should, therefore, be introduced to 'a wide variety of cultural forms and dialects and meet a variety of "voices" – not just geographically varied but also from different age and cultural groups. 'Teachers are encouraged to make use of learners' experiences' – both from their own culture and Denmark to develop further their intercultural communicative competence.

The Ethnographic Approach in Relation to Second Language Tuition and Intercultural Communicative Competence

Developing intercultural communicative competence is a process which requires an awareness of how we perceive others and how they perceive us. Our perception of others in turn influences our understanding of them and vice versa. Our perception of others, however, is formed by our cultural background and its influence on what we consider to be natural and normal. Therefore it will never be enough just to develop our abilities to compare and analyse the culturally determined behaviour of others – we also need to study, become aware of and understand our own.

The learners in our classes come from many different parts of the world, many different cultures and many different walks of life. Their cultural diversity – both *inter*cultural and *intra*cultural – is an asset which should be exploited to the full when working with cultural awareness and intercultural communicative competence, both elements in becoming a successful intercultural speaker (Byram, 1997). A very usable method for acquiring the skills necessary to develop intercultural communicative competence and therefore become a successful intercultural speaker is the ethnographic approach.

The ethnographic approach is a method which bridges the gap between the classroom and the world outside while supporting acquisition and awareness of both language and culture. The ethnographic approach has its roots in classic ethnography and its research methods, which include:

- a preparation phase, building a basic knowledge of the subject;
- fieldwork with observation and the collection of data;
- a presentation phase with time for reflection, collation of data, presentation and setting the newly acquired knowledge in perspective.

The aim of field studies is to describe, interpret and explain both the specific and the universal in human life (social and cultural, past and present, conscious and unconscious), or to put it another way, to interpret what we *think* we have seen.

The use of the ethnographic approach in the tuition of Danish as a second language provides learners with the possibility not only of expanding their knowledge of the Danish language, but also of working with cultural behaviour, perceptions and beliefs – their own as well as others'. As opposed to a more traditional tuition which is centred on language skills, the ethnographic approach allows learners to improve their language skills while broadening their knowledge and understanding of their own and others' culturally influenced behaviour, thus giving them the opportunity to develop their intercultural communicative competence.

Using the ethnographic approach in second language tuition gives almost unlimited possibilities for learning about language and culture in authentic situations – after all the learners are surrounded by the target culture. Fieldwork gives learners the chance to communicate in Danish and practise their language skills while increasing their knowledge of selected areas of Danish culture and language. This in turn gives them the chance to reflect on their newly acquired knowledge, to relate it to their own culture and to act as a mediator between the two cultures.

Furthermore the ethnographic approach gives both learners and teachers the chance to explore new roles in the classroom. Learners take on more responsibility with regard to their learning processes, while the teacher exchanges the traditional role of someone who imparts knowledge for the role of consultant and counsellor.

The labour market in Denmark – in which our learners hopefully will participate – has undergone considerable change in recent years. From a traditional agricultural and industrial nation Denmark has rapidly evolved into a country with a strong emphasis on service industries. These changes are reflected in the skills the labour market requires of its workforce. Instead of working individually in a well-defined area with familiar and routine tasks and little responsibility, employees are now expected to make use of their 'soft' qualifications and be able to collaborate with others, to be flexible and quality-conscious, show initiative, take responsibility, run risks, and work independently. In an increasing number of jobs, having a working knowledge of computers is also a must.

The ethnographic approach with its emphasis on fieldwork strengthens learners' soft qualifications. When researching their chosen areas they work independently yet in collaboration with others, take the initiative when arranging interviews etc., have to be flexible when appointments are changed at the last moment and quality-conscious when preparing and presenting their results. During the whole process they will be 'forced' into new situations, which again involves taking risks.

Finally the whole of the Danish democratic system, educational system and Danish society generally are built on such values as reciprocal respect, joint influence, responsibility and co-determination – all of which can be supported and developed in tuition that uses the ethnographic approach.

Thus, in summary, the main aim of tuition of Danish as a second language is that learners – as well as becoming competent users of the Danish language – become a part of the labour market and play an active role in Danish society. While being well suited in developing intercultural communicative competence, the ethnographic approach can also help develop the skills necessary for a successful adjustment to a new society.

The Project: Life as a Senior Citizen in Denmark

The classes

Two classes on different language levels worked together on the project. There were 21 adults, 8 women and 13 men, between the ages of 20 and 55. They came from Afghanistan, Iraq, Somalia, Lebanon, Sri Lanka, Thailand, Romania and Turkey.

The first class (class A) consisted of learners with limited schooling (approximately three years) in their own countries. They have lived in

Denmark for around ten years, which means they have a wide experience of Danish society and have quite a wide vocabulary. While none of them is totally illiterate (neither in their mother tongue nor Danish), all of them have difficulty reading and writing Danish and make slow, if any, progress. They have been enrolled at the language centre for varying lengths of time over different periods.

The second class (class B) consisted of learners with five–eight years' basic schooling in their own countries. Some of them had gone on to study at technical colleges or their equivalent. They have been living in Denmark for six months to a year. They have a limited Danish vocabulary but read and write at a standard consistent with their expected language level (upper elementary). They have a normal progression, which means that they are expected after two years' tuition to be proficient enough at Danish to be able to sit an elementary examination, qualifying them for unskilled or semi-skilled jobs.

The idea and aims of the project

The idea for the project originated after a classroom discussion. Each week a student from class B held a prepared 'lecture' on a subject he/she chose for his/her classmates. One of the students had related the story of his grandmother who always insisted on waiting up for him, when he was a young man enjoying the night life each weekend in the large city where he lived.

Basically it was the old story of parents/grandparents worrying about the dangers of oncoming adulthood for their offspring, but it led to a general discussion about our relation to our parents and to the elderly in general. This led – not for the first time – to wonder and incomprehension about the apparent lack of interest the Danes have for their elderly relatives, especially their ageing parents. This in turn led to a discussion about how it would be for the class to grow old in Denmark, far away from their culture and homeland. We decided to try and find out how it would be and also to see if the class's somewhat prejudiced views on how Danes treat their elderly were appropriate.

We – the teachers – had been waiting for the opportunity to work together and this was it. While it has begun to be accepted that the ethnographic approach can be used with success in classes of well-educated learners who are used to studying and taking responsibility for their own learning and have reached an intermediate level or higher, many are still sceptical about its worth at lower levels. We wanted to put it to the test.

In relation to our two classes our aims for the project were multiple:

- it was our intention that while the classes gained more knowledge of how life is for a senior citizen in Denmark and expanded their vocabulary, they had the chance to experience Danes and Danish culture in authentic situations;
- we wanted the classes to have the opportunity to compare and reflect on Danish culture and compare it to their own and to describe/explain their own cultures for others (in the class as well as for Danes);
- we hoped that by meeting and talking to different senior citizens the students' preconceived and judgemental views on the elderly and how they are (mis)treated in Denmark would be modified;
- finally we hoped that the project would help the classes to begin to consider how they wanted their life to be when they too become elderly.

At a different level it was also our intention to exploit the different resources in the two classes:

- to incorporate many cultures and perceptions of own and others' cultures, and also differing perceptions within national cultures;
- to build a bridge between the language levels of the two classes;
- to make use of different areas of competence in Danish in the two classes;
- to encourage an equal sense of belonging and participation (one of the classes had tuition in a separate building from the main school and there was a tendency for them to consider themselves as being 'special' – set apart from the main stream);
- to move tuition out of the classroom and into the 'real world'.

We planned the project to last six weeks, using between four and six of our eighteen weekly lessons – a total of about 30 lessons. It would include a preparatory phase building basic joint knowledge, fieldwork with visits, guest visits, interviews and research carried out by the classes and a phase to correlate and present findings before a final evaluation of the whole project.

Phase 1: Building a basic joint knowledge

The first lessons were spent comparing what life was like as a senior citizen in the learners' homelands, finding out how much they actually knew about the elderly in Denmark, establishing what they hoped/

expected to find out, and building a basic knowledge of the situation for senior citizens in Denmark.

In these lessons the classes were divided into national groups and were encouraged to use their mother tongue in their discussions while their results and presentations were, of course, to be made in Danish. We made use of the following questionnaire to compare the different cultures, the results of which were collated after a class presentation/discussion.

Senior citizens in your homeland

Write your answers on a separate piece of paper

(1) Who is considered to be a senior citizen?
(2) When do you become a senior citizen?
(3) Does being a senior citizen have high or low status/prestige?
(4) How/where does a senior citizen live?
(5) How does a senior citizen support himself/herself?
(6) How does a senior citizen pass the time?
(7) Who helps/supports senior citizens?
(8) What happens if a senior citizen becomes ill?
(9) What happens when a senior citizen dies?

The discussion showed a variety of perceptions about the concept of life as a senior citizen, even within the national groups. For example, answers to the question 'Who helps/supports senior citizens?' included the family, the local community and the state. In every culture senior citizens were considered authorities because of their long life experience and were revered and treated with the utmost respect.

The answers to the questions were typed on computers (to ensure the same font and layout) by the learners themselves and pinned on a map of the world next to the appropriate country.

The same questionnaire was used for the learners' expectations of the situation in Denmark, the results of which were noted on an overhead projector transparency for later comparison and evaluation. Here we were surprised – considering the learners' negative opinions and perceptions of the situation for senior citizens in Denmark – that they also expected them to be revered and treated with respect in Denmark. This was somewhat of a contradiction but we attributed it to their cultural backgrounds as they all came from societies that revere senior citizens and their life experience.

During this phase we also made use of videos, pictures, short texts, newspaper articles and television programmes showing different facets of life as a senior citizen, mainly in Denmark but also including examples from other cultures. The materials included subject matter such as an interview with a 99-year-old Dane, who was a winter bather and played tennis on a regular basis; a newspaper article about the (supposedly) oldest man in the world from India and his family and life; a magazine article about a newly wed couple in America – the bride was 101 and her groom a mere 83; a satirical revue song about the 'pleasures' of life as a senior citizen 'forgotten' by their families; and slides with an accompanying tape of an elderly couple who had celebrated their diamond wedding anniversary and talked about their everyday life.

We used the slides and accompanying tape not only to broaden the learners' knowledge but also to practise their listening comprehension and discussion skills. We began by showing the slides in no particular order and without playing the tape. Each slide was discussed at length to ensure a shared vocabulary. The two classes were then divided into groups of three or four, each with a copy of the tape, a set of copies of the slides and a tape recorder. Their assignment was to listen to the tape, find the appropriate picture and set them in order.

Furthermore we scanned and made overhead transparencies of several art paintings and used these to discuss how European artists have portrayed the elderly through the ages – from the Renaissance to today. The two classes worked separately here: class B worked with a more classic form for analysis before relating the portraits to their time historically, while class A merely described the content of the paintings.

We often use artists' portrayals (especially paintings, but also other media) of different situations in our lessons. We do this partly to add an artistic/historical dimension as art has always played an important role in 'Culture' with a capital 'C', partly because paintings tell such good stories, and partly to train our students in how to decode the 'language' used in European art.

To round off the first phase and armed with our knowledge we made our first visit to a local residential home for the elderly, run by the local council (very few homes for the elderly are privately run in Denmark). The home consisted of a main building with 'bed-sits' for the residents, communal television-rooms, workshops, kitchen, etc., and small one-bedroom semi-detached sheltered houses. The houses could be privately owned or rented from the local council. The residents of these were welcome to use all the facilities at the home and in each of the sheltered homes alarms were installed so the residents could call for help in emergencies.

Everyone had their own particular prejudice about these homes, including: the residents had no privacy or financial independence; they were installed there by their children and forgotten; all senior citizens were forced out of their own homes and into homes for the elderly by the local councils.

The two classes prepared questions which were shared out so everyone had responsibility for at least one question. We were met by the warden of the home, who offered us tea, coffee and cake while she told us about the running of it and answered our questions. During this 'question-time' new questions emerged and with goodwill and joint help they were formulated, asked and answered. The warden then showed us around. There was enough time for the learners to stop and visit and/or chat with several of the residents. Back in class we wrote a thank-you letter, evaluated the visit and discussed what we had learned and compared it with what we had expected.

Although the learners did see people sitting alone apparently not engaged in any sort of activity or just sitting and staring, they had to admit that generally everything was not quite as black as they'd expected it to be. In one instance we talked to one woman who had waited two years for a place at the home – she had applied because she was afraid to live alone. Another woman was picked up each Friday by different members of her family to spend the weekend with them. A widower had moved in after the death of his wife – he enjoyed life at the home, playing cards, the good food (which he did not have to prepare himself) and the company of others. One wheelchair-user lived in one of the sheltered houses, thereby retaining his sense of independence while secure in the knowledge that help was at hand if he needed it.

Even though the classes agreed that the facilities were excellent and the residents satisfied with their new lives, they still could not understand why the residents preferred to live there than with their families.

Phase 2: Fieldwork

The next stage was to find out which other areas they were interested in, form groups and decide how to proceed. This was done as a class discussion. Three different groups were finally formed: one interested in the different forms of help available, one interested in folk high schools for seniors[1] and alternative ways for senior citizens to spend their time in their 'third age', and one interested in alternative housing forms to the residential and sheltered homes or family. One more group was discussed – healthcare – but only two were interested and they decided that they would prefer to work in groups with more people.

Normally with learners with a higher proficiency level of Danish, we would have encouraged the formation of more groups with fewer members – three or four at the most. Here we decided that the pooling of resources would compensate for the drawbacks with such large groups. The groups did indeed work well together, taking their roles seriously and sharing responsibility. (The size of the groups also made them less vulnerable if anyone was absent.)

Taking into account the learners' proficiency in Danish, we helped to arrange the visits, transportation and interviews once the groups had decided what they wanted to see and whom they wanted to interview. From there on each group took full responsibility for carrying out the visits and interviews.

The first group visited the local hospital and talked to the woman responsible for the various aids for the disabled that could be borrowed – they were interested in finding out what possibilities for help there are for people who are old and/or disabled, what kind of aids there are, who is entitled to help, what it costs, etc.

The second group visited a nearby folk high school for seniors where they interviewed a teacher and some of the people on a course there. They

Figure 13.1   Students doing fieldwork.

were interested in finding out why the participants were there, how much it cost, why they returned time and time again, whether the participants preferred to be at the high school rather than with their families, etc. The third group visited a commune for people over 50 without children living at home, which was under construction. They were interested in finding out why the inhabitants chose this form for housing, why they did not prefer to live with their families, why they moved from their homes which they had lived in for many years, and so on.

Each visit was carefully planned by the groups and extra information was gathered where necessary (the local library, internet, etc.). Here it was often necessary for us to help, as many of the texts the groups found were too difficult for them to read. Possible questions were discussed and formulated before being distributed amongst the group. The groups took small tape recorders with them as well as a digital camera and/or a video camera. The tape recorders were especially helpful as they allowed members of the group to concentrate on their questions and any following discussion. Back at school there was plenty of time to hear and re-hear the tapes. The groups also had a small gift with them – chocolates, flowers, etc. – on each visit and sent a thank-you note with a photo afterwards.

Phase 3: Analysis and presentation

Back in the classroom the groups had time to analyse their results and decide how they would present them to the rest of the class. The three groups decided to make wall-charts with the pictures they had taken and simple explanatory texts, and to give an account of their visits for the others, giving them the opportunity to ask questions. The wall-charts were hung up as an 'exhibition'. Each group was allowed one lesson to present their results (and show their videos) and to answer questions, and one lesson was also set aside to present the results of the class for another class.

Members of group 1, who had worked with the various forms of aid for the disabled, were very impressed after their visit to the local hospital – both by the variety of aids available and that they could be borrowed indefinitely and without charge when you were referred by your physician and the local council. Group 2 which visited the senior high school, had taken part in morning assembly (including a little gymnastics – the morning warm-up) and talked to a group of participants. Apart from learning about the senior citizens' choices of how to spend their time, group 2 could not resist the urge to ask whether they lived with their families when at home. While a number of the senior citizens were not interested in living with their families – because of their children's busy careers, they did not want to give up their independence, they did not want to be a burden – others expressed the view that they did in fact feel that the younger generation had too little time for them. Group 2 had the impression that the decision to live alone in most cases had been taken by the senior citizens themselves and not forced on them by anybody. Group 3, which had visited the commune, found the idea appealing. People who for some reason could not or did not want to live with their families still had the opportunity to be part of an extended 'family' with people of a like mind. Although all the group members agreed that the whole project was well-planned and exclusive, they also found the prices to be exorbitant.

We rounded off the project by inviting two guests. The first guest was a senior citizen who had stopped working but was still actively involved in the local community as chair of a committee advising the council on questions concerning the elderly in the area as well as still being an active sportsman and working as a volunteer at his former place of work. The other guest was a civil servant from the local town hall who talked about rights, privileges and duties as a senior citizen.

Evaluation

We made external and internal evaluations. As an external evaluation the classes invited a third class from the school for a mini-lecture and a discussion on senior citizens in Denmark – rights, privileges and duties as a member of society – using all the different materials they had produced: photos, wall-charts, videos, etc.

Internally we held a written and an oral evaluation. In class B, there was a written evaluation with questions to be answered individually evaluating both the process and the product. In class A, there was a discussion about the working process, new and interesting things learned, and whether or not they would like to work that way again (and why/why not).

As the final joint evaluation the two classes again looked at the original overhead transparency with the questions and assumptions about life as a senior citizen in Denmark from one of the first lessons. Had they found answers to all their questions? Had their assumptions been confirmed or not? Had they learned anything new about senior citizens?

They all agreed that it had been a new experience working this way and they liked working closely with another class as long as it was not in every Danish lesson and not for too long a period. Especially the visits and interviews with Danes had shown them that they knew more Danish than they thought and that they could easily communicate with Danes in Danish. Working so intensely with Danish culture for a relatively long period and comparing it to their own had made them more aware of their own culture and that of their classmates.

We as teachers also evaluated the project as a success with a lot of intercultural communication, spoken Danish and fact-finding about Danish society. We found that even students with less developed Danish linguistic capacities were very active and motivated to find answers and in their own way were able to contribute to the final product.

Future Perspectives

Using the ethnographic approach in teaching Danish as a second language is pedagogically challenging both for the students and the teachers. We have been told by many that to be able to use this method, making appointments and interviewing Danes, and profiting from it, demands a certain level of Danish comprehension and is too difficult for a beginners class.

To eliminate that problem two classes at different levels and with different Danish competencies worked together and it turned out to be very successful teamwork. We saw only minor problems of a more personal character. We observed that the groups worked very hard and that everybody took part in the process, showing initiative and team spirit and often they did not stop for breaks. We would not normally recommend that groups for fieldwork are so large as there is a tendency for them to split into smaller groups. We realise that it is difficult to evaluate the students' progression when using this method, but our impression – and the students' as well – is that it is a good method to use when you want to improve cultural understanding and intercultural communicative competence, and language skills generally. Of course Rome was not built in one day and no one was suddenly 'converted' and gave up their original beliefs that the elderly should be with their families, but the classes have now a more varied picture of what the situation is in Denmark and have talked to several elderly people who were not interested in living with their offspring and valued their independence. With regard to their own wishes for life as a senior citizen, we hope that when they come to make decisions about their own future, they will now be able to consider all the available choices, including other possibilities than moving in with their children.

The students found working with the ethnographic approach very demanding and time-consuming but a good complement to more traditional tuition. For teachers using the approach for the first time it demands a lot of preparation and adjusting to a new role as consultant not teacher, but these are just a question of time and getting used to a new way of planning and working.

We – the teachers – have also used the method with classes elsewhere in Denmark. Two classes in language centres in different places agreed on a common subject to investigate, carried out their investigations separately and then during the process exchanged findings to see if and how things differed. At the end of the project the two classes visited each other to present their results for one another, and to see for themselves the differences and new locations in Denmark. These types of projects are extremely well-suited to working with the ethnographic approach where investigating conditions in one local community and comparing them with another brings an added dimension to developing an understanding of the diversity of a culture. Working with other schools demands detailed planning and firm commitment from *both* parts. It is frustrating and demoralising for classes when their letters are not answered or they get a very delayed response.

As teachers of Danish as a second language, we are limited with regard to possibilities for exchange projects/visits abroad, which are so often used in foreign language tuition. We are, however, in the first phase of a Scandinavian co-operation between teachers using the ethnographic method. The languages in Denmark, Sweden and Norway are very similar and we plan at a later stage to start co-operation between classes in the different countries.

Note

1. Senior folk high schools (seniorhøjskoler) are private institutions where people can live and take courses (usually 2–8 weeks) in history, religion, handicrafts etc. The schools are open for everyone – no special qualifications are needed.

Reference

Byram, M. (1997) *Teaching and Assessing Intercultural Communicative Competence.* Clevedon: Multilingual Matters

Part 3

Developing Resources

Chapter 14
Cultural Understanding in Danish Schools

LEON AKTOR AND KAREN RISAGER

Changes in the curriculum in Denmark introduced the opportunity to develop an intercultural dimension. There was, however, also a need for suitable materials. This chapter describes the nature of the changes and the ways in which materials were developed for both teaching and assessment purposes. It presents recently published teaching materials for cultural understanding in English, German and French in Denmark, materials which are intended for cross-disciplinary teaching and project work.

The Danish *Folkeskole*

The Danish *folkeskole* covers those stages of schooling which in the English and many other systems are known as primary and lower secondary education. The *folkeskole* is one institution which contains nine forms or grades plus a one-year kindergarten class and a tenth year which is voluntary. The pupils start in grade 1 when they are 6–7 years old, and when they leave the ninth or tenth grade they choose among a wide range of forms of education for young people which last 1–3 years and are equivalent to upper secondary education.

The 1995 education act got rid of the remains of any setting/streaming by ability and pupils now remain together in the same class group for all nine years. On the other hand, a requirement for differentiation in teaching was introduced, i.e. teaching which takes account of each individual's existing, skills and knowledge, and their particular learning style. Simultaneously a requirement that all pupils should have experience of project work was introduced, if possible in the form of co-operation between two or more subjects. All pupils are expected to carry out a project task in the ninth and tenth grades, on which they are individually assessed.

Foreign Languages in the *Folkeskole*

The 1995 education act introduced a number of important changes with respect to foreign languages:

- beginning foreign language learning earlier;
- a strengthening of French to the detriment of German;
- the introduction of a requirement for awareness of language and language learning;
- the introduction of a requirement that they should also address the issue of languages as international languages of communication;
- the introduction of connection with the cultural and societal aspect of languages as subjects, also with respect to assessment.

English is now obligatory from grade 4, a second language, often German, has to be offered from grade 7, whilst French can be offered as an alternative to German in grade 7. A pupil can thus choose not to take a second foreign language but this happens very rarely. Schools also have the option of offering German or French as a third foreign language from grade 8. In practice it is usually French. Furthermore, Spanish and Latin can be offered as non-certificated electives, but this does not happen very much. Typically a Danish pupil leaves the *folkeskole* with two foreign languages, i.e. English and most often German.

The teaching of cultural understanding has acquired a higher priority in all languages and is in principle on the same level as language teaching *per se*. The curricular descriptions for English, German and French in the *folkeskole* are in large part identical but English is different from the other two particularly with respect to examination demands (see below). The overall aims for the three languages are exactly the same and here for example are the aims for English:

The purpose of English teaching is that pupils should acquire knowledge and skills such that they can understand spoken and written English and can express themselves orally and in written form. The teaching shall simultaneously develop pupils' awareness of the English language, of the use of English and of language acquisition.

Para 2. The teaching shall create a framework for experience, insight and co-operation and shall strengthen pupils' active participation. In this way the teaching shall contribute to maintaining pupils' interest in language and culture as part of their further development.

Para 3. The teaching shall give pupils insight into cultural and social conditions in English-speaking countries and thus strengthen their international understanding and their understanding of their own culture.

(*Faghaefte 2, Engelsk*, 1995: 9)

Language learning is thus not given priority over cultural understanding (except insofar as cultural understanding is presented last). In practice, however, it is not the case that these two aims – the linguistic and the cultural – are given equal priority. Both teachers and pupils have a clear expectation that language learning is the first priority. It is that which takes up the time in lessons, and when pupils and teachers think about language teaching, it is far from being the work in cultural understanding which comes to mind first.

The main requirements in respect of knowledge and skills in all the languages include in part the expectation that there shall be teaching in cultural understanding, and in part what basic content the teaching shall cover. In this respect the languages are different; the requirements for French are for example as follows:

- important aspects of cultural and social conditions in those countries where the language is spoken, with the main emphasis on France;
- various written and spoken texts and other art forms which can give pupils experience of French-speaking cultures;
- using the French language to find out about the environment and thereby more generally develop their understanding of other cultures;
- the existence of French language and culture in the world;
- French in a cross-curricular context, e.g. thematic and project work;
- similarities and differences between other cultures and one's own.

(*Faghaefte 18, Fransk*, 1995: 11)

In English and German, there is more specific reference to: living conditions, daily life, values and norms in English- or German-speaking countries respectively.

Requirements for the Assessment of Insight into Cultural and Social Conditions

Before the 1995 act, the specifications for examinations did not contain any requirement that in the final examinations in the ninth and tenth grades pupils should demonstrate their knowledge and understanding of significant aspects of the target language countries' cultural and social conditions. It was the language, not cultural understanding, which was examined. There were therefore very few teachers who seriously felt obliged to introduce systematically cultural understanding as an integral part of language teaching and no inclusion of it as a part of the requirements in final examinations.

However, as a development of the increased requirements in the teaching of foreign languages, the politicians also included new, more precise and more demanding examination requirements. It is now the case for English that cultural understanding must be included as a part of the final examinations at the end of the ninth class and of the 'extended' examination after the tenth grade. In the case of French and German, this only applies in the 'extended' examination after the tenth grade. The 'ordinary' examination after the ninth or tenth grade is an oral examination, whereas the 'extended' examination after the tenth grade is both oral and written. The requirement that pupils shall also demonstrate their knowledge of cultural and social conditions in the countries where the target language is spoken applies to the oral examinations. In the written examinations, pupils are expected to use their knowledge where it is relevant. In addition there is the requirement in the oral examinations that everything should take place in the target language. Pupils are therefore obliged to show their cultural understanding in French, English and German.

A requirement of pupils is also a requirement of teachers. In a decentralised system such as Denmark, the examination specifications represent an effective mechanism for regulating the behaviour of teachers since in effect they too are being examined along with their pupils. In fact changed specifications thus quickly have an effect on what teachers do in their lessons. Now they are obliged to integrate systematically cultural understanding into their teaching, and in the final analysis this has to be documented by their pupils.

Need for Materials to Support Teachers

The heightened requirements for teaching cultural understanding have shaken many foreign language teachers. Even though conscientious teachers have probably always been aware that cultural understanding was a weak point, it was always possible to live with it – like the last little corner in the guest room which never gets the last lick of paint. However, the changed requirements revealed very quickly that there was a major need among teachers to learn about cultural understanding themselves and how to teach it. There also arose in parallel with this a need for material which combined language and culture teaching. Soon after the implementation of the new requirement, there began to appear materials where the aim of the contents was cultural understanding. Suddenly the contents had independent value, at the same time as the link with language teaching was maintained.

As indicated earlier, one of the new elements was that pupils should have experience of project work in the ninth and tenth grades, and so that they shall be ready for this, the ways of working in projects need to be introduced in the younger grades. Teachers are asked to form teams across two or more subjects and to jointly plan their topics, their time-scales, etc. After that, individual classes, together with their teacher(s), decide for themselves how they will organise the process, identify interesting problems, divide into groups, and determine what the final results should look like. The project must be 'problem-oriented', i.e. it must take as its starting point something which awakens wonder, curiosity, frustration, something which needs to be worked on, and which can eventually be formulated as a question, e.g. why do so many animal species die out and what can we do to save threatened species?

There have been experiments for a long time with project work in Danish schools, and English has sometimes taken part, but it was rather rare that French and German participated. With the higher priority given to cultural understanding, this situation will perhaps change and it is in any case the hope in all languages to show they have something to offer in cross-curricular work.

Cross-Curricular Material for All Languages

Even if all three languages have their own approaches to cultural understanding, it is nonetheless interesting to find common problems, e.g. methodology questions which apply across all the languages. Ten years ago it was very rarely that there were conferences including all the languages to discuss common problems. Now it happens often. It was thus not by chance that a publishing house took the initiative to produce cross-curricular material about cultural understanding in language teaching (Risager & Aktor, 1999).

This became a major project in which thirteen people from English, French and German departments were involved in the development work (in addition to the publisher's editor). Five of them, including the editors, wrote introductory articles about various methodological issues, and the other eight decided on themes, planned and described the teaching processes, and piloted them in their own schools. The project started with a meeting about the question of cultural understanding in language teaching and there was brainstorming about possible themes. Then the teachers began their development work in the separate subjects, whilst the authors of the articles wrote. There were meetings between the different groups and the editors throughout the process, and the result was a product which can be used to support work in cultural under-standing in language teaching and also the cross-curricular co-operation with other subjects, including in project work. Furthermore, the materials make visible the different languages' mainly tacit traditions with respect to choice of themes and materials, which is interesting in itself. The publication is in two parts: a theoretical part of 44 pages and a practical part of 111 pages.

The Theoretical Part

The idea behind the theoretical part is to circumscribe and define the concept of cultural understanding in foreign language teaching, and there are four articles which do this. Karen Risager describes in her article the current development towards a new methodology for the integration of cultural and social conditions into language teaching. She gives particular emphasis to the fact that teaching should not give a stereotyped view of target countries. It needs to be based on a broad concept of culture which includes both social conditions and the meanings that different social groups give to their lives and their environment. The teaching should reflect the cultural diversity – regional, social and ethnic – and it can also bring in countries other than the target language countries in connection with the language as an international language, e.g. in connection with international school networks which use the target language. She empha-sises that intercultural competence is not just a question of knowledge, but also of attitudes and cultural behaviour, and that this competence can be particularly beneficial if one can include class visits etc. in the teaching.

Leon Aktor attempts in his article to identify the basic elements of cultural understanding: the work on national stereotypes about the target countries and Denmark (perhaps the country of origin of bilingual pupils), and the work with information about target countries. The article argues that school has a duty to teach pupils to have a critical and rational attitude to cultural understanding. (It also discusses the use of Danish (mother tongue for most pupils) in cultural understanding to ensure a reasonable level of cultural understanding – although the use of Danish is not as necessary in English lessons as in French and German. Aase Rask discusses in her article the interaction between prejudice and curiosity, with the Danish view of Germany as an example, and finally, Kirsten M. Anttila and Mogens Eriksen present the opportunities for further international understanding through the use of information and communication technology in the classroom.

The aims of the subjects include the idea that pupils should acquire knowledge of the distribution of languages in the world and their use as international languages. In connection with this there is finally an article by Karen Risager which gives some statistics and presents some maps showing the geographical spread of English, German and French as mother tongues, official languages and important foreign languages. The article also explains how difficult it is to establish such information.

The theoretical part can be bought separately since it may be of interest for teachers in training and teachers in other parts of the education system.

The Practical Part

The idea with the practical part is to present a model of how a teaching scheme in cultural understanding can be described and prepared, and also to present a few concrete examples which have been tried out in practice. Teachers of English, French and German have prepared a number of 'exemplary' teaching schemes for each language. The themes for these schemes vary but the description of them is common to all. The outline is as follows:

- rationale and aims;
- grade level;
- number of lessons;
- countries;
- aspects of cultural understanding – knowledge, attitudes, skills;
- linguistic skills;
- cross-curricular co-operation;
- practical processes for both pupils and teachers;
- assessment.

For each scheme of work there is a number of pupil pages (for photo-copying) and a list of materials, which includes a series of addresses of organisations and options on the internet.

The fact that the schemes of work are examplary means that they all include methodological indicators of what such work should involve, or at least what the teacher should think about before the work begins. This does not mean that the outline cannot be further developed but it would be difficult to reduce it. On the other hand, the contents, including the concrete examples, are intended as inspiration. One can choose to use a scheme as it is described or to embroider it to make it suit the pupils one has and the situation they are in. Similarly, it is the intention that a scheme from one language can be carried over to the others, even though the teacher will of course need to translate and adapt the pupils' worksheets.

Some of the schemes are planned as cross-curricular opportunities where languages can co-operate with one or more other subjects: religious education, social studies, home economics, drama, music, metalwork, or another language. Most of the schemes are designed as projects, and require pupils to be independent and work together, and they often end in a concrete product. There are together seven schemes, three in English, two in French and two in German.

Themes for English

The themes in English are: youth conference; Great Britain and the former British colonies; life rituals.

'Youth conference' is a very international, creative and practical topic which is best organised as a project with participation from several subjects. The idea is that pupils (in the ninth grade for perhaps four weeks) imagine that they are going to organise an international youth conference on a topic such as religion or music with participants from English-speaking countries throughout the world. The pupils prepare the programme, accommodation, food, parties, invitations and so on, and during the 'conference' they give papers, hold discussion groups, give lectures, have contact with the 'the press', make the food, play music etc. It is important that pupils understand the implications of the fact that the many English-speaking countries in the world are not monolingually English (e.g. India). How much contact does one have with 'Indian' culture via English? This scheme is a pattern for a large-scale project with many sub-projects and with many kinds of activities.

'Great Britain and the former British colonies' is a more historical topic which requires some reading and a wider perspective. The work consists of pupils in small groups choosing a country and describing it to the others. There are also suggestions for various discussion topics, for example on the concept of democracy. This scheme can be done as a project, but otherwise it can be a more traditional reading and reporting approach.

'Life's rituals' provides for a more personal and creative approach (in seventh–eighth grade perhaps in co-operation with religious education).

It focuses on how there are various rituals from birth to death in various religious and cultural contexts, with particular attention paid to entry (baptism and similar things), transfer (confirmation etc.), adult life (wedding etc.) and exit (burial). Here too pupils break into small groups and choose a country and a religion they want to look at. The presentation in front of the whole class can be in dramatised form, with make-up, music, gifts, etc.

Themes for French

The themes in French are: school in France; immigrants from North Africa.

'School in France' has a societal orientation and provides opportunity for comparisons between Danish and French school systems, and daily life at school. The topic can be adapted to different levels from seventh to tenth grade. There are many pupil worksheets with information about school canteens, lessons, free time, regulations and so on. It is particularly suitable for pair work discussions, role plays, etc.

'Immigrants from North Africa' (ninth and tenth grades) is a topic which involves a lot of social and political elements which can be worked on as a project. It deals with an immigrant group which is not much represented in Denmark and thus seems a little exotic to the (native) Danish pupils. They can collect information on many levels: demographic, political (le Front National) social and cultural (e.g. music, religion, food habits). There is, as with the other topics, plenty of information about relevant materials, including material from geography. The teaching scheme includes discussions about cultural differences, racism, equality and tolerance, differences between the position of immigrants in France and in Denmark, etc.

Themes for German

In German the themes are: Landeskundekalendar; a young people's newspaper about football in Germany.

'Landeskundekalendar' is a geographically orientated topic. It is about learning about towns and other geographic phenomena in German-speaking countries (seventh–eighth grade). The pupils decorate a large piece of cardboard (calendar) and make as many opening flaps in it as there are pupils in the class. Each pupil chooses for example a town and finds some information about it from geography books, tourist brochures etc. The information is written on a card the size of a postcard and stuck on the back of the calendar. The flaps are opened on certain days and the pupil in question reads and explains what is on the card. There can also be discussion in class about what other knowledge and experience the pupils might have of the places in question.

'Young people's newspaper about football in Germany' is a practical journalism topic which is suitable for project work (ninth–tenth grade). Pupils are to get involved in football as a sport, in supporter cultures, etc. in Germany, and produce a newspaper on the topic, or a television or radio news programme. The worksheets include for example guidelines for presentations and processes for producing a newspaper (recordings, writing, etc.). The teaching scheme gives opportunity to discuss perspective and presentation and asks questions about the choice of reader group.

Assessment

The last part of the practical section contains a proposal for assessment of the teaching scheme. It is the same for all languages and is directed towards cultural understanding.

In designing the assessment sheets we were concerned to emphasise that the assessment of cultural understanding is not the same thing as checking whether pupils have learnt something about target language countries. The assessment sheets are intended to make the pupils themselves reflect on the processes they have been through, and what has been important for them personally. When we ask them to name five important insights they have had, this involves them in thinking about what is really significant and for whom. Furthermore we emphasise that pupils should think about both what they have learnt about target language countries and what they have learnt about their own country, i.e. they should think about their intercultural competence. Finally we ask them to think about the approach as something which hopefully has played a role in the development of their linguistic skills.

Stereotypes: Come to Stay

Children are good at spontaneously expressing what they think about things which are different. It can sometimes have a provocative effect on well-meaning teachers to hear their pupils' categorical statements about foreign customs and traditions. The best one can do as a conscientious language teacher working on cultural understanding is to pick up on the statements and try to investigate where they come from, and then provoke pupils' curiosity to find out why there are differences. The work on these categorical statements – often what we call national stereotypes – is a constant theme in the material discussed here, and we see it as a significant part of teaching for cultural understanding in language subjects.

For example, one can often find interesting background knowledge by taking one or more television magazines during a period when a specific issue is being debated, or one can ask pupils to work on daily newspapers – in the foreign language where possible but also in the mother tongue. Similarly one can find relevant articles on significant topics in young people's magazines in the foreign language which are published for educational purposes. The very fact of finding that there are reasons why 'foreigners' do things the way they do develops in itself open-mindedness and tolerance. Tolerance does not however necessarily lead to acceptance and positive attitudes towards every phenomenon in the foreign culture. There will inevitably be, in some cultures, differences which are so opposite to the native culture, that the lack of goodwill can only be noted, because in practice this is also an expression of loyalty towards one's own cultural values.

Stereotypes are an important part of the raw material of cultural understanding and it is the school's task to work on them: not to destroy them, since this cannot be done. Working on stereotypes means to get behind them and investigate their substance and their origins. Teachers need to problematise stereotypes, deal with them by always asking why and what and how. Why are things different? How do they really do this or that? What is better or worse than ours? For example for Danish pupils learning French, why is there such a widespread belief that French is a difficult language? And a beautiful language? Why do we feel French people are arrogant, what does it tell us about ourselves? Why is France Danish people's preferred holiday country year after year? Where does the perception that French women are elegant and French men charming come from? What lies behind the French café tradition? Why are there so many French words around us on the street in Denmark, in shop fronts and restaurant signs? By asking these questions we can partly try to find concrete explanations within French culture and partly discover where our perceptions of French people and France come from and what those perceptions tell us about ourselves.

It is important to realise that every time we evaluate and judge others, it is in the deepest sense our own projections we are emitting. In our evaluation of others is to be found our own assumptions of what we feel is right and wrong, good and bad. Work on cultural understanding is thus above all holding up a mirror to ourselves and in this way we gain a deeper recognition of what we stand for, what we like and dislike. In this way pupils learn that there is always an explanation behind the external phenomena. All pupils have to come to terms with these phenomena for themselves, but it can take place on a more conscious level with a basis in insight through work on cultural understanding.

It is precisely here that the teacher's other major task lies. It is important that pupils feel comfortable about saying things about foreign cultural issues and their personal experience of them. Thus it is the teacher's task to ensure that the content of lessons is substantial; not everything is equally important. The topics which are the content of the teaching should be significant and relevant, and it is therefore an important task for the teacher to select material; it is important that teachers and pupils distinguish the trivial from the significant.

One of the pitfalls of work on cultural understanding is for example the tendency to cultivate the anecdotal, the picturesque and the extreme. This is not surprising because it is amusing and easy to exchange major and minor experiences, but in the final analysis this just serves to reinforce our self-esteem by holding on to our stereotypes. Anecdote and amusing experiences abroad can either be used to strengthen our self-satisfaction in being what we are, or to glorify anything and everything in our favourite country.

Teaching Cultural Understanding: Various Contexts

Teaching cultural understanding is an important dimension of general language teaching in many countries but is described differently and in particular has many different kinds of material and institutional conditions. The material described here developed in connection with a school reform which strengthened cross-curricular co-operation through the requirement that there should be project work with cross-curricular teams of teachers. The materials largely allow pupils to work independently, something which has been emphasised in the *folkeskole* for many years in certain subjects. Danish schools are also well supplied with school libraries and access to audio-visual media, computers and the internet. These are relatively good conditions even if stress, social problems and weaknesses in teacher training set limits on what can be done.

We believe that others can find some inspiration in these materials and either develop them or edit them according to need. We would also hope that there could be better opportunities for exchanges across frontiers, so that innovations and experiments in various countries could be spread more quickly. The Danish *folkeskole* could profit from inputs from other countries.

Appendix 14.1

ELEVARK 1

Ungdomskonference

Preparing the conference: organization

1. Programme

Prepare the official, detailed programme for the entire week of the conference. This should comprise:

- the title with reference to the topic you are working with
- permanent daily routine incl. mealtimes, leisure time, etc.
- the time frame for national presentations and discussions, and maybe the time frame for the production of written reports or resolutions
- a farewell banquet Friday evening
- an "Evening of the Nations" one of the other days (see no. 8 below)
- a "Cafe of Poems" (see no. 9 below)
- opening and closing ceremonies
- leisure time opportunities at the Youth Hostel (sports, music, games etc.)
- opportunities for religious services and personal prayer
- an agreement with the local newspaper to come and interview people, and take photographs
- a disco during the week (see no. 4 below)
- out of house tourist programme

2. Menues

Work out the menue for the entire conference, taking into consideration:

- religious as well as vegetarian diets
- presentation of typical Danish dishes
- economy, ecology and health

You need to work out the precise menues for all meals – breakfasts, lunches and dinners. You also need to consider possible picnics or lunch-bags on days out of the house.

The realistic economic frame for this will be 50,- D.kr/day/participant.

3. Rules of behaviour

Work out rules of behaviour for everybody participating in the conference. In this work you might want to consider the following:

- smoking, consumption of alcohol and drugs

- parties and loud music

- visiting in bedrooms

- separation of boys and girls

4. Disco

Plan the disco. You need to consider the following:

- food and beverage
- music, technical equipment
- disco lights, decorations
- economy

5. Invitations

Prepare and design the invitations to the conference. You may want to make use of a computer. The following should be included:

- theme and objectives

- time, place, address, telephone number, e-mail, fax number, how to reach the place by train etc.

- requirements of the entry visa into Denmark

- something about the Danish climate and weather predictions for the duration of the conference

- the detailed programme and elements of the programme which would call for special clothing, equipment brought from home etc.

Preparing the conference:

Topic and culturel activities prepared by the national delegations

Questions 6-8 are compulsory for all.

6. The topic *

Prepare an oral presentation of the topic seen from "your" country's perspective – approx. 30 minutes. You may want to prepare some overheads, photos, drawings, tables etc. Both delegates are to participate in the presentation.

7. Leisure time activities *

Select and prepare 2-3 leisure time activities typical of "your" country or ethnic group. Not only sports but a blend of activities in order to attract all types of participants.

Maybe you will need the assistance of your teacher of gymnastics, a music teacher or other teachers at the school. And maybe you will need to use special facilities at your school or outside.

8. "Evening of the Nations" *

Work out your delegation's national feature for the "Evening of the Nations". This might include food, drink, music and performance.

You should actually hold this evening with e.g. the parents of your class or another class at your school.

9. "Cafe of Poems"

Plan a cafe of poems in which you present poems, myths or other fiction from "your" country. It would add to the atmosphere of the cafe, if you serve beverages and snacks, and music typical of each country would be interesting.

FORLAG MALLING BECK ☞ Kultur*forståelse* Best. nr. 90210   Kopiark

Appendix 14.2   Self evaluation

Translation of pupils' evaluation questionnaire (space is left under each question for pupils to write their answers)

New knowledge

(1) Name five important new pieces of information/knowledge about the country/countries which this topic was about.

(2) Name five important pieces of information/knowledge which you found out about Denmark during this topic.

(3) Which of these surprised you most? Why?

Attitudes and perceptions

(4) Name 3–5 similarities between the country/countries and Denmark in the topic.

(5) Name 3–5 differences between the country/countries and Denmark in the topic.

(6) What do you like best? Why?

(7) Has the work with this topic changed your understanding of the relevant social situation and/or people in the country/countries which you were working on?

     If yes, explain how:

     If no, explain why not:

(8) Did the work with this topic change your understanding of the relevant social situation in Denmark and/or of Danish people?

     If yes, explain how:

     If no, explain why not:

Language learning

(9) Did the work with this topic made you better at:

     • reading and understanding English/French/German texts? If yes, how do you notice this?

     • writing in English/French/German? If yes, how do you notice this?

     • speaking in English/French/German? If yes, how do you notice this?

Practical issues

(10) Write comments and give reasons for them about the way of working with respect to:

- materials;
- time;
- work from books;
- practical work;
- working with other pupils;
- the teacher as guide;
- your own commitment;
- the commitment of the class/group;
- what you learned;
- what the class/group learned.

Other issues for evaluation:

References

Faghaefte 2, Engelsk (1995) Copenhagen: Undervisningsministeriet (Ministry of Education, official guidelines for English in the Folkeskole).

Faghaefte 18, Fransk (1995) Copenhagen: Undervisningsministeriet (Ministry of Education, official guidelines for French in the Folkeskole).

Risager, K. and Aktor, L. (eds) (1999) *Kulturforstaaelse i folkeskolens sprogundervisning.* Copenhagen: Malling Beck.

Chapter 15
'I thought my teacher fancied me'

TANYA MADJAROVA, MAGDALENA BOTSMANOVA AND
TANYA STAMATOVA

This chapter suggests an idea for a cultural lesson designed to raise students' awareness of cultural similarities and differences between school practices in a foreign country and their own. It aims at developing students' tolerance of a cultural phenomenon in the target culture which is alien to them, and therefore potentially threatening. It also encourages students to develop some of the skills needed to analyse social events and account for them. Language teaching becomes part of values education.

Introduction

The idea of this lesson was born in May 1997 when the three of us were intending to trial cultural studies materials (mainly authentic articles from newspapers and magazines) as part of a British Council (Sofia) project which aims to design a cultural studies syllabus for use in the English language schools in Bulgaria – 13–18 highly selective secondary schools where students study English intensively starting from a beginner's level and progressing to advanced proficiency competence. Most of these schools have native British teachers among their staff, and some curricular subjects, apart from English itself, are taught in English.

The material we chose was a problem page in a recent issue of a British teenage magazine ('I Thought My Teacher Fancied Me', from *SHOUT*, March 1997, see Appendix 15.1). It attracted our attention for three reasons:

- firstly, the language level was appropriate for our students, whose competence was between intermediate and Cambridge First Certificate;

- secondly, we liked the story because it was about falling in love, an issue of eternal interest to teenagers (our students were 14–15 years of age), provoking their enthusiasm and imagination;
- last but not least, the article described a social practice which worked differently in Bulgaria and England and we saw potential for exploring cultural differences.

The text is in the form of a letter written by a girl who has had an embarrassing experience at school and shares it with the readers. The girl falls in love with her teacher and sends him a love letter. The cultural aspect which provoked our professional interest was the way the teacher, Mr Hill, resolved the matter. In short, he reports the incident to the head. As a result, the girl's form teacher and guidance teacher are involved, and her parents are informed about the incident shortly afterwards. We were aware that a Bulgarian male teacher would most probably not consult the institution and would resolve such a problem himself, involving friends rather than seniors or parents. To us such modes of behaviour are socially determined and the reasons are embedded in the different value systems of the two cultures.

Naturally, our lesson focused on increasing the students' awareness and sensitivity to culturally different patterns of behaviour. By doing this, we aimed to develop the following skills:

- increasing cultural observation;
- comparing and contrasting;
- interpreting differences;
- developing tolerance.

Besides the above-mentioned cultural skills we expected to practise the four basic linguistic skills too: reading, writing, listening and speaking.

Having identified our aim, we had to decide what framework to apply for the analysis of the cultural issue which was to be discussed. Hymes (1967) in 'Models of interaction and social life' suggests ways of reading a speech act. Adapting his model, we encouraged the students to look for answers to the following questions: WHO did WHAT, WHEN, HOW and WHY? We liked the simplicity of such models which gave clear guidelines for the students to follow in their analysis.

The next issue was how to begin. A good start for analysing cultural differences is the students' own culture. This enables them to draw upon their prior knowledge and past experience and sets the background for comparison of the target culture.

Procedure

Step 1

The students discussed in small groups what they thought a teacher would do if s/he received a love letter from a pupil. The students then listened to short interviews with two Bulgarian male teachers who were asked the same questions, and they then matched their predictions with the information they heard. The groups reported the results to the class and expressed opinions.

These interviews were a fresh point during the lesson. The students enjoyed them: they were emotionally involved because they recognised their maths and arts teacher, and we all had a lot of fun. One thing we should be careful about, however: if we choose to bring into the classroom voices of people familiar to the students they should be credible to them as people with whom students can identify.

Step 2

The students were given the article 'I Thought My Teacher Fancied Me' to find out who did what when and how. Then they identified similarities and differences between the British and the Bulgarian teachers' reactions. The students found it easy to compare and contrast the differences; however, at this point, they could not account for them, even though they wanted an explanation. We had expected this for two reasons: firstly, the students did not know enough about the target culture; secondly, although the article was very informative about the school procedure in Britain in such situations, it did not contain relevant cultural information. Clearly, the piece addressed a different audience, namely British teenagers, who share common assumptions with the girl at the centre of the story about their culture, and for whom the cultural implications of the teacher's reaction are implicitly understood.

Step 3

To bridge the gap, we designed three interviews with two British teachers working in our school. A significant advantage of teachers designing their own materials is that they can compensate for insufficient information in media sources. Native speakers, where available, are an invaluable source of help, especially when it comes to subtle cultural matters omitted from traditional cultural studies books.

In the first two interviews, which the students did as listening comprehension exercises, we asked the same question: 'What would you do if you received a love letter from a pupil?' One of the teachers, Rob, had worked mainly in state schools in Britain. Not surprisingly, his probable reaction would be similar to that of the teacher featured in the article. By contrast, the other interviewee, Michael, had taught mainly in private schools abroad. He said he would try and resolve the matter himself, like the Bulgarian teachers, but unlike them, he would talk to the girl 'in the classroom, with the door wide open'. Also, he would inform one of his seniors afterwards.

The two interviews reveal two different perspectives, and this was important for two reasons. On the one hand, they validated the information from the article, thus pointing to a culturally appropriate pattern of behaviour: a teacher in Britain would probably avoid dealing with such a problem himself and would involve the school at some point. On the other hand, the interviews discouraged stereotyping by showing that not all British teachers would do the same: they would respond to the situation depending on their relationship with the students, the culture of the school (for instance, whether it is state or privately run), the context (the location and the circumstances of the situation) and their own background and experience. The last point is important to consider whenever we try to generalise about people and their ways of doing things, so that we do not fall into the trap of attributing 'false' or tenuous meanings or making simplistic interpretations. Rather, students should be encouraged to explore the diversity which exists within a culture through authentic 'texts'; this should promote their critical thinking and give them a better understanding of a culture and the way it functions.

In the third interview we asked Michael why he thought most teachers in Britain would refrain from resolving such matters themselves, preferring to refer them to the school management. His answer raises two basic issues: namely, the different social roles played by schools in Britain and by those in Continental Europe, as well as the power the British tabloids have in society. First, he points to a prevalent and legally binding attitude in Britain that schools take over the role of parents, responsible for the child's personal and social development. Because of this it is absolutely forbidden for British teachers to be 'overfamiliar' with their students. Second, if newspapers get hold of anything remotely scandalous it can be the end of a teacher's career. There have been cases where teachers have lost their jobs in similar circumstances. So teachers now have a strict procedure to avoid any possibility of jeopardising their own situations. In Michael's opinion, that explains why they would respond in what may seem a rather heavy-handed way of informing teachers, parents and counsellors. This interview came at a crucial stage in the lesson, being both informative and enlightening: it enabled students to find out the reasons for particular behaviour patterns. By helping learners recognise why people do things one way or another, we are actually giving them an essential access to a culture through gaining insight into its value system.

Step 4

The students in small groups discussed possible reasons for the different reaction of the Bulgarian teachers. At the stage of step 1 they were reluctant to do this; now they were much more active and enthusiastic. Obviously, the encounter with an alien phenomenon in the target culture had challenged their assumptions of the validity of their own culture's standards and the principles underlying its value system. They were able to analyse phenomena from a historical perspective and express opinions about the diverse nature of the changing present-day Bulgarian society.

Step 5: Follow-up/evaluation (for homework)

For girls: You are an exchange student in a British state school. Imagine that the story described in the article happened to you. Write a letter to your best friend in Bulgaria.

For boys: A British student is coming to study in your school for a year. Write him a letter about the things you find essential for him to know in order to 'minimise' the culture shock.

Clearly, this lesson can successfully be used with older students. Being more experienced, the students would be able to discuss the reasons for the different modes of behaviour in both cultures more confidently.

Evaluation

This study was designed to investigate possible changes in attitude towards a culture-specific social practice. The evaluation is based both on feedback from the students and our own observations and reflections. There were 78 participating students in the study, aged 14–15 and equally divided between boys and girls, at an English Medium School in Bulgaria.

At different stages of the lesson the students were asked to fill in questionnaires. Peer/teacher lesson observations and post-lesson interviews with students were also carried out. Our aims were to establish to what degree the students were prepared to understand and respect cultural differences, and to ascertain how effective, if at all, our work was in raising cultural awareness and developing tolerance. The data analyses focus on the students' own descriptions of their reactions and feelings. Analysing and comparing students' responses, we tried to examine group patterns of value changes, rather than focusing on individual patterns of response. Monitoring students' feelings proved to be of invaluable help in our further lesson planning.

After being presented with an example of culture-specific behaviour the students were asked what their first reaction after reading the article had been: 10% were curious and interested, 57% were surprised by the teacher's reaction, 10% were shocked. They had expected the teacher to have a private talk with the girl and explain the situation. The involvement of so many people, and especially the head, had been contrary to many students' expectations and that was the reason for their great surprise and 'shock'. Obviously it was difficult for them to distance themselves from their own assumptions and to understand that somebody belonging to another culture may be intending to act in a public-spirited, sympathetic fashion, but may do so in very different ways from those immersed in their own culture. Some 13% clearly expressed disapproval of the teacher's behaviour. They came to the conclusion that English teachers did not care about the students' feelings and were felt to be rude and cruel; talking to the head was described as a stupid reaction. The more judgemental students failed, initially at least, to consider the differences in the target culture. Some 10% were not surprised, but they were quite aware of cultural differences, claiming to have read articles in newspapers and articles describing similar situations.

Although many of our students had failed to understand the implicit cultural message, we were very optimistic, because we had achieved our aim to provoke their interest and make them aware that *our* concept of *good, right* or *appropriate* responses to given situations may not be universally recognised. It was not difficult for the students to observe the surface WHAT, but they found it more challenging to understand the WHY, the reasons motivating the different mode of behaviour. In this respect the article was of less help to them. Some 80% of the students said that the article had not been detailed enough to provide a reasonable explanation of Mr Hill's behaviour – i.e. informing the head. Many of the remaining 20% had misinterpreted the reasons for this behaviour. The following quotation illustrates the sort of interpretation made in most of the students' answers: 'Maybe he hadn't been able to find a solution to the problem, or maybe he wanted this to be an example for all the other girls'.

According to Bulgarian cultural norms, addressing the institution in the way illustrated by the article betrays an inability to solve the problem yourself, which automatically suggests lack of competence. Students were inclined to interpret this story as an isolated case and to blame the teacher for betraying the girl and for being rude to her. The article had only provided the facts about that culture-specific phenomenon without giving any reasons. Being unable to understand Mr Hill's behaviour, as they could not find a reasonable explanation, they tended to reject it. For them this was a personal rather than a cultural reaction because they were trying to give reasons for the behaviour of a foreigner from the point of view of Bulgarian cultural standards.

The interviews with two more British teachers contributed to significant changes in attitude towards the culturally different behaviour. As one of the British teachers said in the interview that his reaction would be similar to Mr Hill's, we asked our students if they thought that all British teachers would do likewise: 56% of the students wrote 'Yes' or 'Probably, yes'. The degree of certainty was different but it was obvious that this mode of behaviour (which they generally found unacceptable) was associated with the representatives of a certain culture, which was, possibly, a step further to cultural awareness.

We were quite prepared for the fact that stereotyping was inevitable in such cases and it was interesting to find that 18% of the students thought that most, but not all, British teachers would do likewise. Data analysis showed that the third interview was extremely valuable, illustrating a kind of reaction different from that described in the article and thus showing that individuals within the same culture do not necessarily behave according to the assumed cultural norms – a fact very often ignored in favour of cultural stereotyping. Students found this interview the most useful because it clearly described the reasons for the culture-specific reactions of British teachers – in other words, it provided the answer to the question 'why do they do it that way?' and helped them most to understand the British perspective.

After so many authentic materials and discussions we were eager to find out whether the students' attitude to the British teacher's behaviour had changed. Being realistic we did not expect the students to approve of it, and the questionnaires proved we were right. With very few exceptions, the students' answer to the question 'Did you like Mr Hill's behaviour?' was 'No'. In order to find out how far from or how close to tolerance we were, we asked our students if they would try to change the British teachers' views or would rather think 'OK, they are different but I understand them and respect their opinion'. Some 75% of the students answered that they were ready to understand the cultural differences and to show a degree of respect, although 'we would never behave that way'. These results were rewarding for us, in that our basic aim to help students understand and respect a culture-specific phenomenon had been achieved. Despite this respect, the attitudinal judgements of some of the students revealed their own cultural standards. One student wrote: 'I respect them being different BUT I think sometimes they are too cold and ignore students' feelings'. Different degrees of tolerance could be identified in the answers of the other 25% of the students who were eager to change the British teachers' views in accordance with their own standard of 'right' behaviour.

> I'd try to tell them my opinion but I wouldn't argue.

> They are different and I respect their opinions BUT in that situation I think they could solve the problem in better ways e.g. involve as few people as possible, have a short conversation with the girl, etc.

> I'd tell them they shouldn't be so cruel and selfish.

> They think only about themselves and don't really care how the student feels. I would definitely try to persuade him not to tell the Head.

It should be noted that although in the questionnaires students demonstrated willingness to accept the culturally different behaviour, in their letters (the follow-up activity) they strongly rejected it. The quotation below is from the letter of a girl who had written in the questionnaire that she was ready to respect and accept Mr Hill's behaviour.

> I am so angry with this idiot and coward Mr Hill. I hate him! How could he have done this to me! Hadn't he known what would happen when he told my form teacher! But, of course, his job and career were more important than my feelings. He could have just ignored my letter or told me he was engaged or something, you know that stuff.

Data analysis showed that tolerance was not an inseparable part of their value system and when they were emotionally involved, they reacted spontaneously and ignored all cultural explanations and tolerance.

This study has revealed some interesting insights that have broadened our understanding of the long and difficult process of changing attitudes. The data analyses suggest that we might usefully work with our students to develop in them important intercultural qualities: a greater awareness and acceptance of the idea that the target culture may have a system of values that differs from our own; and a growing realisation that people always have a purpose behind their behaviour. Even if it seems strange and unacceptable to us, we can be certain that it makes sense and is acceptable to them.

Conclusion

The introduction of a cultural component into the foreign language class enriches its content: it promotes students' curiosity about the target culture and raises awareness of their own culture. This does not impede students' language acquisition; on the contrary, it provides a meaningful context for language learning, thus enhancing motivation.

Authentic materials can be an invaluable source of culture teaching and learning. Designing their own materials, teachers can make up for the insufficiencies in existing coursebooks and achieve unexpected rewards in provoking students' interest and emotional response.

The focal point in the methodology we used was the skills-based approach: students observed, analysed and made conclusions using their prior knowledge of their own culture and comparing and contrasting it with the target culture. The main problem they encountered was the attribution of meaning to a culture-specific behaviour. One reason was their insufficient knowledge of the target culture. Another was their judgemental attitude towards an alien cultural phenomenon. Bridging the gap was crucial for an in-depth understanding of the behaviour under discussion. It is important to bear in mind that ethnocentric attitudes – the tendency to believe that 'our way is the right way' – is pretty universal. As a result, people tend to reject something which they do not like or understand. The factors which influence and govern people's actions are personal but are also embedded in society: what people do in a particular situation is, by and large, an expression of the cultural norms of the community to which they belong or with which they identify. When we encourage students to interpret the reasons behind people's actions we actually enable them to gain better insight into the target culture and its ideas, beliefs and value system.

Raising students' cultural awareness means widening their horizons and thus helping them to acquire an international outlook. Modern language teaching is fundamental because its role has developed from language instruction to a values education. Our aim is not to 'brainwash' students, to make them like or agree with a particular point of view; rather, it is for us to help them to accept the validity of the target culture. This is an essential part of intercultural competence and one towards which we should work consistently because it is one step towards achieving tolerance of 'otherness'. This may present us with what seems like a daunting task, but it is well worth the effort.

Reference

Hymes, D. (1967) Models of interaction and social life. *Journal of Social Issues* 33(2) 8–28.

Appendix 15.1

BRANCHING OUT · A CULTURAL STUDIES SYLLABUS

I THOUGHT MY TEACHER FANCIED ME

Clare poured her feelings out in a letter to her teacher, thinking he felt the same way . . .

A Problem Shared...

I couldn't believe it when Mr Hill started at our school. He was totally good-looking, young and unlike any other teacher I'd ever seen before.

It didn't take me long to start really fancying him — as soon as I saw him I thought he was gorgeous. Of course, I wasn't the only one — nearly all the girls in our class thought he was lovely, but I was sure my feelings for him were stronger than theirs. They just had crushes but I really loved Mr Hill and I'd never felt so strongly about anyone before.

I tried really hard to get him to notice me and I always put my hand up to answer questions. A couple of times he told me that I was doing really well and I was so pleased because I thought that must mean he liked me.

After a while in fact, I really began to think Mr Hill fancied me. A couple of times when I looked up in class, he seemed to be looking at me and he'd smile then look away, almost as if he was flirting with me.

I confided in Hannah, my best mate, and I think if she'd laughed and told me not to be stupid, I would have realised that I was living in a dream world. She didn't, though — she said I could be right and he did always seem to single me out in class. She really seemed to believe that he fancied me, too, so I thought it must be true.

It got so I spent most of my spare time daydreaming about what it would be like to go out with Mr Hill. I imagined what it would be like to kiss him and go out in his car with him.

Then one day, me and my little sister, Jenny, went swimming and we met Mr Hill at the pool. He gave me a big smile and spent a few minutes chatting to me. I had on a new swimsuit that I'd got for going on holiday and I was sure he was looking at me in it. I tried to keep him talking but Jenny got fed up and I had to go after her, which made me really annoyed.

Afterwards, I couldn't stop thinking about meeting Mr Hill. He'd come over to me, after all, and he'd seemed so pleased to see me. I was positive that meant he fancied me, and I thought that maybe he just didn't want to ask me out in case I said no or he got into trouble for it.

I discussed it with Hannah and she said I should tell Mr Hill how I felt. That way, she said, I'd at least find out how he felt and we might even get together. I considered it, but the thought of actually telling Mr Hill to his face that I fancied him was too nerve-racking. Besides, I'd never be about writing him a letter — that way, I'd be able to let him know that I fancied him without actually having to speak to him.

I wrote a letter that night on really nice notepaper I'd got for Christmas. In the letter I told Mr Hill that I loved him from the first time I saw him and that I knew he felt the same way about me. I went on to say that it wasn't fair that we couldn't be together, just because he was a teacher. I said we could go out with each other in secret and he shouldn't worry because I wouldn't even tell Hannah.

I took the letter to school with me the next day and managed to sneak it on to Mr Hill's desk as I left his class. For the rest of the day, I felt really nervous and excited as I waited for him to get in touch with me.

When I went into school the next day I was still feeling quite nervous. I even put some make-up on, just in case we managed to sneak some time together. But nothing could have been further from the truth.

Once my form teacher and I had done the register, she asked me to stay behind. She looked so serious that I immediately knew I

He'd smile then look away.

was in trouble.

Once me and my form teacher were alone, she told me that the headmaster, Mr Jackson, wanted to see me in his office right away. I asked what for, but she said she didn't know. I knew, though, that it must be about the letter.

I walked up to Mr Jackson's office feeling so scared, but I kept thinking to myself that surely Mr Hill wouldn't give me away and even if he didn't want to go out with me, surely he wouldn't have to involve the headmaster in it all?

Mr Jackson looked really serious.

When I went into the head's office, Mrs Gold, my guidance teacher was there. Mr Jackson looked really serious and he told me that it'd been brought to his attention that I'd developed a crush on a teacher and had written him a letter. He didn't exactly give me a row but he said there was no way Mr Hill felt the same way about me and I'd placed him in a very awkward position. Mr Jackson was going to get in touch with my parents to get them up to school to talk about it. Then Mrs Gold stepped in and said if we went to her office, we

could talk it all through.

It was so embarrassing. Mrs Gold wasn't horrible to me — in fact, I think she felt sorry for me. She said I'd humiliated Mr Hill and I'd left him with no choice but to go to the headmaster. I tried to say that he'd encouraged me but when she asked how, even I had to admit that he hadn't really — I mean, I'd thought he was trying to give me hints when he smiled at me and praised me, but he'd done exactly the same with other girls, too.

Mrs Gold said I could move classes if I wanted to, but Mr Hill had said it was up to me — I didn't have to. She said if I stayed in his class, he'd act as if nothing had happened and she also pointed out that if I moved, I'd have to put up with questions from other people in the class.

I agreed and so I stayed in Mr Hill's class. Facing him was just about the hardest thing I'd ever done, but he acted like nothing had happened. Facing my mum and dad was awful, too — Dad went mad at me, but Mum just said she was disappointed in me for being so stupid. It was awful.

I know that fancying a teacher isn't that unusual — loads of people still go on about how good-looking Mr Hill is. But if anyone's reading this and thinks that their teacher might fancy them, they should let my story be a warning. Just because a teacher is friendly to you, it doesn't mean he fancies you, — and if you tell yourself that he does, you just end up making a big fool of yourself . . .

Cathy Says . . .

Clare learned the hard way that it can be painful and embarrassing when a crush gets out of control. Her feelings were strong but they *were* a crush because you can't fall in love with someone without getting to know them first.

Teachers are placed in a position of trust with their pupils and know that if they take advantage of that they could lose their job, their reputation — maybe even end up being prosecuted by the police — so don't let your feelings get out of hand.

Chapter 16
British and Bulgarian Christmas Cards: A Research Project for Students

KRASSIMIRA TOPUZOVA

Inspired by a chance observation of changes in Bulgarian customs at Christmas, this chapter describes how simple artefacts such as Christmas cards can help students with advanced language skills to analyse, compare and contrast different cultural values. It links non-fiction and literary texts as a basis for both empirical observation and textual analysis.

Introduction

The 1990s will probably go down in the history of English language teaching as the decade of world expansion and globalisation, which in itself has brought the ever-increasing demand for intercultural communication and understanding between people. This process has changed the focus of English language teaching, directing it to culture teaching and learning. It has revolutionised schools syllabi and created new approaches and methods in the teachers' practices as well as challenging students' understandings of education and the world.

My school has readily responded to these new changes by adopting the new cultural studies syllabus in English language teaching approved by the Ministry of Education in Bulgaria (1998). The teachers from the English department have undergone training in using the syllabus in their classrooms and exploring its skills-based approach to culture teaching.

The school itself is a specialised foreign language school with English, French and German departments. It offers a five-year course of education in English, French and German respectively. This type of school is considered to be 'elitist' in the sense that it offers advanced language teaching and learning and the student body is well above the average level of ability and performance. The age of the students is 14–19. They come to our school after successful completion of an examination in Bulgarian literature or mathematics, and their motivation for studying English and other languages is very high. They begin with a preparatory year in which English is studied extensively and in the next four years they study their main subjects (biology, chemistry, geography, etc.) in English, as well as English literature and computer science.

I teach courses in English literature and advanced English language and I developed my project as part of my literature course. My class consisted of 26 students at the age of 17–18 and it was their fourth year of studying English. They had an advanced level of spoken and written English and in a year's time most of them were to sit for exams in English to go to university.

Background of the Project

Like all new democracies in Eastern Europe, Bulgaria has opened itself to change – change in the political, economic, social and cultural spheres of life. Governments have been replaced, the economy has been reconstructed, and education and the media have undergone significant changes. Even the celebrations and habits of people have started to change. A completely new celebration appeared: Bulgarians started to celebrate St. Valentine on the same day as St Triffon's day, 14 February. Christmas has become more commercialised with a stronger emphasis on Christmas shopping and decoration. Many new symbols of Christmas have been introduced: the Christmas wreath of mistletoe, Christmas turkey, Christmas presents. Even the Christmas cards have started to change. How did I find out?

Shortly before Christmas 1996 I was standing in a queue in the bookshop of the American University in Bulgaria. A Bulgarian woman in front of me asked for Christmas cards with English greetings on them. I have never made that distinction. My concept of the traditional Bulgarian Christmas cards didn't include foreign greetings. So, I decided to organise some research with my students and explore the issue.

My aims were:

- First, to show whether the Bulgarian Christmas tradition has changed in the years of change and make students aware of these changes.
- Second, I wanted to compare it with the British tradition and introduce other cultural issues, which the students might raise.
- Third, it is generally accepted that in the field of cultural studies 'research' is a keyword, be it ethnographic, anthropological,

historical, linguistic, etc. It is through analysing compiled data that one forms concepts and draws conclusions about cultures. Getting the students involved in such a venture is challenging both for the teachers and students and does yield amazing results.

I am convinced that Christmas cards as products of society can fit well in Brøgger's (1992) model of cultural studies which envisages three levels of analysis: social, cultural and textual.

- On the social level, the students are introduced to 'the general infomational framework about different areas in British and American society' (Brøgger, 1992, quoted in Benson, 1994). This would include, for example, some discussion of the social structure, the economic system, religion, history, geography, etc.
- On the cultural level, the analysis would focus on how these structures are products of the dominant assumptions and values of the society.
- Finally, on the textual level, it is possible to analyse texts as linguistic expressions of the culture in question. Here, through a careful reading of a literary or non-literary text, the underlying cultural values will be revealed.

Organisation of the Project

It was Christmas time and Bulgarian Christmas cards were available in the shops. As for the British ones, I received a whole collection from a friend in the UK. In the preparation stage of our project, I asked each student (26 altogether) to go to a shop and buy one Christmas card they'd like to post for Christmas. While in the shop, I asked them to observe the following:

(1) Who buys Christmas cards? Their age, sex, nationality?
(2) How many Christmas cards do they buy?
(3) Which cards sell more and which less?

At school, they exhibited the cards and each student explained why he/she had bought a particular card. Some of the answers were connected with the price, size or colour of the cards, others pointed to their images and messages. They also reported on the observations at the shops and their answers to the above questions.

We split into groups of five or six in order to analyse the cards. The analysis focused on three major groups of questions:

Who buys Christmas cards?
(1) What age, sex, occupation are they?
(2) Are they local people or tourists?
(3) How many cards do they buy?

What Christmas cards?
(1) What size and format are they?
(2) What images are included?
(3) Who printed them?
(4) What price are they?
(5) What is written on them?
(6) Where are they sold?

Why buy Christmas cards?
(1) What do Christmas cards mean to Bulgarians?
(2) Why do they buy them?
(3) Who do they send them to?
(4) What do they write on them?

All groups prepared written and oral presentations of their answers. Here I have included the answers of one of the groups to illustrate the kind of work the students produced:

Who buys Christmas cards?
(1) *What age, sex and occupation are they?* People of different age and occupation but mainly women and young people (young mothers with their children or grandmothers with grandchildren). Women in Bulgaria have more free time (young mothers are on maternity leave and grandmothers are pensioners) to do the shopping.
(2) *Are they local or tourists?* Almost always they are local people. Sometimes tourists (Americans who work in the American University in Blagoevgrad) buy them as a souvenir which has impressed them.
(3) *How many cards do they buy?* Usually not many – three or four cards according to their finances.

What Christmas cards are bought?
(1) *What size and format are they?* There is a variety of sizes – very small and rather big ones but most popular have average size 11×16 cm. They are usually rectangular. Rarely they have an irregular format – a Christmas tree for example – but these are more expensive.
(2) *What images are included?* Most often the cards contain Father Christmas, Snow-White, beautifully decorated Christmas trees, snowy winter scenery, bells, decorated Christmas table in the Bulgarian tradition.

(3) *Who printed them?* They are printed by private publishing houses and international organisations like UNICEF, whose main goal is collecting money for homeless children.

(4) *What price are they?* There are different prices but altogether they are not so expensive. They are rather expensive when they are not ordinary ones, like melody-cards for example.

(5) *What is written on them?* Some kind of Christmas greeting like 'Merry Christmas' and 'Happy New Year' in Bulgarian (mainly) and in English (not so often).

(6) *Where are they sold?* In the bookshops, newsagents or merely on tables in the main streets of the town made especially for them.

Why buy Christmas cards?

(1) and (2)   *What do Christmas cards mean to Bulgarians and why do they buy them?* They are an old tradition – a sign of attention and respect to whom you send them.

(3) *Who do they send them to?* They are sent to friends, colleagues, relatives, to everybody one wants to greet for Christmas.

(4) *What do they write on them?* Greeting for the holiday and wishes for success, health, luck, happiness in the New Year or maybe something more intimate.

The second stage of the work in the classroom included the classification of the Christmas cards into types, according to the images and messages. As a result, the following types emerged:

(1) *Traditional Bulgarian Christmas cards:* illustrating the traditional Christmas table with the round bread and coin in it; the traditional *buklitsa* (a wooden vessel for pouring wine) and the cornel tree, placed on the traditional embroidered tablecloth. Some other traditional foods are *banitsa* (baked pastry with pumpkin or leek), walnuts, dried or fresh fruit, garlic and also typical *surovachka* (a piece of cornel tree), decorated with popcorn, sesame rings and dried fruits.

(2) *Religious Christmas cards with Biblical images:* connected with the Bible's story of Christ's birth. The students regarded this type of cards as a relatively new development in our country, due to the official rejection of the church before the changes.

(3) *Children's cards:* typical cards, depicting children making snowmen, playing with snowballs, skiing, skating, as well as Santa Claus.

(4) *Winter-landscape cards:* commonly presenting snowy woods or fields, i.e. nature at winter-time.

Figure 16.1 Bulgarian Christmas card.

(5) *Christmas-tree decorations:* typical Bulgarian cards, showing traditional decorations for the Christmas tree. An interesting observation for this type was the fact that some of the cards contained images of the holly-wreath with ribbons, which the students regarded as untypical of our tradition.

The third stage included a discussion of the cultural implications of each type of Christmas card. We found out that the traditional Bulgarian Christmas cards haven't changed and are being sold along with some recently introduced innovations, like the religious cards or UNICEF cards with 'Merry Christmas' in English and not in Bulgarian.

Comparisons

Having completed the research on Bulgarian Christmas cards, we proceeded with similar research on British Christmas cards.

First, I brainstormed ideas and expectations from the students about British Christmas cards. I asked them to write one or two questions about British cards which they would like to know about. Some of the questions overlapped with those asked about the Bulgarian cards but others were different. For example: Who printed them? Is the habit of sending Christmas cards still going on in Britain? Are the cards only British or foreign?

After distributing the British cards to the groups, they started analysing them, following the same procedure as before. We rotated all the cards between the groups, and the students answered the questions they had written. They were also asked to arrange the cards in types. Four types were outlined which the students labelled as follows: religious cards, winter-season cards, children's cards, Christmas decorations.

The fourth stage included the comparative analysis of the Bulgarian and British Christmas cards. The students were asked to make two columns: one for the differences and another for any similarities between them. The following summarises the findings.

In general British cards are more varied in size, shape and format. Some of the images were not expected to be there on a Christmas card – like the House of Commons, or Westminster. British cards have no price marked on them. The most striking difference, however, is the amount of information written on the cards, referring to what charity printed them and what material they are made of, or written extracts from the Bible, as well as some religious or funny texts. In contrast, the written text by the sender of the card is very short, just one or two lines which is in most cases a repetition of the printed wish 'Merry Christmas and a Happy New Year'. In the Bulgarian Christmas cards it is just the opposite – very little printed on them, only a discreetly marked publisher and the greetings 'Merry Christmas and a Happy New Year' in Bulgarian or recently in English. The sender is expected to write a longer text inside, sending his/her wishes to the receiver. A common text may sound like:

Dear . . .,

Happy New Year!

Please accept my greeting for Christmas and the New Year,
sent from me with the kindest feelings. I wish you luck, happiness and most of all health during the New Year. May all your wishes come true and all the best things happen to you.
Yours . . .

The students guessed that the short British text written by the sender may be due to the restrained and cool British character or may be because the cards themselves expressed everything the people wanted to show – respect, love, friendship. Or the sheer volume of cards sent by some people spoke of their feelings and attitudes stirred by the spirit of Christmas.

The students found it difficult to accept the idea of buying Christmas cards to support a charity. This is a very interesting point of cultural difference that the students raised. The concept of charity didn't exist in our culture before 1989. Under communist rule people were 'ideally' equal – we got equal wages, we had equal rights and obligations. There were literally no starving people. It was a 'classless' society, people had their bread and homes without fear of losing them. We went to the same shops, selling nearly the same things at the same price. Now, ten years later, the concept of charity has emerged with a clear shape and meaning. The 'classless society' has practically become non-existent. Instead, two distinct classes have formed – those of the rich and the poor. Homeless and unemployed people started to appear. At the same time, the first charity organisations appeared, usually founded and sponsored by people with money and power. Probably, this accounts for the fact that some of the Bulgarian cards had a printed price and none of the British had. British cards may have a price either written in pencil or on a stick-on label, which British people always remove before sending them.

At this point we had a discussion on British charities, their role and value in society. The students learned about some of the well-known British charities – the Samaritans, the Salvation Army, Oxfam, etc. They were surprised to find out that these charities got their funds from public donations, not from state or private businesses as is the case in Bulgaria. They explained this by reference to the centralised social service system in our country which is still surviving, though quite neglected by the state due to its financial and economic crisis. However, they came to the conclusion that the charities in Bulgaria would develop in very much the same way as West European charities because of the guidance they received from them, and the expertise they followed in organisation and activities.

In contrast, most of the Bulgarian Christmas cards are simpler in design, format and shape, without printed wishes inside, advertisements for charities or details of the materials they're made of. Instead, the Bulgarian cards have some typical, national Christmas images and a lot of empty space to be filled by the sender.

The work and the completion of this stage of the project suggested wonderful ideas for further discussions of cultural issues raised by the students themselves. These issues came up naturally in the brainstorm activity which the students had at this final stage. I asked them to look at the whole selection of British cards and, accepting them as products of culture, think of the cultural aspects of life encoded in them and list any possible topics of interest for further discussions of British culture. These included Easter celebrations, British character, how religious are the British, art and architecture. The latter was suggested by a student who was interested in a Christmas card which was a picture of the House of Commons and had the following lines above: 'Christmas Greetings from the House of Commons'. The discussions were planned as long-term events which took place at different times of the second term (for example, during Easter we had a discussion on Easter celebration in Bulgaria and Britain), or were incorporated as short-time activities to accompany the main English textbook.

Literary Dimensions

Since my project was carried out with students taking their course of English literature, I thought it worth trying to explore the third level of Brøgger's model of cultural studies. This is the textual level which allows for comparing literary texts and analysing them as linguistic expressions of a particular culture. In our case, the literary texts I chose were linguistic expressions of British and Bulgarian cultures, describing the Christmas traditions of these countries. In order to expand our comparison, I decided to include a third writer, Dostoevsky, and his short story 'Child Under Christ's Christmas Tree'.

This last endeavour of our project was extremely challenging for the students. Having in mind that they were students with a considerable knowledge of English literature, they accepted the idea enthusiastically because they could have another chance for discussing a novel by Dickens. Second, they felt challenged by the task of comparing a Bulgarian classical writer of Dickens's stature and a world-famous Russian writer who they've only heard about. They were surprised to find out that these three writers had written on the same topic of Christmas, sharing a common level of interest which could be used for making cross-cultural comparisons.

The three pieces of literature we had in mind were the following:

(1) An excerpt from Dickens's *Christmas Carol* – in particular the conversation between Mr Scrooge and his nephew just before Christmas Eve.
(2) A short story by the Bulgarian classical writer Ivan Vazov, called 'Christmas Present'. This is a story about a rich, newly married couple preparing to celebrate Christmas Eve.
(3) A short story by the Russian writer Dostoevsky, 'Child Under Christ's Christmas Tree'. It is Christmas Eve in St Petersburg. In the cold basement of a poor house lies a dead body of a young woman. Next to her lies her 6-year-old boy. The child is dying of hunger and cold. In this state between life and death he sees a beautiful Christmas tree, lots of toys and happy children, a warm and pleasant fire and plenty of food. This is Christ's Christmas tree and he has been invited to Christmas with Christ's children.

It is generally accepted that literature is a reflection of society's views, values and beliefs: a reflection of the social, political, cultural development of any society. It reveals the people's ideals and dreams in the most creative and imaginative way. Literary works live in time – in the past, in the present, in the future; there is also a certain continuity of time. This continuity can be interpreted in the following way: in the literature of the past we can find the roots of the present; in the literature of the future we'll see the traditions of the past. Literature contains and expresses both the transition of time and social reality as the agent of change. This motivates the reader to seek for some real truth about time in the literary works and justifies literature texts as reliable, truthful resources of cultural representation.

That is why we chose to compare the description of Christmas in classic texts. Our objective was not the comparison of the literary texts as such. It was rather to compare the images and characters the writers used in describing Christmas as a symbol of a particular culture, in our case English, Bulgarian and Russian cultures. My intention was to shift the students' attention from the purely literary analysis of the texts to a more culture-oriented analysis. Accordingly, I wanted to place the emphasis on the contrast with the students' known 'home' literature and culture rather than 'establish literary and cultural parameters, especially where the difference between the learner's own culture and the target culture is large' (Durant, 1997: 20)

The students worked in groups of four or five. They were given three extracts to read and discuss. The guidelines for the comparison were not strictly set. However, for the sake of clarity and time-saving, I advised them to compare the images and the characters used in the description of Christmas, which were then presented orally. They were surprised to find out a great number of similar images of Christmas in the three texts. Some of the most important are: the Christmas fire, the cold Christmas weather, the Christmas tree, the description of poor and rich characters, money as an image connected with Christmas, and the description of children versus old people. Even the number of characters in the extracts is the same – two main characters: Scrooge and his nephew, Tsanko and Verka, and the child and his mother.

The outward similarities, however, masked big differences in ideas, values, beliefs. The students noticed a profound difference in the attitudes of the characters to Christmas. For the characters in the Bulgarian story, Christmas was a time for thinking about the poor and making them happy. The wife feels sorry for her poor neighbour in the cold winter night: 'It's Christmas Eve. They have no fire, they'll celebrate Christ's birth without food. Oh, God, why have you made some people poor?' She is rich, and her husband is rich. She wants to be happy on Christmas Eve, expecting a rich present from her husband. But her happiness is blighted by the sight of extreme poverty opposite her house. Shortly after, the doorbell rings and Verka opens it to see the poor widow and her children looking happy and contented in their new warm clothes and behind them her husband with his generous heart, making his wife the happiest person in the world, giving her the strangest Christmas present.

The wife's feelings are 'charitable' indeed and they point to a period in Bulgarian history when charity had existed as a vital part of social life. It was considered inseparable from the religious and moral norms of a society which was a monarchy supported by a strong orthodox church. When the communist rule was established in the 1940s the social structure was radically changed, the existing class-hierarchy was destroyed and a 'classless' society was built, thus destroying the need for charity and charitable activities.

On the other hand, Scrooge's attitude to Christmas is connected with money: 'What's Christmas time to you but a time for paying bills without money; a time for finding yourself a year older, but not an hour richer; time for balancing your books . . .'. He finds happiness in his money and doesn't view Christmas as a source of joy and inspiration: 'What right have you to be merry? What reasons have you to be merry? You're poor enough'. Surely, Dickens is highly critical of such an attitude but he was building a type representative of certain aspects of social reality and he could not but remain truthful to reality.

Dostoevsky's story describes a gloomy picture of St Petersburg with the extreme poverty of two poor creatures – the young dead mother and her little child. The child is dying in the cold freezing night. Suddenly, there's a warm light coming from a Christmas tree. There are many children like him, flying around, inviting him to their Christmas tree: 'This is Christ's Christmas tree – they answered. On this day, Christ always decorates a Christmas tree for the children who don't have one . . .'.

The students concluded that Dostoevsky's description of Christmas was the most 'socially biased' because it described the social and economic problems of St Petersburg at that time. At the same time it was the most religious and the most 'Christian' and spiritual. The Bulgarian text is closer to the Russian because it is religious and social in general. However, the students defined it as 'more philosophical' because it deals with the philosophical opposition of good and evil: 'It is not enough to have desire to do good – you must have courage to do it. Because to do good means to be brave for it. Only evil could be done easily, almost unconsciously, that's why it has spread nearly everywhere.'

The English text, according to the students, reflects the social events most profoundly. The religious nature of Christmas, however, is secularised and put in the background. Reading the students' responses, I could judge that they were beginning to build up the skill of comparing and contrasting cultural values:

> In my own opinion Christmas is the day when all Christians should be together. Even more, we should help the helpless, be good, make other people happy and forgive each other, no matter if it is a Bulgarian, English or Russian Christmas.

> I think the three texts deal with the same universal topic – that of social poverty which becomes even sharper at times of celebration.

> 'The three extracts are more contrasting than similar. They describe three types of characters who have three different opinions about

Christmas: humanistic opinion expressed by Verka; materialistic opinion expressed by Scrooge; religious opinion expressed by the narrator in Dostoevsky's book.

It is not easy to establish general procedures of the comparing and contrasting method in cultural studies. Still, this method can inspire cross-cultural interest in the students by raising their own cultural awareness and using it as a basis for intercultural communication. The students' responses illustrated, though on a smaller scale, the possibility of fulfilling some of the aims of the cultural dimension in language teaching as stated by Byram and Risager (1999), namely:

* giving students an understanding of their own cultural identity;
* developing their ability to see similarities and differences between cultures;
* helping students to acquire an interested and critical attitude towards cultural/social issues;
* breaking down prejudices and developing pupils' tolerance;
* making language teaching more motivating.

Clearly, the comparison of the three texts could go deeper if the teacher decides to include historical and social texts describing the time when they were written.

This part of the project proved that literature could be used as a successful tool in the teaching of culture. The usefulness of the literary texts can be justified by the importance attributed to literature in a more recent view of cultural studies which unlike the 'civilization' view is labelled 'cultural studies as practised by British scholars'. It combines, 'sociological, *literary* and historical approaches in order to investigate the changing formation of British society from a critical standpoint, and explores assumptions, traditions and conventional attributions of value' (Durant, 1997: 21). Literature could provide a good basis for developing the cultural skills of the students and achieving the ultimate goal of culture teaching – the skill for 'reading' another culture, 'interpreting' what you've read and 'understanding' it.

Conclusion

To sum up, I refer back to Brøgger's model of cultural studies and illustrate its application in our project. On the social level of this model, we interpreted the cards as religious, historical, economic products of society and discussed issues such as religion, charity, market forces, etc.

in the two cultures. On the cultural level, the analysis focused on how the cards represented the dominant assumptions and values of the respective societies. The lack of religious cards and charities in Bulgaria before the changes reflected the dominant attitudes and values in our society. On the textual level, we analysed the texts on the cards and literary texts describing Christmas as linguistic expressions of two cultures.

We used only two of the vast amount of resources in British cultural studies: cards and literary texts. Despite the complex nature of the debate about the essence and content of cultural studies and the controversial opinions of experts on these issues, they surely agree on the traditional sources of cultural knowledge: cards, books, surveys, histories, interviews, photos, maps, films, television programmes, trips, adverts, etc. No matter which source or approach in cultural studies teachers and students take, they are bound to interpret cultural artefacts or data. In doing so they have to bear in mind that these are 'representations' of culture, and as such are already 'mediated' by previous interpretation. Bearing in mind their mediated character, teachers and students have to be aware of the 'means of representation' including the 'viewpoint' of the representation. This involves the learner in plunging below the surface of cultural texts and interpreting the discourse behind their meanings.

Where cultural situations are discussed, the learner has to go beyond the surface behaviour into fuller analysis of the intentions, strategies and codes which give such behaviour significance. Finally, teachers and learners must acknowledge the question of viewpoint in their discussions of culture. Cultural artefacts are loaded with meanings which reveal various veiwpoints (ironic, critical, tolerant, etc.) that need to be decoded. In order to do this one has to answer the following questions. How is the meaning created? How is it circulated? And how is value attached to it?

References

Benson, M. (1994) Review of F.C. Brøgger: *Culture, Language, Text. ELT Journal* 48(1), 92–94.

Brøgger, F.C. (1992) *Culture, Language,Text: Culture Studies within the Study of English as a Foreign Language*. Oxford: Oxford University Press and Scandinavian University Press.

Byram, M. and Risager, K. (1999) *Language Teachers, Politics and Cultures*. Clevedon: Multilingual Matters.

Durant, A. (1997) Facts and meanings in British cultural studies. In S. Bassnett (ed.) *Studying British Cultures*. London: Routledge.

Chapter 17
Study of Landscapes as an Approach to Openness to Others

FRANÇOISE VIGNERON

> *This chapter describes the development of an approach to the teaching of geography in the French primary school which enhances children's intercultural competence. This is an interdisciplinary project combining geography with mother tongue lessons.*

> *Chacun appelle barbarie*
> *ce qui n'est pas de son usage.*
> *(Montaigne)*

The rapid acceleration of progress in transportation and the world-wide rise of media and information networks have established a new environment in which our local and also our national worlds disappear into a global space. It often seems as though we can communicate more easily with New York, Tokyo or Buenos Aires than with our next-door neighbour. Human beings have become citizens of the world and have to face extremely complex changes towards an open and plural world, founded on knowledge of and respect for others.

However, even if it is incontrovertible that our world is becoming smaller and is globalising, it is also obvious that the unknown of wider frontiers initially creates anxiety and fear in many of our co-citizens. Old prejudices re-appear and new xenophobic mistrust arises.

Of course the return of attacks of nationalist fever can be explained in terms of circumstantial difficulties, above all economic difficulties, but this phenomenon is also the consequence of basic problems which we cannot ignore, and especially of the reality described by Dominique Wolton (1993): 'il n'y a rien d'évident et de naturel dans le fait de s'intéresser à l'autre'. To construct the world of tomorrow, simultaneously respecting differences of identity and capable of sharing the same destiny, we need a truly Copernican revolution in perceptions, intellectual attitudes and mentalities. Education is without any doubt the decisive means by which such a radical change in ways of thinking and reasoning can succeed. It is education which shapes cultural customs and mentalities. It is through education that new identities will be created.

It would of course be unreasonable to think of educational activity as taking place only in school, but school remains an essential place of education in many cultural systems. Thus different educational communities find themselves charged with a major responsibility and role in this process of creating a global awareness and a recognition of otherness. It is at the institutional level above all that we need to facilitate encounters and contacts with foreign cultures (Janitza, 1989).

Thus teachers, including primary school teachers, cannot ignore any longer their responsibility to sensitise their pupils to the relativity of customs and to give them, as Marc Bloch says, 'le sens du différent'. On the other hand, they need to know that mere knowledge of behaviour and social customs from another culture is not sufficient in itself for true cultural competence (cf. Zarate, 1986). It is actually necessary to *learn* to accept other people and their difference.

Thus in order to allow pupils to understand better 'the other' and 'elsewhere' and gradually to develop a true competence in foreign culture(s), we need to develop approaches deliberately based on reflection and on a decentring from knowledge and values which have hitherto been considered undeniable and universal.

Methodological Principles

It is in fact difficult for pupils to accept that there are several ways of seeing the world. Doubtless this is due not so much to a real belief in one's own cultural superiority but rather to a naïve assumption that the values in which one believes are universal, and therefore absolute. It is true that they have always been presented and taught as such. Furthermore, it is precisely because they have this assurance of self-evidence that they are effective in creating a sense of confidence in one's own values, in Geneviève Zarate's view. She also argues that it is this very lack of distance from one's own values which leads to us feeling inadequate in facing otherness, when the sense of what is self-evident is in fact challenged and breaks down.

If we wish to avoid pupils simply rejecting behaviours in other cultures which are for them indefinable and therefore bizarre, we have to show them that one of the roots of the problem lies in the subjectivity of their own responses, which have been unconsciously conditioned by the system in which they are profoundly involved participants.

The acquisition of (inter)cultural competence must therefore be organised on the basis of two principles which are of equal status and significance:

(1) *Extending the range of contents which are taught.* When a particular concept is taught, it is necessary first to extend the domain of the knowledge which is transmitted, i.e. the elements of one or more foreign cultural systems. This knowledge provides the reference points by which one can orientate oneself in foreign cultures. We can only approach what we know even if we know it only partially

(2) *Ridding oneself of the illusion of the universality of one's own culture.* Although it is extremely important to familiarise pupils with some foreign cultural realities, it is insufficient to combat the negative effects of natural ethnocentrism. It is not sufficient simply to attempt to improve general knowledge of other cultures. If pupils show interest in this, it risks being simply anecdotal curiosity about folklore and local colour. It is therefore necessary to create at the same time the conditions which will really give them the opportunity to relativise their own native system.

If we really wish them to accept all existing systems, without pre-established priority of one over the other, it is not simply sufficient to express, throughout the process of learning, the discovery of cultural facts combined with accounts of knowledge about the native culture. It is also necessary to make the latter the object of study and questioning, in parallel with and equal to the target culture. It is only in this way that the native culture will gradually lose its status of being the basis for universal reference, and that we will be able to make pupils conscious of the relativity of their native system.

Approach

In order to link the presentation of ideas in the syllabus for geography with the discovery of foreign realities and the requirement of questioning values hitherto taught and received as if definitive and indisputable, we used the reflexive framework for teaching cultural facts developed at the Institut National de Recherche Pédagogique under Albane Cain. However, as far as we know, there had been no work with children in primary schools and we needed to re-work the techniques.

The approach we propose is based on the principles we explained above. It includes a comparative dimension, juxtaposing elements from the native culture with facts from the same domain in one or more foreign systems, and also a reflexive dimension. However, this approach would be built on sand if it did not first establish the pupils' existing state of perceptions and knowledge of the topic in question (Meirieu, 1995).

Establishing perceptions of the topic to be studied

Before we can guide pupils towards relativisation of their own system, we need to know what is their vision, more or less stereotypical of the domain to be studied, both in the foreign and in the native cultures. In fact pupils often already have perceptions and even knowledge of the topic which is going to be studied. Some are negative, others positive. Most have quite neutral connotations. All are, however, possible sources of hindrance to a proper construction of knowledge about the topic unless they are brought to light and then integrated into the work.

Organising a collection of documents around a 'leitmotif'

The methodology used is always developed from a collection of documents which should be organised around a schema which Cain (1988) calls a 'fil conducteur' or leitmotif.

Cultural competence is acquired in part through access to a framework for reading phenomena in the foreign system. This presupposes, as we said above, that a certain number of traits of the foreign culture are known. However, there is then a danger of limiting oneself to an accumulation of points of knowledge, dealt with one after the other, without a preconceived structure. In this case, the probable range of elements presented to pupils cannot give them the means to orientate themselves properly in the foreign culture.

Instead of such a picturesque and exotic kaleidoscope, what is needed is the gradual construction of a system of coherent reference points. One needs to go beyond the simple observation of a phenomenon taken in isolation and be capable of placing it in its context and in the continuity of which it is a product, if one is to access the hidden order of a world which initially appears strange. This is why we present several documents and we choose these so that they create a network of relations. The pupils are thus able to (re)contextualise the different elements in relation to the vast jigsaw puzzle of the foreign culture, which in fact is in no way arbitrary.

The concept of a 'content gap'

All these documents need to be realisations of the concept of 'content gap', so that they can facilitate a proper construction of knowledge. This concept, taken from Gauthier (1981), is defined by Cain as follows:

> Par écart de contenu, nous entendons toute différence porteuse de sens entre, d'une part, les références implicites que constitue le système de données au sein duquel tout natif est intégré, et d'autre part, l'information apportée par plusieurs documents. (1988: 8)

> (By 'content gap', we mean any meaningful difference between, on the one hand, the implicit references which constitute the system of assumptions within which every native-speaker is integrated, and on the other, the information provided by several documents.)

In other words, all the documents to be used should all provide the reader with one or more items of new and significant information.

Choice of topic

The choice of topic was determined by two factors. We needed to deal with a topic which represents a national identity and for this reason creates stereotypes, and this topic also needed to be in the syllabus of the class working with us. The study of landscapes was appropriate in both respects.

Following the syllabus and transmitting knowledge

The 'Documents d'application des programmes de l'école élémentaire' state very clearly that on leaving the second phase of primary schooling, pupils should know several types of French landscape. They get to know France by studying these different landscapes.

However, our work was not conceived simply as a means of facilitating pupils' construction of competence in a domain of geography. It was also to develop the (inter)cultural education of the future cyber-citizen.

One of the traits representing national identity

The two objectives could only be realised, in our view, if the topic chosen involved two kinds of presupposition. First, it had to be the source of stereotypes. Second, since cultural traits, far from being contingent, in fact are part of a process, the topic for study has to be linked as much to the historical and economic development of a country as to physical and geographical criteria of the country. The study of landscape meets both these conditions.

First of all, landscape is part of a list of symbolic and material elements of identity which every nation needs (Thiesse, 1999). One only needs to look at a few tourist guides to see this and to find in the list of contents repeated mention of landscape as one of the distinctive traits of the country in question. Thus, the representation of different national landscapes is the opportunity for the production of stereotypes. From the Norwegian fjord to Dutch tulip fields, via American canyons or Scottish lochs, the examples are legion.

In a similar way, one can imagine that books about France will bring out the idea of 'typically French', and so the question is whether there exists in fact a national principle which allows all, natives or foreigners, to identify France at the first glance, distinguishing it unambiguously from every other country.

The study of landscapes also meets our second criterion. Landscapes as they now exist have been created by man, and therefore in every case we can attempt to distinguish what has been created by people from that which is natural. Landscapes, as true palimpsests, are simultaneously reflections of a way of life and of a socio-economic history.

Taking multiple purposes into consideration

We wanted our work to be related to several disciplines in the primary school. The study of landscape easily provides links for cross-curricular teaching. It allows the establishment of links between geography teaching on the one hand, and other disciplines such as the plastic arts and French for example.

Implementation

Learners involved

The École Molière, where we worked, lies on the edge of a medium-sized town in the west of France and takes pupils from varied socio-professional environments. Half the parents belong to the middle class and are in the service professions, technicians, nurses, teachers, etc. Other children, approximately a quarter, come from more modest backgrounds. Their parents are manual workers, sometimes unemployed. The final group in the school are from more advantaged origins. The parents of these children are in the liberal professions and as such are members of a wealthier middle class.

Whatever their origins, all these families still have a certain respect for schooling although they also have expectations of what schooling should offer them and their children. As a consequence, their children accept quite willingly the constraints of our school system. On the whole they conform to the expectations of the teachers not always very quietly but reasonably motivated to work.

The CM1 class with which we worked comprised 24 pupils aged 9–10, and was composed in the proportions described above for the school as a whole.

Conditions for the work

This project was carried out in the second half of the second term of the school year. However, this is not an obligatory period for this work, which can be carried out at any point in the year. What is significant in fact is on the one hand the progression and the coherence of the learning in the discipline in question, here geography, and on the other hand the opportunities for integrating the work into an interdisciplinary project.

Furthermore, the objective here of developing in children an (inter)-cultural competence is not related at all to foreign language learning. The medium of instruction was the mother tongue throughout. Nevertheless, certain activities can be done in a foreign language if the pupils are capable, but it is not the aim of this project.

The process

The implementation of our project was organised in two phases of unequal length.

In the first stage, two sessions, our purpose was to give the pupils the opportunity to express their perceptions of the chosen topic. In this case the teacher asked all the pupils to draw the landscape which in their eyes represented France (first session). In the following session, the pupils' products were first shared. The pupils were divided into four groups of six. Each group was asked to sort and put in piles the 24 drawings according to criteria which each group decided for itself. Then the different solutions were compared in the whole class. This produced two large categories which were then refined and sub-divided. One collection of drawings comprised 'natural' things: quiet places, presence of water, of animals, trees or meadows. Then the mountain landscapes were separated

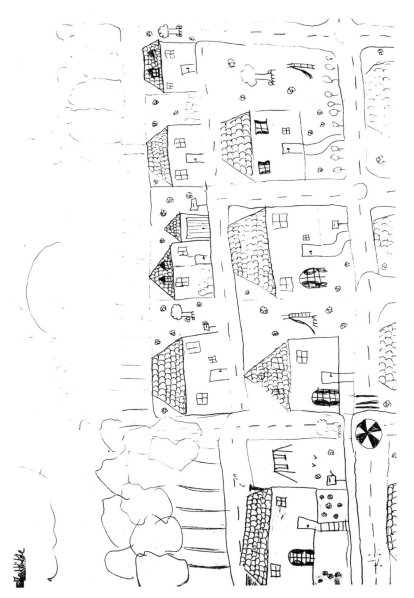

Figure 17.1 Student's drawing of an urban landscape.

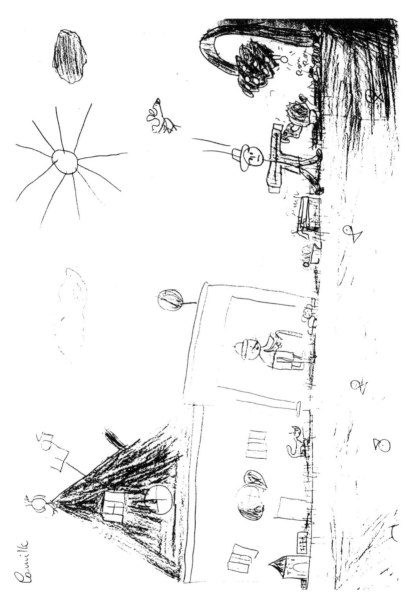

Figure 17.2   Student's drawing of a rural landscape.

from the country landscapes for example. This first group was in contrast with a pile comprising more urban landscapes. This second pile included what the pupils considered to be drawings representing the town, identified in their eyes in terms of a roundabout, a supermarket, roads and cars, blocks of flats, and lots of houses, or by electric pylons or traffic lights. The teacher clarified a few ideas and introduced the specific vocabulary she wanted to teach: urban landscape, country landscape, coastal, mountain, etc. Furthermore pupils noted the large variety of illustrations; there were five or six piles depending on the group. At this stage, this point was noted in order to return to it at the end of the second stage when the notion of stereotype would be addressed with the pupils. No commentary was made at this point.

The second stage begins here and was organised in five sessions. Our first concern was to conform to the syllabus and give the pupils some geographical knowledge. We decided to teach them to read and characterise two types of French landscape: the urban landscape starting from the town where they went to school and where many of them lived (Coulaines near Le Mans) and one type of rural landscape, the one in their region (le Maine). They learnt a basic vocabulary useful for describing each of these types of landscape – 'bocage' (hedge-lined fields)/open field; 'barres' (low-rise apartment blocks), areas with detached housing and housing estates etc. – then they worked on the evolution of these landscapes in order to see in particular that the same rural landscape has been managed and modified by man (three sessions).

The first session was organised as follows:

Session 1: Characterisation of an urban landscape

Objectives and competences
- read and describe an urban landscape with the help of appropriate vocabulary
- read aerial photographs of a familiar urban landscape and identify the recognisable features

Material
- children's drawings, plan of Coulaines, aerial photos

Plan
(1) Starting point
- put up children's drawing they classified as 'town'
- ask them to say how they classified these landscapes in this way
- note the vocabulary they use

(2) Study of the historical and geographical evolution of Coulaines
    (a) Start with the plan of the main road, the origin of the village
- what do they recognise: street, church
- why did the village begin on the road to Ballon: main road from le Mans to Ballon (need for a means of communication)

    (b) Extension and organisation of the town, shown in aerial photos taken before the school was built
- identify the church and the original main roads – find extensions: where, in what form (low-rise buildings, high rise flats – why they were needed – increase in population)
- what extensions are missing: new housing estates (what are the advantages and disadvantages of urban housing estates)

(3) The organisation of the town centre
- where do people buy their newspaper, consult the doctor, fetch their money, etc.
- list the different shops etc.
- discuss the significance of the town centre

(4) Extension work
- colour the different parts of the town to represent their different periods of construction
- contextualise the children's drawings in the lesson as a whole
- compare with other towns.

In the second and third session, ('Reading and study of a rural landscape' and 'Characterisation of two rural landscapes: the bocage and the open field'), further vocabulary was learnt and the functions and periods of development noted.

In the fourth session the nature of the work changed to focus on a first questioning of pupils' perceptions.

Session 4: Landscapes and Stereotypes

Objectives and competences

- evocation of stereotype landscapes and first stage of challenging them
- re-use of descriptive vocabulary learned in previous sessions

Material

- colour photos taken from geography textbooks and some publicity material

Figure 17.3 Aerial photograph of town.

Figure 17.4   A 'Stereotype' landscape.

Plan

(1) Identification of stereotypes and/or hypotheses linked to the pupils' cultural references
- task: you are going to look at photos and say if they are French or non-French landscapes – you need to justify your answers (French bocage; hunter constructing an igloo; windmill and tulips; French village etc etc)

(2) Questioning the stereotype
- show again the Algerian oasis: ask why oases are inhabited (emphasise human activity developed around water points in arid regions)
- show the photo of an oasis in the Colorado desert (USA) (introduce vocabulary needed; explain the irrigation system; emphasise the landscape is entirely constructed by human beings; ask what there is in common with the Algerian oasis

Emphasise that oases are not limited to North Africa – they are found in many parts of the world, similar or different – the landscape depends on the techniques of the particular civilisation – the same question can be asked about other types of landscape.

In the final session they were asked to compare their perceptions with reality in order to challenge their rather reductive views of this reality.

Session 5: From the stereotype to the reality of landscapes

Objectives and competences
- challenge the children's representations of reality
- undermine stereotypes
- understand that stereotypes are a cultural code

Material
- colour photos from the previous session and further photos taken from geography textbooks

Plan

(1) Similarities
- take photos from previous session and similar landscapes for other countries
- task: compare each of the familiar photos with the new ones introduced in this session: similar landscapes are found throughout the

world; we often characterise a country by a type of landscape, a stereotype; why is a particular stereotype attached to a particular country when it is also to be found elsewhere?

(2) Diversity of landscapes in one country
  • provide several landscapes for one country(the stereotype: igloo, and other: Inuit village, etc.)
  • emphasise that there are similar landscapes in two countries and also variety within one
  • question: why is it that there are diverse landscapes in one country, for example in the USA and France: since landscapes are human constructions, they are linked to climate and relief and human beings have to adapt

Conclusion: stereotypes exist but they are not the only form of landscape in a country because all countries have a variety of landscapes. Stereotypes are useful because everyone knows them – they are *a cultural code*

(3) Reflecting on auto-stereotypes
  • put up again drawings pupils did in the very first session and ask them to think about their representations and to consider how far their drawings are auto-stereotypes
  • compare with well-known paintings – *L'angélus* by François Millet, *L'entrée du village de Voisins* by Camille Pissaro, *Vue d'Auvers* by Paul Cézanne – and ask what if we saw our landscape through the images painters have given us?

This fifth session finished with getting the pupils to think about the functions of stereotypes. They saw the use of sharing common cultural references in order to facilitate rapid mutual comprehension. (We have begun to think about a prolongation of this work with respect to this function of stereotypes by including the study of advertisements. Advertisers use a lot of stereotypes precisely because they have to get to the essence of things quickly.) We then took some of their drawings, those which illustrated a first stage of stereotyping, and compared them with several classic paintings. We had more than enough to choose from, and decided on *L'angélus* by François Millet (1859), *L'entrée du village de Voisins* by Camille Pissaro (1872) and *Vue d'Auvers-sur-Oise* by Paul Cézanne (1873). The aim here was to begin to raise their awareness that we have constructed our perceptions of a typical landscape through what we know and what we remember, but also through the images that painters have given us. It is a shared capital.

So as not to neglect the interdisciplinary dimension, we took further this work begun in the plastic arts. We chose to study the multiple pictorial representations of three emblematic landscapes: Fujiyama, Big Ben and some views of London, and the Eiffel Tower.

In the mother tongue teaching we wanted to help pupils to make their understanding of stereotypes more precise. There are many opportunities in French literature and we chose to focus on the vision of black people, wild, brutal and obtuse, as represented in two texts: an extract from *Five Weeks in a Balloon* by Jules Verne and some vignettes from *Tintin in the Congo* by Hergé. Pupils were able to see that these are not recent works and this representation is perhaps out of date. Now that we are able to communicate with the whole world, we have surely finished with simplistic and reductive stereotypes! Reading two children's albums, however, showed that the opposite is true and that there is a long-lasting effect of certain clichés (the rainy weather in Britain, the English as tea-drinkers, wine and camembert in the French home, etc). Pupils were even able to see that these two stories were based entirely on the use of a few widely held stereotypes. They noticed that the use of a few ready-made ideas aimed to make us laugh at the other because of his otherness. They nonetheless realised that this could be reversed and that people could laugh at us too.

Conclusion

There is no human society without culture and there is in each culture a specific capital which links together the members of a particular community. Without doubt, national identities will still remain an essential element for a long time at the heart of our being and our personality. But each culture is particular and these identities are primarily constructed as differences, and it is the case that difference awakens most often *a priori* reactions of resistance, and even of exclusion. Pier Paolo Pasolini said that 'we have a tendency to express an irreducible racism with respect to those who live in another culture' (1976).

However, when the new communication technologies allow us to surf a web which covers the whole planet, the opportunities for contact are infinite. Even if there are fundamental questions for our future when faced by this communication revolution, and if the growth of these networks does not meet with universal consent, the connection of isolated terminals creates a world where distances and geographic, political, economic or cultural frontiers will be relative. The internet, as the experts of these new electronic networks of information tell us, allows us to weave universal links. We are able to travel in real time from one country to another, following our personal research or willingness for openness and communication. This extraordinary historic change, which we have to face up to, will transform our lives as other inventions, the automobile or the telephone, have done in their time, and our education sitemaps risk falling into crisis if they do not manage to incorporate the international dimension which the evolution of our contemporary world is creating.

Education on a global scale is therefore an absolute necessity, and a real advantage, for the common future of young and future citizens of a *global* world. We were conscious of these issues as we set out to develop this work from one of the elements which constitute a sense of identity and belonging, i.e. landscapes. We ensured throughout the process, therefore, that it operated on the basis of the two axes we had defined. On the one hand, we brought out the perceptions, and perhaps the knowledge, pupils had on the theme we studied. We took these into consideration as new knowledge was transmitted, i.e. the orientation points for finding one's way in both cultures, the native and the foreign. Parallel to this, we also ensured that the native culture should remain an object of study in its own right together with the target culture. We think, then, that these two conditions allow us to provide the pupils with conceptual tools which permit them to rise above national prejudices and self-interest. These two conditions enable us to develop in pupils a true capacity to open up to others in their difference, and to give them a true intercultural competence.

References

Cain, A. (ed.) (1988) *L'enseignement de la civilisation (langues vivantes, seconde cycle.* Paris: INRP.
Gauthier, A. (1981) *Opérations énonciatives et apprentissage d'une langue étrangère en milieu scolaire. L'anglais à des francophones.* Paris: APLV.
Janitza, J. (1989) *Rapport de la commission de réflexion sur l'enseignement des langues étrangères.* Paris: Ministère de l'Éducation nationale.
Meirieu, P. (1995) *La pédagogie entre le dire et le faire.* Paris: ESI.
Pasolini, P.P. (1976) *Ecrits Corsaires.* Paris: Flammarion.
Thiesse, A-M. (1999) *La création des identités nationales en Europe.* Paris: Le Seuil.
Wolton, D. (1993) *La dernière Utopie. Naissance de l'Europe démocratique.* Paris: Flammarion.
Zarate, G. (1986) *Enseigner une culture étrangère.* Paris: Hachette.

Further Reading

These are books recommended by authors of chapters in this volume with their comments on why they found them useful.

Agar, M. (1994) *Language Shock: Understanding the Culture of Conversation*. New York: William Morrow. This is a most valuable reading as it manages to pull together and put in place any fragmented understandings that we may have of the relationship between language and culture. He introduces the term 'langua-culture', which reinforces the idea that culture is something that happens to us and that we experience instead of something which others just have.

All Different – All Equal, Education Pack (1995) Strasbourg: European Youth Centre. The book focuses on racism, xenophobia and intolerance, but it has as its starting point issues such as awareness of one's own and other cultures, identity, stereotypes, prejudice and ethnocentrism. These are dealt with in a very clear way enhanced by questions relating the issues to the reader's personal experience. The book contains a wide range of materials, which, with a certain adaptation to suit a particular context, can prove very useful for language teachers interested in giving a cultural dimenion to their language teaching.

Bennet, M. (1997) How not to be a fluent fool: understanding the cultural dimension of language. In A.E. Fantini (ed.), *New Ways in Teaching Culture*. New York: TESOL. A useful text applying the principles of Whorf's linguistic relativity to meaning, e.g. why it is possible in Turkish to count in two different ways, why colours are distinguished differently in the lexis of different languages, etc., and the implications of this aspect of culture for the classroom.

Byram, M. (1995) Acquiring intercultural competence: a review of learning theories. In L. Secru (ed.), *Intercultural Competence: The Secondary School*. Aalborg: Aalborg University Press. Gives a brief but comprehensive introduction to inter-cultural communicative competence in theory and practice and the intercultural speaker in language tuition.

Byram, M. (ed.) (1997) *Face to Face: Learning 'Language and Culture' through Visits and Exchanges*. London: Centre for Information on Language Teaching and Research (CILT). A collection of articles centred around learning and culture through exchange visits. Includes a description of transformative learning in relation to adults (as a supplement to Piaget's work with children's learning processes).

Byram, M. (1997) *Teaching and Assessing Intercultural Communicative Competence.* Clevedon: Mulitlingual Matters. A description of the type of competence needed for intercultural encounters, theoretical enough to 'feed the souls' of researchers and educational policy-makers and practical enough to help teachers develop their own practical tools for measuring whether students have developed the competence. Byram includes proposals for assessment of intercultural communicative competence which is an area from which many authors shy away. Very useful as a reference for those setting up courses with an intercultural element.

Byram, M. and Fleming, M. (eds) (1998), *Language Learning in Intercultural Perspective: Approaches through Drama and Ethnography.* Cambridge: Cambridge University Press. Although of recent date, already a 'standard classic' offering several approaches to the teaching of intercultural awareness in secondary schools.

Byram, M. and Zarate, G. (1997) *Young People Facing Difference.* Strasbourg: Council of Europe Publishing. Helpful to direct teachers how to develop non-confrontational awareness of the 'foreign' other as a part of teaching. A document of guidance, 'animated' by activities illustrating the principles with classroom application.

Byram, M. *et al.* (1994) *Teaching-and-Learning Language-and-Culture.* Clevedon: Multilingual Matters. This book has been an invaluable source of insight into the affective aspect of culture teaching and learning. The section 'Empathy' has given us the incentive to design activities to break stereotypical attitudes, reduce ethnocentrism and work towards tolerance of 'otherness'. The book contains excellent examples of classroom practice illustrating an integrated approach to language and culture teaching and learning.

Davcheva, L. and Docheva, Y. (eds) (1998) *Branching Out: A Cultural Studies Syllabus* Sofia: British Council and Tilia. An example of a cultural syllabus overarching the linguistic one, containing both the theoretical 'backbone' and lesson plans for the classroom. The (Bulgarian) culture-specifics serve the purpose of exemplification of the principles of applying an intercultural approach to presenting cultural matters.

Delanoy, Werner (1995) Cultural learning in the FL-classroom: From 'Landeskunde' to 'New Cultural Studies'. In N. Wadham-Smith (ed.), *British Studies Now.* London: British Council. The article outlines the main characteristics of the two approaches to culture teaching: 'Landeskunde' and 'New Cultural Studies', offering good examples to illustrate the main differences between the two. This could help a language teacher design a course of cultural studies focusing around the idea of teaching intercultural communication skills.

Doyé, P. (1996) Foreign language teaching and education for intercultural and international understanding'. In *Evaluation and Research in Education* 10, 2–3. A useful part of the 'survival tool kit' of the teacher whose headmaster keeps asking 'What do newspapers have to do with language teaching and culture?' Traces the evolution of the goals in language teaching from linguistic competence, through sociolinguistic competence, to intercultural communicative competence.

Doyé, Peter (1999) *The Intercultural Dimension: Foreign Language Education in the Primary School.* Berlin: Cornelsen. Geared to the needs of primary school teachers, this is an easy-to-read and very interesting introduction of general interest.

Dutton, W. (ed.) (1999) *Society on the Line.* Oxford: Oxford University Press. This is a rather academic text but it does cover the use of the new technologies in a wide variety of areas and has an excellent bibliography that is as current as can be expected.

Fantini, A. (1997) *New Ways in Teaching Culture.* Bloomington: Pantagraph Printing. This book is interesting for exploring in the classroom. The activities suggested introduce innovative ways of integrating language and culture teaching. The practical orientation of the book is well balanced with useful theoretical input.

Fisher, S. (1997) *Creating Dynamic Web Sites.* Berkeley: A-W Developers Press. The technology in this book is a bit dated now, but the general approach to using the new technologies is extremely valuable.

Freedman, T. (1999) *Managing ICT.* London: Hodder and Stoughton. This is the book I wish I had when we first started to work with the new technologies. It sets down sensible practical ways in which to ensure that the most common disasters of using new technologies in schools or colleges are avoided. It is centred on meeting the needs of UK secondary school teachers but the overwhelming majority of the book is useful wherever you are.

Gookin, D. and Ratbone, A. (1999) *PCs for Dummies.* San Maeto: IDG. The title does not build confidence but the 'Dummies' series real does what it says, i.e. gives simple straight guidance on becoming familiar with the new technologies. It allows you quickly to mutter words that leave 'techies' wondering at your wisdom.

Hadfield, J. (1992) *Classroom Dynamics.* Oxford: Oxford University Press. A book from the series 'Resource Books for teachers'. This series has a standard format for activities, giving, for example, the level of students for whom the activity is intended, materials needed and timing. Practical ideas for promoting a positive class culture in your classroom through, for example, activities which enable students to learn about each other and empathise: both components of inter-cultural competence. The book has come out of the British EFL teaching context (though the author has taught elsewhere) but I think the activities can be integrated into other contexts of communicative language teaching.

Hartley, J. (1993) *Understanding News*. London: Routlege. Although rather academic, this is the book teachers cannot do without. With its simple language, detailed classification of the different elements, modes and codes of presentation of television news and accompanying shots, it will be extremely useful for understanding some basic media terminology.

Hymes, D. (1967) Models of interaction and social life. *Journal of Social Issues*, 33(2), 8–28. This article offers ways of reading a speech event. As an aid to organising the information that is collected in an ethnographic research project, Hymes suggests that observers look for eight groups of components, grouped under labels whose first letters spell out the word SPEAKING to make them easier to remember. Adapting it, we designed our framework for analysing cultural phenomena, i.e. who did what, when, who with, how and why.

Kramsch, C. (1993) *Context and Culture in Language Teaching*. Oxford: Oxford University Press. A useful supplement to Byram's theories on the intercultural speaker. Focuses on the interaction between language and culture and describes 'the third place' where learners construct their own meaning.

Kramsch, C. (1998) The privilege of the intercultural speaker. In M. Byram and M. Fleming (eds), *Language Learning in Intercultural Perspective: Approaches Through Drama and Ethnography*. Cambridge: Cambridge University Press. This text is an eye-opener for teachers of foreign languages as it challenges the long-established orientation of language classrooms towards the monolingual native speaker norm and proposes that we encourage our learners to develop as intercultural speakers.

Mascull, B. (1995) *Collins Cobuild Key Words in the Media*. New York: Harper Collins Publishers. A very useful reference book for all who need explanation of some basic terms used in newspapers, radio and television news. Arranged in eight topics, the first being 'The Media', the key words are followed by various practical exercises.

Masterman, L. (1985) *Teaching Media*. London: Routledge. This book covers most of the techniques in shooting and camera work with a number of illustrations and explanations. It helps the readers to understand better the operating codes and modes of television, i.e. to 'read' the messages sent from the screen.

McRae, J. (1991) *Literature with a Small 'l'*. New York: Prentice Hall. Useful in the way it adapts linguistic theory, e.g. R. Jacobson's functions of language, for classroom application. Another helpful aspect is that 'text' is treated broadly and includes pictures, posters, proverbs, etc.

Negroponte, N. (1996) *Being Digital*. London: Hodder and Stoughton. Nicholas Negroponte has been working on using the new technologies in innovative ways longer than possibly anybody else and this book is a provocative overview of where the new technologies may take us.

Raw, L. (1997) *The Country and the City*. London: British Council. A collection of activities created to present Britain to foreign (mainly university) students, effectively illustrating the use of geographical topics for the purposes of cultural learning.

Robinson, G.N. (1985) *Crosscultural Understanding*. Oxford: Pergamon. I really like this book because it is the first one I read with both an anthropological and a language teaching background. It is accessible, and enlightening.

Tarasheva, E. (ed.) (2000) *Lessons of the Mountain*. London: British Council. A collection of lessons taught by Bulgarian student teachers to English pupils as a part of an intercultural project, presenting various aspects of Bulgarian culture. The problem of presenting own culture from a cultural perspective is illustrated in a practical aspect.

Tomalin, B. and Stempleski, S. (1993) *Cultural Awareness*. Oxford: Oxford University Press. An 'evergreen' collection of classroom activities developing the skill to understand oneself as a being made up of multiple cultural components and to approach the other as a different but similarly complex creature. A particularly clear and useful foreword explaining the rationale.

Valdes, J.M. (ed.) (1986) *Culture-Bound: Bridging the Cultural Gap in Language Teaching*. Cambridge: Cambridge University Press. This book is a collection of papers concerned with ways of integrating cultural learning and language learning. The authors start from the assumption that since language is never culture-free, learning a foreign language inevitably has cultural implications. Thus the book's title could perhaps be understood as 'bound to teach culture'.

Wresch, W. (1996) *Disconnected: Haves and Have-nots in the Information Age*. Piscataway: Rutgers University Press. This book deals amazingly well with the threat the new technologies offer of a world and societies permanently divided between those who have access to the new technologies and those who do not.

And from the web . . .

tandem-schule@tandem.uni.trier.de

They will be able to find tandem partners for your students.

Web Skills for Language Learners http://www.well.ac.uk

A compilation of case studies of web-supported language teaching and learning.

Index